DATE DUE

SE 22 '98		
NY 20 '99		
OC 25 '99		
NY 2 9 01		
OC 30 02		
DE 7 03		
NO 6 05		

DEMCO 38-296

A WOMAN SCORNED

by the same author

FEMALE POWER AND MALE DOMINANCE:
ON THE ORIGINS OF SEXUAL INEQUALITY

DIVINE HUNGER:
CANNIBALISM AS A CULTURAL SYSTEM

FRATERNITY GANG RAPE:
SEX, BROTHERHOOD, AND PRIVILEGE ON CAMPUS

A WOMAN SCORNED

ACQUAINTANCE RAPE ON TRIAL

Peggy Reeves Sanday

D O U B L E D A Y
NEW YORK   LONDON   TORONTO
SYDNEY   AUCKLAND

PUBLISHED BY DOUBLEDAY
a division of Bantam Doubleday Dell
Publishing Group, Inc.
1540 Broadway, New York, New York 10036

DOUBLEDAY and the portrayal of an anchor with a dolphin are
trademarks of Doubleday, a division of Bantam Doubleday
Dell Publishing Group, Inc.

Author's Note: In keeping with the dictates of anthropological ethics, the names of the defendants in the St. John's case
have been abbreviated.

Book design by Jennifer Ann Daddio

Library of Congress Cataloging-in-Publication Data
Sanday, Peggy Reeves.
A woman scorned : acquaintance rape on trial / Peggy
Reeves Sanday.
p.   cm.
Includes bibliographical references and index.
1. Acquaintance rape—United States.   2. Acquaintance
rape—United States—Case studies.   3. Trials (Rape)—
United States.   I. Title.
HV6561.S253   1996
364.1'532—dc20   95-22774
                                                    CIP

ISBN 0-385-47791-0
Copyright © 1996 by Peggy Sanday
All Rights Reserved
Printed in the United States of America
March 1996
First Edition
10 9 8 7 6 5 4 3 2 1

Heav'n has no Rage, like Love to Hatred turn'd
Nor Hell a Fury, like a Woman scorn'd.

WILLIAM CONGREVE, *The Mourning Bride (Act III. Scene I)*

Why then, he was asked, did the woman press the case? The juror answered:
"What was that thing that Shakespeare said? 'Hell hath no fury like a
woman scorned.' "

INTERVIEW WITH ST. JOHN'S JUROR. *Newsday,* JULY 24, 1991

Each person has the right not only to decide whether to engage in sexual contact
with another, but also to control the circumstances and character of that con-
tact. No one, neither a spouse, nor a friend, nor an acquaintance, nor a
stranger, has the right or the privilege to force sexual contact.

SUPREME COURT OF NEW JERSEY, 1992

We need to get away from wordless sex. The brain is the most powerful sexual
organ. It works by being verbal. If your mind isn't in it, if your heart isn't in
it, then your body doesn't respond.

ALYSIA TURNER, BROWN UNIVERSITY STUDENT, 1994

FOR SERGE WITH LOVE

CONTENTS

A WOMAN SCORNED

HOOKING UP AT THE TRUMP[1]

IT WAS MARCH 1, 1990, ABOUT TEN O'CLOCK IN THE EVENING. A CAR *pulled up and parked in front of a house in Fresh Meadows, Queens. The temperature at nearby Kennedy Airport registered 36 degrees. The house was rented by members of the St. John's lacrosse team. As testimony to their carefree life, the house was nicknamed the Nugget. Another lacrosse-team house was called the Trump.*

Three young men were crowded into the front seat of the car. The backseat appeared empty. Two of the front-seat passengers got out of the car. One of them was wearing a mask pushed back from his face on top of his head, a clown mask with large eyeholes. The hair on the mask was blacker than the night. An unusual sight for late winter, a sight you might expect to see in front of this house on Halloween. But this wasn't Halloween.

The masked figure looked like the residents of the house, a strong, athletic type. He was taller and more muscular than most of the residents, a commanding figure who, by the sound of his voice, was used to giving orders. Shorter and broader, the second male figure looked more boyish, just out of high school. His blond hair and pale skin shone in the dark. He opened the back door of the car. There was someone lying in the backseat. Maybe a drunk friend. The guys in the house frequently stumbled out of their cars, helping each other into the house on party nights. This drunk friend couldn't move and had to be pulled out instead.

The figure dragged from the backseat wasn't a guy at all. She was a light-skinned black girl, about five-three. She looked like she was about sixteen or seventeen. She was completely limp, a rag doll. Her head fell back as she was taken from the car and carried into the house. Her arms hung at her sides. Her clothes were disheveled. No coat. She must have been oblivious to the cold because her white shirt was hanging out of her gray pants, and the sleeves of the shirt were crumpled up around her elbows. It was too cold to be without a coat.

Angela (pseudonym) didn't look her age. When I first met her she seemed more a sweet sixteen than an adult twenty-one. After listening to her testimony on the witness stand nine months later, Sheryl McCarthy of *Newsday* described her as "a tiny blue bird," "tentative and nervous . . . more like a teenager than a 22-year-old."

At the time she was carried into the Nugget, Angela was one of a small percentage of minority students who went to St. John's University in Queens, New York. In early 1990, the St. John's student body was mainly white and Roman Catholic. Many members of the nonwhite student population did not feel welcome on campus. They complained that they were treated differently both by the administration and members of student government. In the month before Angela was taken to the Nugget, students of color had marched silently through campus dressed in black to protest discrimination. Angela was not among them.

Angela had grown up in rural Jamaica, part of a proper Catholic family. Her mother came from an extended family of college-educated landowners, which included Rhodes scholars and graduates of Cambridge University in England. Both of Angela's parents were college graduates. Angela's mother was a schoolteacher until her children were born. Her father worked as an accountant for a hotel chain in Jamaica. Angela remembered watching her father play polo on weekends. As in other former British colonies, cricket, croquet, and tennis were popular sports. White was the required color for play.

Angela identified more with the English than the African tradition of

4

her roots. In this, she was definitely not politically correct. She liked to think that she was made by nature and nurture, not by politics. She had grown up hearing people sing "God Save the Queen" and drinking tea. In the U.S. people were always telling Angela that she was too Catholic. She didn't agree. Being Catholic was an integral part of her mother's family tradition. She would always be Jamaican and always be Catholic. In Jamaica, she had gone to church every Sunday and looked up to the priests, even though they were American. She and her cousins were all baptized by the same priest. She would never forget him. He was more than an authority figure; he represented faith, hope, and trust.

From an early age Angela had been conditioned to respond to authority with complete obedience. Discipline at home and school had always been very strict. Educated by nuns who wore traditional habits, Angela had been required to wear a uniform to school—blue skirt and white blouse with dark shoes. Socks were worn around the ankle. Drills were announced unexpectedly to check for cleanliness. Fingernails had to be clean and cut, shoes polished at all times. No fighting or swearing was allowed in school, and students were expected to mind their manners at meals. The home environment for the kids at this school was just as strict. If they were punished at school, they knew to keep it to themselves, because if their parents found out they'd misbehaved, they'd get into even bigger trouble at home.

When they first came to the U.S., the family lived in the New York area, where Angela attended high school. Her mother tried to preserve the discipline of Angela's childhood environment, and Angela continued to lead the sheltered life of rural Jamaica. She was virtually cocooned, her older brother told the press. She was not a party-goer, and her inexperience added to her trusting, almost gullible nature. Her brother described her as a "prime candidate for some people who have psychological deprivations . . . to work out their inferiority complexes and what-have-you on her."[2]

Before she entered St. John's, Angela's parents moved out of town, while Angela stayed behind to continue her schooling. She had been admitted to Syracuse, Rutgers, and New York University, but chose St. John's because it was affordable. She also liked the seclusion of the Queens campus and the fact that Governor Cuomo had gone to St. John's and made something of himself. Cuomo once said that St. John's was "the place where the children of people with no degrees are able to get an excellent education." He graduated from St. John's in 1953 and received his law degree there three years later. In his commencement address at St. John's in 1989, Cuomo attributed whatever success he'd enjoyed in large measure to the university.

Angela began at St. John's in the fall of 1987. On March 1, 1990, she was a second-semester junior, a marketing major. She was a member of the rifle club and participated in events sponsored by the Saint Vincent de Paul Society, a Catholic social organization for students and faculty. Occasionally, she joined in the activities of the Caribbean Students Association.

Angela got to school in time to have lunch before class on the day that would end for her in a nightmare of sexual abuse and assault. She ate quickly: a cheeseburger and french fries washed down with fruit punch. After classes and studying at the library, she went to the rifle club for practice. She had joined the club that winter, thinking that maybe one day she would get involved in some aspect of law enforcement. She got to the rifle range at about 6 P.M.

Michael was already there. Michael came from a blue-collar, Italian-American, Catholic background. His father was a retired firefighter for New York City. Michael's well-groomed, jet-black hair framed a large face with a prominent aquiline nose. He carried himself with pride—back straight, shoulders back, chest out, head up. He wore cowboy boots with heels, and his regular shoes also had heels. He was new at St. John's, having transferred there in the fall of 1989, and he was doing very well, earning a B+ average.

Angela first met Michael when she had become more active in the club in January. They had teamed up as shooting partners. Angela thought he was something of a gossip, always talking about everyone else and their business. He had told Angela about a girl on the rifle team who drank with him and his friends. Once she got sick and Michael cleaned her up, he said. Another time, after they all had got drunk together, one of his friends had woken up to find her next to him. The way Michael told this story, Angela got the impression he disapproved.

Angela thought of Michael as an older brother who looked out for her. Often he would tell her what to do, who she should stay away from, when she should be careful about walking alone on campus, and so on. She liked him, but not as a boyfriend. His Catholicism—he had once told her he had thought of the priesthood —inspired a feeling of comfort in his presence. Michael was a criminal justice major, so they also had a mutual interest in law enforcement. Angela was flattered because Michael seemed to rely on her friendship.

When she got to the rifle range, Michael was leafing through the pages of the Sports Illustrated *swimsuit issue*. Angela wasn't too surprised, because she had gotten used to the posters of girls in bikinis all over the walls of the rifle range. Turning the pages of the magazine, Michael pointed to the breasts of a bikini-clad figure and asked Angela if she looked like that. All she could think to say was "Michael, please."

As they were waiting to shoot, the subject turned again to sex. Angela was comfortable talking vaguely about a person's love life, but not about sex. She tried to get Michael off the subject of sex by asking him about his love life, but he didn't take the cue. When he asked her about her love life, he meant sex. "How's your love life, Angela, did you lose it in the backseat of a car or are you wholesome?" he asked.

Her response was a polite "You can say that."

That should have been the end of it. But, in jest, she mimicked Michael and asked him the same questions in return: "Are you wholesome?" Later, she hated herself for doing this. If she had just shut up, maybe the whole thing would have ended right then.

After they finished shooting practice, Michael offered her a ride home. She gladly accepted because she lived three bus rides away from campus and had an important economics test the next day. On the way out of the rifle range, Michael made a phone call that lasted five to ten minutes. She wondered about the call.

Why was he so long on the phone; who did he call? Michael told her he had called his mother out on Long Island, because he was going there after driving her home. As they drove off campus, Angela didn't think anything of it when Michael said he had to stop by his house to get gas money. It was the house called the Trump. Of those who lived there, all but Michael were on the lacrosse team.

On the way to the house, Michael returned to the subject of sex. He said he had sex four or more times a week. Explaining his sexual philosophy, he said, "You know, Angela, I don't think you have to know a person that well to have sex with them." He asked her if she had ever had sex with a white guy. The only response she could think of was to ask in return whether he had ever had sex with a black girl. Michael proudly answered that he had had sex with a black girl and a Chinese girl.

The sex talk continued. Michael asked if she liked oral sex. She quickly said no. When he kept on in this vein, Angela became confused and vaguely anxious. His words were crass and unpleasant, yet he spoke them as a friend. Her need for his friendship, coupled with her innocence, blinded her to the moves he was making.

At his house, Michael pulled his car into the driveway in back of two other cars. It was a nice residential neighborhood, with well-built single homes. The house itself was picturesque, dark brick with a slate roof. It was a solid, middle-class, trustworthy-looking house.

Michael invited her in, but she stayed in the car. She felt embarrassed to go into a man's house alone. She waited for a while, wondering how much longer he would be. Just as she was opening the car door to get some air, Michael came out on the porch and asked her to come inside and meet his roommates. She decided to go into the house, partly out of curiosity and partly because she felt it would be unfriendly to refuse his invitation a second time.

It was very dark inside the Trump. The living room was full of broken-down furniture. A cardboard stand-up figure of the actor Jack Nicholson dressed as the Joker in the movie Batman *stood in one corner. Food scraps littered the floor. Seeing no roommates, Angela headed for the light, which was in the kitchen. No roommates there, either. She wondered how she could meet roommates if they weren't there. She nervously opened the refrigerator door. All she could see inside were a bottle of liquor and a carton of milk. She thought to herself, These guys don't have a proper diet. She looked at the stove. Food all over the place. It was a mess.*

After about five minutes Michael came into the kitchen. He invited her up to his room to meet his roommates. It was a bedroom-den arrangement: a couch on one wall, two beds at the end of the room on either side of a window, some shelves with books, and a TV against the other wall. Near the steps was a refrigerator. The room was neatly arranged, compared with the kitchen and living room on the first floor. The nude posters on the walls, however, made her feel uneasy once again.

There were two people in the upstairs room. Pointing to them, Michael said, "That's Walter and that's Andrew."

Walter was sitting on the sofa eating ravioli. He looked like an athlete. He was tall, muscular with a thick neck. His thin lips, pointed nose, and smooth face caused some to remark that he looked like Sean Penn. He had a wound-up, tightly harnessed, almost growling kind of bodily energy. His words tumbled out as if he were running somewhere and didn't have time to stop. Munching on his ravioli, Walter wanted to know Angela's age. He asked if she was eighteen. When she said no, he wondered if she was nineteen.

As she was about to answer, another guy came into the room. He was tall, good-looking, Angela thought. He had dark, neatly trimmed wavy hair. Angela didn't catch his name. It was a short, one-syllable name, which she couldn't hear. The only thing she could remember about him later was that he was wearing a white T-shirt and he was just a little shorter than Walter. He stayed in the room a few minutes and then went downstairs.

Shortly afterward another guy came in. He was introduced as Tommy. Angela remembered him because he had such a baby face. Guys don't look so innocent and childlike beyond age twelve, she thought. She concluded that Tommy was Michael's roommate because he sat down on one of the beds as if it were his. It was bad manners to sit uninvited on someone else's bed. Tommy was very friendly. He asked where she was from and she said Jamaica. He said that once he knew someone from Haiti. He added, as if Angela didn't already know, that they spoke French in Haiti. Their conversation was also very brief. Tommy stayed a few minutes and then left the room.

Walter took charge of the conversation once again. His questions were brisk, to the point. "Do you like parties?" he asked.

Of course, who doesn't? Angela thought, as she said yes.

"Do you and your friends hook up?" he shot back.

"Sure," she said. "We do it all the time."

Walter's smile brought momentary relaxation to his coiled tension. Pointing to the two beds, he said, "We do that here all the time. You see those two beds, we use them and switch the girls back and forth by going from bed to bed."

She acted as if she hadn't heard what he said. She was far too embarrassed to say what was on her mind: "That's not what I meant." She had never heard the term used like that before. She thought hooking up meant getting together somewhere with your friends. Not knowing what to say, not wanting to seem impolite, she said nothing. She thought her silence would more than amply convey her disapproval.

Silence was the only response possible for Angela. Between Angela and the jock culture she encountered on March 1, there was not just a racial gap, there was also a gap in cultural understanding. For Angela sex was something reserved for love, marriage, a committed relationship. For the young men she encountered that night, sex was a group sport played with teammates. The name they had for it—"hooking up"—conveyed its casual nature. It was a game you played with your buddies. One teammate set it up, others played, while still others watched.

After Walter made the remark about hooking up, Angela had the feeling of being pulled into the dark stream of fate. She dimly heard the boys in the room joking about their sexual escapades. Rendered almost completely passive by the straitjacket of her background, Angela became an easy target.

She accepted a drink from Michael. The drink tasted terrible; it was bitter and stung her throat. When she asked what was in it, Michael said he put a little vodka in it. When she explained that she never drank, because drinking made her sick, Michael didn't listen. Then she tried to tell him that she hadn't eaten anything since lunch, but this did not move him. "Vodka is a before-dinner drink," he explained, insisting that she drink it.

Finally, she gave into his pressure and downed the contents of the first cup in a few gulps because of the bitter taste. When she finished, Michael went over to the refrigerator and brought back a large container, which he said was orange soda with vodka. He placed the container on the floor beside her feet. When Michael poured another cup, she told him, "But, Michael, I couldn't finish the first one. I don't think I will be able to finish another." Michael said again: "It's only vodka. It can't do anything to you, Angela." He also said, "You know, Angela, in college everyone does something, something wild they can look back on."

"Something wild?" Angela asked quizzically.

"Something wild," Michael said again. "Something you can look back on and talk about later in life." With the beer can that he was holding in his hand but never drank from, he hit her cup and said, "Here's to college life."

Later, Angela blamed herself for accepting the drinks from Michael. She was caught between wanting to please the host and wanting to assert her own needs. She had tried to please him by finishing the first drink. Now, she drank the second.

Then, he poured a third drink. When she balked at drinking this one, he started getting upset and annoyed. He told her it was a special drink, made just for her. He accused her of making him waste it. He started pushing the drink up to her mouth. He put his hands over the cup and pushed it to her lips. He said, "Oh, Angela, don't make me waste it. It's only vodka. A little vodka can't do anything to you."

By now, Angela felt dizzy and her hands were shaking. She felt lost, unable to move. She had spent a lifetime doing what she was told, to avoid being punished. Here was Michael upset with her because she didn't want the drink he had made for her. She thought to herself, If he wants me to drink it, I'll drink it for him. After she drank most of the third cup, Michael went to put the container back. Her head was spinning and she began to feel really sick, like she was going to vomit. She tried to tell Michael that she was sick, but he didn't seem interested in how she was feeling.

Michael sat next to her and massaged her shoulder. She would never forget his pseudo-seductive voice. She hardly knew him, and here he was talking to her like he really cared for her. He kept telling her, "You need to relax. You are too tense. If you relax, you will feel better." She tried to get up but she was too weak and she fell back down.

Later she recalled what happened next. "He kept telling me I was too tense, that I had to relax. He started massaging my shoulder. I tried to get up, but I couldn't, I fell back. I was sick and he was telling me I was tense. Then he started to kiss me. He put me to lie on the sofa. I couldn't make a scene because of the people downstairs. When he started to kiss me, I did tell him no. I said, 'Michael, not now. If you want this some other time, it's all right, but not now.' "

She felt she had to say something like that. It was the only polite way to get out of the situation without making a scene. In her mind she knew there would never be another time.

But Michael didn't listen. He just kept going, doing dirty things. First he started with her neck, down her neck and everything, and then down her chest and everything else. . . .

She couldn't find the words to describe what the everything else was. She remembered that Michael reached under her shirt and started unhooking her bra. She was flooded with embarrassment. Why was he doing this? Michael was never interested in her and she was never interested in Michael. He pulled off her white shirt, over her head. It came off quickly, which was very unusual, he just took it off, and then he threw it down. He unhooked her bra and threw it across the room. And then, it really started . . .

It all happened in slow motion. Throughout she felt like she was at the bottom of a deep pit. Far, far away she heard Michael's voice and felt his movement. She tried to get up, to struggle with him. But she couldn't move. She couldn't see. Her head was spinning. She felt sick. She wanted to vomit. She blacked out and then came to, as if she were reaching up from a deep well. She would be conscious for a moment and then slip back into the well. She was terrified because she had no control over her neck or her body. She couldn't hold up her head. Her body slumped on the sofa.

She was able to remember only a part of what he did. The memory made her feel small, like a hurt child. Whenever she thought about it a terrible sense of guilt tugged at her. What had she done in life to deserve this? How could she be so stupid as to get into a situation like this? She asked herself these questions a million times. The only control she had over what happened was to blame herself. If she blamed herself, then she could ask God's forgiveness.

But how could she blame herself? It wasn't her whom God had to forgive, it was Michael.

She remembered that he started with her chest and everything else with his mouth and all of that . . .

Her breasts . . .

With his hands, his face or whatever . . .

And then he started to pull down her pants.

And his hands were all over her. She struggled with him, trying to get up, but couldn't. She blanked out. Michael kept saying the same thing: "You're fighting too much. You're not relaxed, you're too tense."

But she wasn't *tense, she told herself. She just wanted to go home. But she passed out again. When she woke Michael wasn't dressed. And then he stood up and started putting something in her mouth . . . it was his penis. He sat down and put her head on his lap. Again he put his penis in her mouth. She tried to lift her head, but it fell back in his lap. He put his penis back in her mouth.*

She heard him speaking to her, ordering her. His words weren't loving, or even sexual. The tone was aggressive, angry, demeaning. He said, "Go ahead and suck that white cock."

She passed out again. When she came to, Michael was sitting next to her. His hands were still going everywhere, all over her breasts. He said something like "Open your legs." She remembered that he was touching her with his hand below her waist.

Each time she came to it was the same. She kept asking him to stop, but it was useless. He never answered her. They struggled. He told her she was fighting too much, she was too tense. He didn't seem to understand that she was struggling against him. It finally ended when she heard someone say something about a phone call. Maybe it was Michael who said, "I have a phone call. I have to go." She hadn't heard the phone ring and there were two phones in the room.

She felt very weak, unable to move. She thought to herself, When I feel better, I'm going to get up and get dressed. I won't bother with the ride, I'll just find my way home. But she wasn't able to move. She lay there waiting for Michael to leave. She was exposed from the waist up. When he left she thought it was all over.

As she was lying on the couch alone, Angela felt a hand on her back and someone said, "Are you all right?" It was Walter. She thought he asked how she was because he was concerned. To get rid of him, she said she was fine. She didn't want anyone's help. She didn't want to admit what Michael had done. She only wanted to sleep and forget. When she woke up, she would go home. So she told him she was fine, thinking that he would leave her alone if she said she was okay. She had no idea that he had been watching all along and was there now to take his turn.

What happened after Michael left was a blur. Angela was unconscious through most of it. It started with Walter. He put her head on his lap and his hands on her breasts. She passed out. When she woke, it seemed as if there were five or more boys in the room. There was a guy sitting on the chair in front of the sofa and another sitting on the bed that she had been told was Michael's bed. These two were just watching. Andrew was to her right and the guy in the white T-shirt was to her left. They hit their penises against her face. Walter put his penis in her mouth. When she gagged on Walter's penis, she heard him say, "Do it, choke on it." She heard someone say, "She is dead. She is not doing anything for me. I have to get a hard-on."

They had propped her up to a sitting position, but her head wouldn't stay up. Walter held her cheeks to force her mouth open so his friends could put their penises in her mouth. She tried to get up several times. Once her nails scratched Walter. He slapped her hands. She passed out again. When she came to, she screamed. Walter ordered her to stop, telling her it was a residential neighborhood and she might alarm the neighbors. When Walter put his hand on her neck, she felt that she had to be careful not to upset him. She didn't know what he might do to her. Dazed, she fell back on the couch. One of the guys in the room left and she heard someone say, "Her pupils are dilated. She doesn't know what's going on."

She passed out again, and when she woke her vision was blurry. It seemed like the room was shaking. There were people wearing masks. One of the masked figures really scared her. The eyes behind the mask were bulging out and she couldn't understand how these could be human eyes. There was another figure wearing a Lone Ranger mask, which covered half his face. She thought the person wearing this mask was either Tommy or the guy in the white T-shirt. Walter was wearing the mask with the bulging eyes.

There were three people in the room at the time. She knew that two of them were Walter and Andrew. She was not sure about the identity of the third. Walter ejaculated in her mouth, but it dribbled out of her mouth onto the sofa. Andrew and the other boy ejaculated on her chest. Someone in the room told Walter to slap her. She vaguely heard someone telling Walter to fuck her up the ass. She tried to get up, but was unable to because Walter pinned her to the sofa with his hand and knee.

Finally, it ended when Walter told the guy in the white T-shirt to get her dressed so that they could take her to a party at the Nugget. This guy stood her up to dress her, but she fell to the floor. He propped her up to get her shirt on, managing only to get it on backward.

Once she was dressed, Andrew and someone else carried her outside and put her in the backseat of a car. She was unable to sit up. Walter, Andrew, and the third person rode in the front seat. Walter was still wearing the mask with the funny eyes. On the way to the Nugget, she remembered that she almost vomited when she started to cough. She thought she heard Walter tell the driver, "If she vomits in my car I'll kill her." She passed out.

Angela was semiconscious when Walter pulled her out of the backseat of the car and carried her bodily into the Nugget, where another party was just about to begin.

INTRODUCTION

WHEN ANGELA WENT TO THE TRUMP WITH MICHAEL ON THE NIGHT OF March 1, 1990, got drunk, and passed out, she was caught up by the cult of male sexual license that ruled life at the house. The boys saw nothing wrong in what they did to Angela. It was part of being wild at college—get girls in for a party, get them drunk, and go for it. Consent was determined by a girl's coming to the house. Getting her drunk was part of the seduction. The sex capped the conquest. For the boys at the Trump, the night with Angela was just another one of the party games they often played together.

The libertine excess of their games and the religiously inspired restraint of Angela's innocence and naïveté are archetypically American. From the time that the colonists landed in Virginia and in Massachusetts, the divided nature of the American sexual culture was evident. We inherited sexual restraint from our Puritan heritage and sexual license from the Faustian exhilaration with freedom characteristic of the frontier. From the birth of the nation on, it was common for aristocrats, rakes, rogues, and Indian fighters to treat certain classes of women as sexual toys and property. Yet, these same men expected to marry women who exemplified the cultural ideal of passionlessness that marked the morally superior woman.

The polarization of the American sexual culture is reflected not only in the sexual behavior that took place at the Trump but in the subsequent reactions to that behavior in the courtroom and in the media. What the Trump boys treated as fun and games sent Angela into a downward spiral of despair and progressive emotional deterioration. To redeem her self-esteem Angela sought vindication by going to the police. According to the New York State penal code, a sex offense is defined as lack of consent because of "forcible compulsion" or "incapacity to consent" due to such factors as physical helplessness caused by alcohol or drugs, for example. The investigation determined that Angela was unable to consent at times because of physical helplessness and at other times because of forcible compulsion and unlawful imprisonment. Six male students were indicted on charges ranging from unlawful imprisonment and sexual abuse to sodomy. A seventh defendant pleaded guilty and agreed to testify for immunity.

Disgust, ambivalence, and disbelief characterized the public reaction to the St. John's case from the moment Angela's charges were made public by the press. Opinion was divided as to whether the sexual behavior should be classified as seduction, exploitative sex, a bad night, or rape. The conflicting voices heard during the two trials—those of the judge, jurors, defense lawyers, prosecutors, courtroom observers, defendants, St. John's students, and reporters—rose like a Tower of Babel in modern America. The public's response was split between those who thought a crime had been committed and those who blamed Angela for going to the house and taking the drinks.

In acquaintance rape cases, this divided response is a recurring theme, and to attempt to understand it is the subject matter of this book. When caught up in the immediacy of stories like Angela's, many of us side with the emotional trauma of the complainant; yet as the sordid story of Angela's night at the Trump spun out in the courtroom before the parents of the defendants, one cannot help but also identify with their obvious suffering. In order to take an intelligent stand on the current "date rape" controversy, it is important to step back and try to gain a broad historical perspective of the American sexual culture.

Informed by my experience as a cultural anthropologist, this book is an attempt to bring this perspective to our understanding of acquaintance rape by examining the sexual culture that victimizes women and seduces males with its addictive power. By acquaintance rape I mean sexual activity that meets the legal definition of rape, and involves people who first meet in a social setting, a scenario that the woman would have no reason to think might lead to acts of forced sex. This definition is broad in including dates as well as casual acquaintances. However, it excludes relatives and spouses, topics deserving separate treatment.

What follows is primarily a study of the popular ideas and legal history shaping the way we treat women and sex, with particular focus on acquaintance rape. Because the judicial response to acquaintance rape is as relevant as popular opinion in shaping the American sexual culture, the way justice has been historically meted out in the American courtroom and the degree to which it serves both sides or is biased toward one provide an important piece of the overall puzzle.

I journey through the centuries to look at the origin of the American legal tradition with respect to rape and ask why sympathy for the defendant so often rules America's response to acquaintance rape. With the exception of earliest Colonial times, rape has been a crime notable for placing the complainant on trial. To explain this response, I examine the legal and social subordination of women as well as attitudes regarding female sexuality. The female sex drive has had a peculiar trajectory, recognized as relatively equal to the male drive early in our history, then denied certain women in the nineteenth century while assumed to be natural to others, after which it was returned in the twentieth—but only under certain conditions. The relationship between the checkered history of the female sex drive and courtroom outcomes in cases of acquaintance rape is part of the focus of this book.

Broad as my reach may be, it cannot pretend to be an exhaustive history of acquaintance rape; that would take an even broader palette, one that probes the political, economic, and technological changes (among others) that also have a bearing on how we deal with sex. While I allude to various factors that have shaped America's response to rape, I am mostly concerned with clarifying the relationship between legal practice and popular sexual attitudes, and with showing that with respect to sex crimes, we have not abided by our constitutional commitment to equal justice for all. In my opinion, the principle of equal justice for both sexes must be inserted into the heart of the current national debate over date rape, just as equal rights is at the heart of the woman's movement.

ACQUAINTANCE RAPE AND THE HISTORY
OF AMERICAN SEXUALITY

The phrase "acquaintance rape" was coined in the 1970s to distinguish forced, nonconsensual sex involving people who know one another from rape involving strangers. The distinction, however, was evident as far back as the early fifties and grew out of the concern with sexual psychopaths in the 1930s. Before that the distinction between stranger and acquaintance played a minor role in rape trials.

In the 1970s, rape allegations involving strangers were the most likely to win a conviction, for reasons to be discussed. However, surveys showed that most incidents of forced, nonconsensual sex involved acquaintances. Today, most women don't report acquaintance rape to the police, fearing that there is not enough evidence or that no one will believe them. The farther one goes back in time, however, the more likely one is to find that the majority of rape cases have involved acquaintances for the simple reason that more people knew one another in the smaller, less anonymous communities of the past.

The American historical response to acquaintance rape can be partitioned into four general periods. The first period—that of Colonial New

England—was the most rape free. A woman's no meant something in Puritan New England. Interestingly, given our current way of thinking about "puritanism," it was a time when males and females were thought to have the same sexual appetite, and sexual desire was conceived of as explosive and in need of a vent for both sexes. It is true that the laws of the colonies kept passion in check, forbidding "fornication" outside of marriage, but within marriage sexual passion was encouraged. A woman married to an impotent husband could sue for divorce on those grounds alone. If a woman was raped, community officials tended to side with her because of the belief that a woman would have no reason to lie. If she said no, a man was more likely to desist from making sexual advances.

The nineteenth century saw the flowering of the cult of "true womanhood" and a radical change in the conception of female sexuality. At a time when licentiousness in the cities was well known and poor women often turned to prostitution as their only source of income, chastity became the dominant symbol of a polite, refined America. True womanhood gave women of means moral superiority but, as we shall see, its definition robbed them of the right to a sexual appetite. Wielding new power and influence, some of these women reached beyond the feminine sphere of the home and entered the arena of public debate, where they took up abolition, temperance, and social purity as causes and founded the women's rights movement.

As much as the ideology of this period extolled the moral superiority of righteous women, the growing importance of the culture of pornography and prostitution deepened belief in the inherent lustfulness of men and their female companions in the bawdy houses of the times. If a woman was raped, her past was carefully examined for evidence of prior lustful acts on the grounds that once "fallen," a woman was always ready for sex. The complainant's credibility might also be impeached by the suggestion that she was a false accuser, a scorned or vindictive woman. The tenacity of these suspicions is seen in the expectation for more than a century that complainants provide evidence of having resisted to the utmost.

The third period, which began in the early twentieth century, was in large part a reaction to the sexual restraints on proper women of the previous, Victorian era. Basing his position on Darwinian thought, male sexual aggression was glorified as a biological, evolutionary necessity by Havelock Ellis, one of the founders of modern sexology. The female sex drive was defined as inherently passive but responsive to forceful male seduction—even rape. Freud defined the sex instinct as a basic biological drive, which in its active form was masculine and in its passive form was feminine. This way of thinking returned the sex drive to women, with the restriction that the proper female was to be a sexually passive, though willing, recipient of male passion. This new version of the true woman still had to say no when she meant yes, not because of moral superiority but in obedience to her alleged biological desire to be dominated. Under her demur demeanor, however, Freud assumed that the raging fires of desire still lurked in the female breast, giving her an overactive sexual imagination that sometimes led to false accusations of rape.

In the courtroom, the concept of the false accuser was first introduced by English judge Sir Matthew Hale in the seventeenth century. His belief in the likelihood that most rape complainants were false accusers was redefined in twentieth-century psychoanalytic jargon. At midcentury, the noted jurist John Henry Wigmore cautioned the legal establishment to beware of the female hysteric and the pathological liar and advised that all rape complainants be examined by a psychiatrist for nefarious complexes of a Freudian nature.

Investigation of the sexual ideology associated with these three periods shows the cumulative impact of historical attitudes on modern myths of male and female sexuality. For instance, today's understanding that no means yes can be traced back to the nineteenth-century cult of true womanhood and to the Freudian concept of female sexual passivity in the twentieth. To preserve her reputation, a woman still has to say no so that a man can take pride in his seduction and assure himself that she is not "loose." Turning a no into a yes by getting a girl drunk or through aggressive seduction continues as a common practice on college campuses, as Angela's night at the Trump illustrates.

Today's blame-the-victim attitude derives from the twin notions that women are sexually stimulated by force and that male sexual aggression is primarily biological. The assumption that "she wanted it" reflects early notions of female sexual voracity dating from the seventeenth century. The Rhett Butler-Scarlett O'Hara scenario suggesting that women harbor a secret desire to be raped derives from Havelock Ellis's proposition that women and men are sexually stimulated by force. The biological argument put forth most recently in Camille Paglia's assertion that hormones rule male sexual behavior dates from Ellis also. Since a man can't help himself, she holds, it's up to the woman to look out for herself. The implication is that women who are in the wrong place at the wrong time have it coming.

The fourth and most recent phase in the history of American sexuality developed in reaction to the increasing rape rates that began after the sexual revolution of the 1920s and soared during the sexual revolution of the 1960s. This period was a watershed in the history of American sexuality because, for the first time, the proportion of young women engaging in premarital sex went from a minority to a majority. Although the women of the sixties were having sex in greater numbers, they were not seen as equal sexual partners with the enforceable right to say no. The revolution freed them to have sex, but only on male terms.

The feminism of the 1960s, a rebirth of the women's rights movement of the nineteenth and early twentieth centuries, sought to return passion to women on a par with men. The role of the clitoris, well known, as we shall see, in seventeenth-century sexual culture, was rediscovered, and women rejected Ellis's and Freud's belief that female passion needed to be passive to spark the fire of male lust. Women lobbied to reform rape laws that had remained on the books since the seventeenth and eighteenth centuries. For example, in many states the death penalty for rape persisted up to the 1960s, making convictions highly unlikely. Another holdover from the seventeenth century, abolished in the 1970s, was the practice of reading to the jury the cautions of Sir Matthew Hale. By giving semi-legal status to the fear of the false accuser, Hale's instructions to the jury created a pro-defense bias.

The innovation introduced by feminism to the American sexual culture was female sexual choice. The basic proposition was that a no means no and "earnest," "sufficient," or "utmost" resistance shouldn't be necessary to indicate nonconsent. The legal reform was an attempt to equalize rape trials so that fear of false accusers and examining a woman's reputation would no longer play a decisive role. Although articulated in the 1970s, these ideas only began to reach the American public in the 1990s. The media attention given to the St. John's sex case, as reporters called it, helped bring this message to the general public, as did other high-profile cases of the times.

As the first St. John's trial went into jury selection in May 1991, William Kennedy Smith was arrested in Palm Beach, Florida, and charged by Patricia Bowman with sexual battery. During the St. John's trial, Mike Tyson, the boxer, was accused of raping Desiree Washington in Indianapolis. That same fall, Anita Hill testified before the Senate Judiciary Committee. The common denominator for Anita Hill, Angela, Desiree Washington, and Patricia Bowman was the degree to which sexual stereotypes permeated the proceedings. All were labeled scorned women. The venerable phrase "Hell hath no fury like a woman scorned" played a prominent role both in the jury debate over whether Angela was telling the truth and in the Senate debate over the veracity of Anita Hill's charges against Clarence Thomas. This phrase, misquoted from a seventeenth-century play by William Congreve, comes from the same century in which Matthew Hale expressed his fear of women accusers. It seems that the intervening centuries have not dealt a more nuanced understanding of women's motivations in accusing a man of sexual transgressions. The outcome of the Mike Tyson case was reminiscent of still another common pattern: only certain kinds of men are likely to be convicted in acquaintance rape cases.

As a group, the cases of the early 1990s teach us a great deal both about America's response to acquaintance rape and contemporary notions of female sexuality. I begin with the St. John's trial because more than the others it combines all the elements of our nation's highly conflicted ideas about sex rights for women, including the role played by race and class. Despite the rape law reform of the 1970s, Matthew Hale played an unseen but determinative role as the St. John's case unfolded in the courtroom. Though never read verbatim, Hale's cautions were present in the opening and closing statements of the defense lawyers.

To illustrate how little has changed during the course of history, I compare the outcome of the St. John's trial with that of a famous case tried in the early seventeenth century. The complainant in this case was Margery Evans, an illiterate fourteen-year-old serving girl who pressed charges against the men who raped and abducted her in 1631. Like Angela, Margery Evans struggled against enormous odds to seek vindication and punish the men who violated her. At every step of the way, she experienced setbacks, including being thrown in jail after pressing charges. She, too, was blamed for being where she was late at night. And, like Desiree Washington, Anita Hill, and Patricia Bowman, it was implied that she was a scorned woman; she brought charges in retaliation for being seduced and then casually dropped.

Separated by more than three centuries, these cases and others like them open a window on the past, providing a vision of the problems, the possibilities, and the hopes we inherited when the American colonies adapted English rape law to their own. By examining the continuity as well as the change in the American response to rape, my goal is to move modern discourse from fruitless debates over restraint versus freedom and the assumed "naturalness" of male sexual aggression to the subject of the "rightfulness" of female sexual choice.

My approach does not deny the biological component in sexual desire;

in fact, I look to the nexus between social relations and biology to under-stand rape in human society. All human societies have found it necessary to constrain, shape, and channel the sex drive due to two major biological facts. The first is the lack of estrus, the biological property of other mammalian females of coming into "heat." Estrus is the biological ex-pression of readiness for sexual union. When the female is "in heat," all systems are go for both sexes, and rape is an impossibility.

The second biological fact unique to humans is the long period of parent-child bonding necessary for the human infant to survive. If men used their greater physical strength to exploit the continuous receptivity of women at will, social relations necessary for nurturing and educating children, providing shelter for the mother-child bond, and transmitting culture from one generation to the next would break down in the interest of self-gratification. Social relations transmitted from one generation to the next and symbolic templates governing sexual behavior are as impor-tant to human social survival as the operation of genetic templates are to the survival of other animal species. Thus, all known human societies have been observed as recognizing rules regarding appropriate sexual practices.

The same is true with desire. While we can say that desire resides in the body, the expression of desire—its intensity, its focus on self-gratifi-cation or upon mutual pleasure and consent, and a host of additional factors—is determined largely by nonbiological factors, namely culture and the social relationship between the sexes. If biology constituted both the necessary and sufficient conditions for human sexuality, we would do it as other animal species do—quickly and seasonally. We would not display the polymorphous capability of being sexual in our thousand different ways.

All the evidence gathered by nearly a century of anthropological field-work demonstrates variability, not homogeneity, in the way humans have found to channel the sex drive. In a study of 95 band and tribal societies, I found that 47 percent were what I called "rape free," while only 18 percent were "rape prone." By rape free I do not mean that there is no rape, only that there is very little. Comparing the position of women in rape-free as opposed to rape-prone societies, I found significant differences. There was more violence in the rape-prone societies, more emphasis on male toughness and competition, and a low respect for women as citizens. In the rape-free societies, on the other hand, both sexes held exalted positions in public decision-making and both were integrated and equal in the affairs of everyday life.

Differences between rape-prone and rape-free societies are the products of cultural selection, not biology. It is the task of the anthropologist to describe these differences and place them within the larger historical and cultural framework of the society being studied. We must look at the historical attitudes that shape the expression of male and female sexuality over time. The analysis that follows of the different periods of thought and behavior shaping the American response to acquaintance rape is directed to this task.

My research and that of psychologists and sociologists demonstrate that human sexual behavior cannot be divorced from the larger system of beliefs, values, and attitudes—what I call the sexual culture—that I suggest motivates our response to rape in the courtroom. As Susan Brownmiller shows in her landmark study, *Against Our Will,* sexual behavior cannot be separated from male dominance and the American culture of violence. The backlash discernible in response to each gain of greater sexual autonomy by women during the course of American history demonstrates that males have enforced dominance through increasingly aggressive definitions of male sexuality. To maintain a belief in the exclusively biological (or natural) determinism of sexual behavior, against which society or the law is powerless, is itself part of the politics of male sexual dominance.

I ask how we as a society can give women the enforceable right to sexual self-determination, and thereby give them the status of more equal citizenship. From the documentation of the roadblocks and the successes women have experienced in the courtroom, I hope a picture will emerge of how complainant and defendant can achieve justice in acquaintance rape, for it is only through the fair application of justice that women can hope to find autonomy. When we examine the outcome of Angela's ordeal in the courtroom, it will become clear that changing attitudes is one of the answers. A reconsideration of the legal definition of consent is another. I do not claim to have all the answers, but I do hope to provide many of the right questions.

ONE

THE ST. JOHN'S CASE GOES TO TRIAL

ACQUAINTANCE RAPE RESEARCHERS FIND THAT MOST VICTIMS ARE NOT PRONE to report forced sex, but would like to see their assailants punished. At the least, they would like their assailants to realize that what they did was wrong, so that the behavior won't be repeated with others.[1] At first, Angela had no intention of going to the police. She was sure that if she told anyone what happened they wouldn't believe her. The boys indicated as much. Before taking her home early Friday morning, she overheard one of them telling the others, "Remember Tawana Brawley? No one believed her. So what if she says something, no one will believe her." In the car on the way to her house they grilled her with their version of the story. She went to the Trump, got drunk, and passed out. Nothing else happened.[2]

After a sleepless night of going over and over in her mind what had happened and blaming herself, Angela decided to see her most trusted school advisor, a nun who reminded her of the nuns in Jamaica. Not finding Sister Faith in, Angela told a school friend the whole story. The friend suggested she go to the police, but Angela could think only of getting the school to punish the boys—kick them off the lacrosse team or something like that.

When Angela saw Sister Faith the first thing Monday morning, she pleaded with her to do something. But Sister Faith was unable to help. She was critical of Angela for accepting the drink and told her that there was nothing the school could do because it happened off campus. The sum total of Sister Faith's advice, according to Angela, was the suggestion that she see a counselor and confront Michael to ask him why he did it.

Believing that she had no other recourse, Angela called Michael. After many tries she finally succeeded in getting him to the phone when she used another name. He denied everything, claiming that he had done nothing wrong. According to Michael, Angela had started the whole thing. She was coming on to him and the rifle team coach. At the Trump, she asked him for a drink and this meant she wanted sex. "Angela," he said, "I didn't put a gun to your head and make you drink. You were the one who came to the house and wanted something to drink." When she got drunk, he said, she fell all over him.

Seeing Angela's progressive deterioration, her friends from the Caribbean Club at school took her to the office of the dean of students. When he heard Angela's story, Jose Rodriguez started an investigation and advised Angela to go to the police. She decided to take this step only after it became clear that the boys would not cooperate with the school's investigation.

Despite all the pulls to the contrary—Sister Faith's lectures, the rifle team coach's indifference when she went to see him, Michael's refusal to confront her accusations—Angela could not shake her sense of having been wronged. Due to her religious background and its emphasis on forgiveness, if the boys had confessed, she would have forgiven them. If Michael had agreed to see her as she asked, it is unlikely that she would have gone to the school administration. Had the school investigation succeeded, she most assuredly would have let the matter drop. But the boys continued to avoid facing up to what had happened. They came to see Jose Rodriguez once and cancelled their next appointment. If she wanted some sort of vindication, going to the police was her only remaining option.

THE POLICE INVESTIGATION

At approximately two o'clock in the afternoon of March 30, Detective Vito Navarra was beeped by his commanding officer, Lieutenant Stanley Carpenter. His partner, Matthew Fogarty, returned the call, and the detectives were instructed to go to the St. John's University student affairs building. They arrived in Dean Rodriguez's office soon after and took Angela back to the precinct for questioning.

Fogarty and Navarra were long-time veterans of the New York City Police Department. Fogarty had worked on special assignment in the Queens Sex Crimes Squad for six years and Navarra for nine years. As members of the squad, their job was to investigate all sex offense felonies, namely, first-degree rape, sodomy, sex abuse, and abuse of children under the age of eleven. Fogarty and Navarra had interviewed thousands of women and kids over the years. From these years of experience, Fogarty felt he had developed a sixth sense about victims and knew, usually immediately, when someone was lying or telling only part of the story. He estimated that about 20 percent of adult complainants were false accusers. (However, studies show that the actual frequency of false rape reports is much smaller, about 2 percent, the same number of false reports as those of other crimes.[3])

When Fogarty first met Angela at St. John's, he thought she was fifteen years old. She was polite, but very withdrawn and hostile. After hearing her story, however, Fogarty felt a great deal of compassion for her. He concluded that she was sexually immature and trusted Michael too readily. "You couldn't pay her to lie," he said after talking to Angela many times.

When Navarra heard the details of Angela's story from Fogarty, he was skeptical. It was too outlandish, it didn't sound right. How could St. John's students be involved in such behavior? he wondered. His superiors were telling them to be sure this was not another Tawana Brawley case.

"Make sure this is not a pack of lies," the detectives were told. "We don't want a body crawling out of a bag."

In time, however, as all the details of her story checked out, Navarra came to believe her completely. Michael's account of what had happened corroborated Angela's story in part. Michael admitted that he gave Angela three drinks. He described Angela as becoming like a "rag doll," which fit Angela's claim that she had passed out. Michael's admission that Angela didn't know her address or where she lived at the end of the evening was also consistent with Angela's story.

Walter's version of what had happened was slightly different. Walter said that after Michael gave Angela the drinks, she freaked out and started screaming and yelling. He claimed that Angela was on drugs. He also said they never took her out of the house.

Several events helped break the case. A search warrant of the Trump yielded a mask, like the one Angela described as having been worn at the Trump and when she was taken to the Nugget. Lab tests of the couch in Michael's room showed positive presence of spermatozoa at the place on the cushion where Angela's head would have been. The big break in the case came when Todd M., who had been identified through the lacrosse team photograph by Angela, admitted that she had been brought to the Nugget. He described her as sick, drunk, and out of it, just as she had said. He, too, thought she was on drugs. The downside was Todd's tendency to protect his friends without outright lying. His story was full of exits and entrances. He described coming into the room, leaving, and then coming back. He saw and heard some things but not all. At the trial, Peter Reese, one of the prosecutors, called such lapses in memory and convenient absences "the anti-rat factor." It was a factor that plagued the case even as it broke it open.

The next big break came when Tommy admitted that he had driven Angela from the Trump to the Nugget. In exchange for immunity from prosecution, Tommy agreed to testify at the trial. His story was also full of exits and entrances. He was like a yo-yo, going up and down the steps to Michael's room at least four times to watch.

He said he watched Michael and Angela from the landing, along with Walter, Andrew, and Matthew. He described what happened after Michael left. His story implicated Walter, Andrew, and Matt in acts of sodomy and sexual abuse. He said he saw Andrew hitting the girl on the top of her forehead and on the left side of her face with his penis. This was an important detail because it corroborated Angela's description.

Tommy implicated himself and two others, Adam G. and Joe R. The three of them "touched the girl's breast," he said. Adam lived at the Trump and Joe at another lacrosse team house called the Jewel. Joe came with two of his roommates after receiving a telephone call from the Trump telling them to come over because they had a girl in the room.

Tommy confirmed what the investigators suspected. There had been a cover-up from the beginning. Walter had called a huddle of the lacrosse team in the middle of the field out of earshot of coaches or other school officials to tell everyone not to involve the people at the Nugget. The Nugget guys were told to tell anyone who asked that Angela had not been at the house.

In response to questions about alcohol and drugs, Tommy said that Popov vodka was occasionally kept at the Trump in one of the refrigerators, including the refrigerator in Michael's room. Tommy swore that no drugs were ever used in the house, including steroids. Only alcohol and maybe marijuana. Despite their suspicion that Angela's drink had been drugged, the investigators were never able to find evidence of drugs at the house.

Tommy talked about the attitude toward women at the Trump. His description of this attitude helped Reese put the events of March 1 in the larger perspective of a common sexual pattern. The guys went to bars and picked up women. When they got them home one guy would score and let the others look in on it. Watching was an important part of the sexual behavior. There were holes in one of the closet walls in a downstairs bedroom so the guys could watch without the girl knowing. If the upstairs room was used, they watched from the landing. If the basement was used, the guys had yet another place where they could watch without being detected. During the sex act, girls' bras were removed in order to add them to the house collection of bra trophies. If possible, photographs were also taken. Tommy talked about one picture showing two girls naked and retching in the bathroom. He also talked about a girl he knew who woke up at the house to find someone masturbating on her.

Tommy's account of group sex at the Trump was confirmed by a number of women who called the DA's office after the story broke in *Newsday.* At least a half-dozen women called, and two came in for an interview. One woman said she met one of the defendants at a bar and went home with him. At the Trump she asked for something to eat. He refused to feed her, saying he wanted sex. She got angry and told him to forget it. He got aggressive. Another defendant "rescued" her and took her downstairs. They started necking and petting. She heard noises and asked what was going on. Nothing, she was told. After they went back to petting, some naked guys jumped out from behind a curtain and started to touch her. She fought them off and ran upstairs. When she tried to call a cab they pulled the phone line out of the wall socket. They finally yielded to her demand to leave and let her call a taxi.

Other women described getting sick and passing out after drinking at the house. Taking advantage of a drunk woman seemed to be an accepted part of the house sexual code. As Tommy talked about women getting drunk at the house, Reese remembered him saying that it was when Angela screamed that the people from the Jewel house left the room. Reese concluded that according to their code, it was okay to do what you wanted, or were told to do, to a drunk woman. It was not okay to do anything if a woman resisted. As long as Angela was drunk, whatever happened was within the code. The code did not include using force, at least in the minds of the people who left the room. Later, other eyewitness testimony would confirm Reese's theory.

Tommy minimized the seriousness of the sexual code involving drunk, sick women. Sure, he said, girls came to the house and got drunk. Yes, there were mistakes. Misunderstandings. But, he vowed, nothing like what happened on March 1 had happened before. He said this despite the incidents he himself had described of girls getting sick, vomiting and retching in the bathroom half-naked, or of girls waking up in the house to find someone masturbating on them.

The stories told by Todd and Tommy, along with the evidence collected at the Trump, resulted in indictments against six male students on offenses ranging from sodomy to sexual abuse. Two trials were scheduled. The defendants in the first trial were Walter G., Andrew D., and Matthew G. Michael C. was to have a separate trial, as were Adam G. and Joe R., who were charged with minor offenses. The week before the first trial opened, however, Joe R. pleaded guilty and agreed to give testimony on what he saw at the Trump.

THE PUBLIC RESPONSE

If Angela had been hit in the head by black teenagers wielding their penises in an alley or on a subway, the case would have been open and shut, a conviction virtually assured and public opinion 100 percent behind her. The many comparisons between the St. John's case and the 1989 Central Park jogger case showed that the public still thought that rape involved strangers. The jogger case was a classic jump-from-the-bushes, stranger-rape type case. The jogger was found, near death, in Central Park at one-thirty on the morning of April 20, 1989. Six black and Hispanic teenagers, some of whom had made videotaped statements concerning their roles in the attack, were charged with her assault and rape.

After the St. John's case broke in the news, it was inevitable that the two would be discussed on radio talk shows. Call-ins on one show angrily rejected any comparison between the plight of the jogger and that of alleged victims in the numerous cases of campus gang bangs reported in the 1980s. The jogger defendants were dismissed as marginal males, members of a "teen wolfpack," a "roving gang," "park marauders," and "thugs." Reporters were fascinated by the fact that they called what they did "wilding." People expressed fury over the life-threatening assault on the jogger. Although many thought that she should not have been running in the park alone at night, they did not blame her for the attack, while many blamed Angela for going to "an all-guy house."

Students at St. John's called it "sick" but "seeable." "Anyone can picture that happening," one student said. "She shouldn't have been where she was," another said. "It's just like walking down the street in the city by yourself. You know better than to go into a dark alley."[4] This attitude explains why out of more than one hundred cases of alleged campus gang bangs during the 1980s, only one ended with anyone going to jail. And that case involved lower-class black defendants on football scholarships.

The truly violent nature of the sex acts in the Central Park jogger case fit easily into the category of absolute evil. The sexual behavior confronting Angela, on the other hand, fell into the category of seduction. *The New York Times* reportage, for example, never described the sodomy acts as forced. In the courtroom, one of the court artists repeatedly expressed doubt that forced fellatio was even possible. Despite the graphic testimony heard from eyewitnesses of Angela being poked in the mouth or hit in the head by masturbating males, the reporter for the *Times* preferred to describe the sodomy acts in terms of Angela *giving* oral sex.[5]

Unlike the complainants in other high-profile sex cases, reporters did not dig into Angela's past and transform her overnight into an archetype. She was neither virgin nor vamp, heroine nor hussy. Perhaps because she was black and a student, as well as foreign born, she didn't stand for anything that touched the collective imagination of reporters. She didn't represent the youthful, striding energy of a young woman on the move—a symbol of the great and glittering metropolis—that reporters saw in the Central Park jogger. Nor was she symbolically infused by the press, as were Patricia Bowman and Jennifer Levin (victim in the "Preppy Murder" case), with the aggressive sexual energy of a woman at the forefront of the sexual revolution. Perhaps because they didn't understand her path in life, or how it was thwarted by the events on March 1, the press left

Angela alone. In the early history of the case, Angela was seen only through the eyes of Walter's lawyer, Stephen Scaring, who was masterful at shifting jury sympathy from the complainant to the defendants.

Studies show that jurors are affected by class and racial bias. Jurors assume that males who look like college boys are not capable of rape.[6] They are even less likely to believe the complainant if she is black. "Negroes have a way of not telling the truth," a juror quoted by Gary LaFree in his study on rape trials said. "They've a knack for coloring the story. So you know you can't believe everything they say." In the case of black victims, jurors are also more ready to assume that they probably consented to sex or are more sexually experienced and hence less harmed.[7]

After the indictment, Stephen Scaring described Walter as a middle-class college student with an "impeccable record." "He was on the scholastic honor role," he told reporters.[8] When reporters learned that Walter and three of the defendants had grown up together in the same hometown, they interviewed their friends and teachers, who described them as the "fabulous four," who shared a "stand-by-me friendship" since childhood. Their high school lacrosse coach called them sons of "hardworking," "blue-collar" parents, boys who "led by example," "leaders on the field and off." They were the kind of kids "you would want your daughter to go out with," he concluded.[9]

About Angela's allegations, Scaring told the press, "It's not unusual for a young woman to make such an accusation and juice it up."[10] Scaring's suggestion that Angela was "juicing up" her story raised the specter of Tawana Brawley, yet another black woman coloring the truth. He also questioned why it took Angela one month to go to the police. "If this was such a horror story as she described it," Scaring told the Daily News, "it is difficult to believe the accusations would not have been made earlier."[11]

Scaring struck several times at the fear of false accusations. While the jury was deliberating, he gave an interview to Newsday pointing out that there was a high percentage of acquittals in rape cases. This, he said, was evidence that too many cases which didn't merit prosecution were being brought to court. Men accused of rape are victimized by scheming females who manage "to manipulate and control the entire criminal justice system," he claimed ominously.[12]

THE FIRST TRIAL

The first trial opened on May 28, 1991, the beginning of a long, hot New York summer. Court artists sat in the first row with their large sketching pads spread on their laps. News reporters from the Associated Press, the *Daily News, The New York Times,* and *Newsday* sat in the section reserved for reporters. Outside the courtroom, news photographers and TV cameramen waited for a sight of the defendants and an interview with the defense lawyers. The defendants in this trial were Walter G., Andrew D., and Matthew G., the guy in the white T-shirt Angela remembered meeting at the Trump.

The trial was held in the Long Island City courtroom of Queens County instead of the usual Kew Gardens or Jamaica courthouses, where most criminal trials in Queens take place. It seemed that all embarrassing cases involving white defendants ended up in Long Island City. However, the trial was probably moved to Long Island City in the event it turned into a racial case. If that happened, demonstrations would be easier to control and less likely to get out of hand. Being a bleak area of factories, warehouses, auto repair shops, and rail yards, there was no neighboring black community to swell the crowds that might be attracted by the trial.

One's first impression of Long Island City is of utter drabness. Getting off the subway from Manhattan after tunneling under the East River, one finds two buildings to provide aesthetic relief. Facing each other in the shadow of the Queensboro Bridge is the stately, historic courthouse and the modern Citicorp building across the street from it. The two buildings bridge the centuries: one reaching to life in the twenty-first century and the other facing backward in time to the nineteenth century, when the Queens county seat was moved to Long Island City.

A small park sets the squat, red-brick, four-story courthouse off somewhat, giving the viewer a chance to sit on one of the several benches and contemplate the courthouse, first built in 1876 and declared a Queens landmark in 1976. The park also provided a good vantage point for observing the lunchtime activities of the jurors during the long, hot days of the trial.

One of the most famous trials that took place in the courthouse during the first half of the twentieth century was the murder trial of Ruth Snyder and her lover, Henry Judd Gray, in 1927. Both were convicted for murdering her husband with a window-sash weight. She became the first woman to die in the electric chair and the first to have her picture taken in the process. A newspaper photographer got a picture of Ruth Snyder in the throes of death by strapping a concealed camera to his leg. Snyder's trial took place in the great, two-story trial room on the third floor, which is lighted in part by a splendid green stained-glass skylight that tops the recessed dome in the middle of the ceiling, reminding one of the time when the first courthouses in Queens doubled as churches.

The first St. John's trial was conducted in the same third-floor courtroom. Inside the room, one is immediately struck by its size and by the skylight. The observer section is more wide than long and stretches between two window-lined walls. At the center, separated from the observer section by a waist-high wood partition, is the jury box, two conference tables, a clerk's desk, and a judge's bench, which faces toward the entrance. On the wall above the bench, in letters that are slightly askew, are the words IN GOD WE TRUST.

On the opening day of the trial, the defense lawyers sat around the larger of the conference tables, with their clients facing the judge's bench. Stephen Scaring and his client Walter sat at one end of the table. Of all the defense lawyers, Scaring was the most experienced in defending against charges of rape. Lawrence Silverman, Andrew D.'s lawyer, sat at the other end of the table. He was second, so to speak, in terms of throwing his weight around in the courtroom. He was a Manhattan lawyer, but not as fashionable as Scaring. He let Scaring carry the ball in terms of the argument. However, he had his share of hits in what became a game of wearing down the judge. Matthew G. and his lawyer, Benedict Gullo, were in the middle of the table. Gullo was the most approachable. Short, handsome, and friendly with parents and observers, he was always willing to explain what was going on. Gullo often took something of a backseat. He had less to worry about because the evidence against his client was the weakest.

Sitting at the judge's bench was a little, soft-spoken lady who looked to be in her early sixties. Judge Joan O'Dwyer had been appointed to the bench in 1959 by Mayor Wagner. With her gentle ways and low voice, she was unable to maintain order during the increasingly raucous proceedings, made so by the daily demonstrations by black protestors, who flooded the courtroom. O'Dwyer had only one rule in her courtroom: no one was allowed to read the newspaper while she was on the bench. Otherwise, she seemed oblivious to the bizarre little scenes that developed before her as the trial progressed. The most appalling of these scenes unfolded as Scaring cross-examined Angela.

It is often said that the complaining witness in a rape trial relives the experience, not just in the retelling but in the way she is treated by the defense lawyers. Now, in the courtroom, just as one set of teammates had stood on the landing leading to Michael's room at the Trump watching the alleged sex acts on March 1, another set stood in the back of the courtroom to watch Scaring's cross-examination. Shoulder to shoulder, with arms folded and legs spread, four jocks positioned themselves directly in the line of Angela's vision. Whenever they saw an attractive young woman walk up one of the aisles, they smirked and nudged one another with their elbows. The noise from this part of the courtroom became particularly evident, turning many heads, when a short-skirted TV reporter leaned over in front of them to talk to a colleague.

When court officers took no action after the situation was reported to them, several young black men and one woman rose and stood on either side of the line of athletes. The stir of hostility that rippled through the courtroom eventually led the court officers to ask everyone to take their seats. However, very soon a new defensive line of mutually hostile black and white supporters would regroup in the same location. After the prosecutors, Peter Reese and Vincent Gentile, were alerted to the behavior, they asked Judge O'Dwyer to request that standing not be permitted in the courtroom on the grounds that it was not conducive to proper decorum. But, by the time the disturbance in the back of the courtroom finally ended, Scaring was well into his cross-examination of Angela.

During his cross-examination, Scaring put everything Angela had said or done under a microscope, looking for contradictions, inconsistencies, or anything else that might fit his characterization of her as a liar and a scorned woman. Bit by bit he wore her down. At first she tried to answer politely, then she got angry and confused because many of the questions seemed to have no bearing on the alleged sex acts. When Angela tried to explain why her statements appeared inconsistent or why she had used a false name in trying to reach Michael on the telephone, Scaring cut her off sharply. "I'm only concerned about whether or not you told a false story," he said coldly one of these times.

At one point, after Scaring quibbled over whether Angela had first identified Walter as the person who pulled her by the hair, she lashed out in utter frustration.

"I'm trying to tell you that your client Walter [G.], who is sitting over there looking like a saint, pulled me by my hair, picked me up by my hair," she said, nearly yelling.

"When you spoke to Dean [Corlisse] Thomas, you said 'they,' " Scaring replied.

More exasperated, Angela shot back, "Well, they did, too. You know, there's nothing here that I made up."

It was just what Scaring wanted to hear.

"I see," he replied meekly.

"This is getting too much for me," Angela continued.

Playing the gentleman, Scaring offered her a break.

"I don't want no break, Mr. Scaring. I can handle myself quite well," she said gamely.

As the cross-examination continued, dwelling on minor inconsistencies and repetitively drumming on certain points, Angela's mother yelled out from the audience, "Stop badgering her. She's suffered enough," at which point Scaring spun around and glared at the section in the courtroom where the voice had come from.

Emboldened perhaps by her mother, Angela gasped in desperation, "I'm not on trial.

"You know he is putting me on trial," she repeated, turning to the judge.

In his final summation Scaring repeatedly referred to Angela as aggressive as well as a liar and a scorned woman.

"Was she timid or aggressive?" he asked.

Referring to the testimony of rape-trauma expert Dr. Anne Burgess, he exclaimed, "Traumatized? Baloney! . . . Scorned? You bet!"

Driving his point home, he gave all the reasons why he concluded that she was "arrogant." "She fiddled with things on Rodriguez's desk. She rummaged in the refrigerator at the Trump. She called Michael. She made up a story about a death threat. She persistently questioned Collins," he said.

"Passive? Not likely!" he concluded.

To convict a defendant of rape in New York, the state has to show three elements: (1) that a sexual act occurred or was attempted; (2) the victim, if adult, did not consent either because of force, the threat of force, or because of physical helplessness or mental incapacity; and (3) the person charged has been correctly and properly identified.

The evidence for the sex acts was presented through Angela's testimony and that of Tommy, Joe R., and Joe's roommate, who went to the Trump with him but was not charged with any crimes. These witnesses described various sex acts ranging from sexual contact to sodomy. The testimony was graphic and sent a gasp through the courtroom, with the defendants at times blushing a beet red.

There were inconsistencies in the description of Angela's degree of nudity and in whether people saw Angela lying on the couch, sitting backward, or slumped forward. The prosecution explained the inconsistencies by noting that none of the witnesses saw everything that happened. Angela was in and out of consciousness and the males picked up different details. One of the defense lawyers suggested that perhaps they didn't see all that was happening because they were otherwise preoccupied. They weren't in the room to drink coffee and chitchat, he suggested. Although he didn't say so, he implied that they were there for sex—either to watch, masturbate, or participate.

Angela and these witnesses as well as Todd M. testified to her physical helplessness. Her condition was variously described as dizzy, nauseated, lightheaded, unable to lift her head, slumped over, unable to talk, and passing in and out of consciousness. Tommy testified that Angela had to be carried out of the room because she couldn't walk on her own, and others noted that her eyes were rolling back into her head. When Reese listed these symptoms for the benefit of Dr. Yale Caplan, an expert witness and chief toxicologist of the State of Maryland, he testified that such symptoms were compatible with "very acute, marked alcohol intoxication." Caplan estimated that the alcohol concentration was somewhere between .25 and .30, which creates a condition known as "alcoholic stupor."

THE JURY

The mainly white jury treated jury duty as party time from the beginning of the trial. At the lunch recess, groups would be seen drinking together. Judge O'Dwyer did not suggest a dress code, and the jurors often came dressed in shorts and T-shirts. One seasoned court observer commented that it was the sloppiest jury she had ever seen.

The pace of socializing among the jurors quickened as the trial wore on during the hot, steamy summer. They no longer hid their drinking, imbibing in the park or at nearby cafés. After lunch, the red face and glazed eyes of one juror explained his occasional nodding off in his seat. Michael Fahid, the foreman, drank from a bag in the park and sat bolt upright during the long afternoon sessions. One of the younger female jurors sprawled in her seat, face upright, contemplating the heavens through the stained-glass skylight. Leslie Burke, the one black female juror, celebrated her birthday in the jury room with a chocolate cake baked by juror Karen Lehr. On the day of the party, Judge O'Dwyer recessed early for lunch, telling the jury "to enjoy."

As Angela's supporters observed these activities, they grew progressively pessimistic. The cake was the last straw. "It's not a good sign," one man exclaimed. The more the jurors get chummy, he reasoned, the less likely they would be to disagree with one another when it came time to deliberate. Black observers concluded very quickly that the trial would end in a mockery of justice.

The Monday after the cake incident, Leslie Burke arrived in court wearing a T-shirt that proclaimed in bold letters: NO PLACE BUT TRUMP PLAZA. The court watchers were dumbfounded. Some hoped it was only a bad joke. Others were certain Burke was trying to send a signal to the defendants that she was on their side. The T-shirt messages got worse. During jury deliberations, juror Howard Stovall came to court dressed in shorts and a T-shirt that read UNBUTTON MY FLY. On the same day, another male juror wore the words of Bobby McFerrin's top-of-the-chart song of a few years back—DON'T WORRY, BE HAPPY.

THE VERDICT

Although the jury was out deliberating for six days, it turned out that they voted quickly to acquit by a margin of 10–2. They took six days to convince the one holdout, Theodore Lynch, the second black juror. Lynch argued for the conviction of Walter G. and Andrew D., though he was willing to go along with the acquittal of Matthew G. As soon as Lynch relented the jury voted to acquit on all charges, giving no consideration to the lesser charges. As Howard Stovall explained to Nicholas Varchaver, a reporter for *Manhattan Lawyer,* they decided that if she wasn't "forced or drunk," it was acquittal across the board. "It's either all or nothing," Stovall said.[13]

Speaking for the jury in general, Michael Fahid published a statement in the *Daily News* for which he was paid, claiming that the jury's decision was based primarily on lack of evidence and the twenty or so inconsistencies between "the girl's" testimony and that of witnesses.[14] The jury gave no credence to the chief prosecution witness corroborating Angela's testimony, Tommy, calling him a "complete liar." They dismissed the testimony of the other eyewitnesses on the grounds of "inconsistencies."

The jury listened to Joseph R.'s testimony on physical helplessness, but decided that he changed his testimony to please Reese. But Joe R. had never changed his testimony about Angela's physical helplessness, only that it could have been due to alcohol and not drugs, as he first testified. Fahid's reasoning in the *Daily News* article demonstrated that the jury was diverted by Scaring's courtroom tactics designed to suggest that Joe R. had changed his testimony on physical helplessness. Judge O'Dwyer did not give Reese the opportunity to question Joe so that he could clarify for the jury that he had not changed his observation that "she was out of it."

The jurors who talked with Varchaver explained their rationale for acquittal. Denise McDermott and Kathleen Finn said that Angela was too combative and angry on the witness stand. She wasn't "what we felt a victim should behave like." "The way she was described [by the prosecution], we expected to see this shy, withdrawn woman come in," McDermott told Varchaver.[15]

Kathleen Finn was suspicious because Angela didn't show the right emotions. "She tried to cry but she couldn't," Finn said. "She didn't shed one freaking tear up there. . . . I thought she was very arrogant. The first day she was there she did nothing but look at these guys and laugh like, 'Well, here we are.' " Finn indicated that she and other jurors felt no sympathy for Angela when she asked for a break. It was just a way to escape rough cross-examination, she told Varchaver. "One day we said, 'S———, three-thirty. It's time for her to bail out,'" Finn recalled.[16]

Finn was of two minds on guilt or innocence. Echoing the sentiment of several other jurors, she told Varchaver, "Something definitely happened in that house. But the way the law was given to us, it didn't add up to criminal behavior. They were a bunch of bastards, those kids. I really think they did it."[17]

Finn's theory was that Angela had a crush on Michael and later acquiesced to Walter's advances "to spite [Michael]," and then "found herself in a situation where," as Finn said, "it got out of hand." This was an entirely new take on the proceedings, one that was never mentioned during the trial.

Theodore Lynch described to me jury behavior that broke nearly all the rules. Sympathy for the defendants was expressed from the very beginning of the trial. Contrary to Judge O'Dwyer's daily instruction not to talk about the case, the jurors started discussing it from the beginning, expressing a fear of ruining the lives of the defendants. "They weren't concerned about justice," Lynch observed. "They were more concerned about making a mistake than about listening to the evidence and going by what the law says." "This was the big umbrella over all of their heads," Lynch said. "They didn't want to be guilty for putting the boys away for a long time."[18]

Denise McDermott became convinced that Angela was a woman scorned from the time Angela got on the witness stand, Lynch told me. Even before Angela took the stand, McDermott talked about how when women are hurt they will do anything to get revenge. Lynch remembered her saying, "When a woman is scorned she'll do anything for revenge. *Anything.*" McDermott's theory was similar to the one expressed by Finn. It was simple: Angela really wanted Michael. After he gave her the drink and she passed out, nothing happened between them. She got mad because Michael left her there so that the other boys could do whatever they wanted. She was scorned because she only wanted Michael, not the other boys. Angela was so hurt she brought the whole thing to court to get revenge.

Buying this theory, or perhaps contributing to it, one of the jurors, who wanted to be identified only as Juror No. 10, told *Newsday*, "What was that thing that Shakespeare said? 'Hell hath no fury like a woman scorned.' "[19]

McDermott based her theory of the scorned woman on Angela's "smirk" when she was on the witness stand, Lynch said. He remembered McDermott saying in the jury room, "Look, look at her. Is this the face of a woman who has endured such an ordeal with these guys?"

Lynch told me that his reaction to Angela's expression was quite different. Her face showed "she had the boys where she wanted them, where she could tell her side of the story and have people listen," he said. "She was staring at them in order to communicate to everyone that something happened and she was the victim in the crime." According to Lynch, however, Denise McDermott was so adamant in her belief that a woman who is hurt will do *anything* that all the jurors, especially the women, were infected by her certainty.

Lynch said that he argued vehemently with McDermott, going "head-to-head" with her in the jury room during their deliberation. "She wouldn't go this far to get revenge," he told McDermott. "Bring charges, come to court, get humiliated. I don't think she would do that. Maybe a woman will go the distance, but they're not going to go that far."

But McDermott only dug in further, telling him, "Ted, you're not a woman. You don't know."

The jurors did not buy Dr. Caplan's testimony because they were convinced that a person can't be in and out of consciousness when in a drunken stupor. Lynch tried to argue against this by saying that Angela was drugged. Howard Stovall agreed that it was possible to be in and out under the influence of drugs and alcohol. However, they couldn't consider this possibility, Stovall said, because "it wasn't brought into evidence."

Although he agreed it was possible, he told Lynch, "I don't want to judge these kids and ruin them."

Lynch also remembered Finn talking about how much the trial was costing the parents. Lynch noted that Finn seemed to know a great deal about the financial status of the parents. Once she told everybody that the parents had to take a second mortgage on their homes to pay their lawyers and one of them had to take out "a second mortgage on his boat." Lynch never found out where she got this information, but was amazed at the degree to which sympathy for the defendants and their families came into play during the deliberations.

When it was all over it left a bad taste in his mouth. According to Lynch, no one really understood the charges. Four people did most of the talking and arguing, he said. The others went along with Denise McDermott. Whatever she said was fine. When Finn and McDermott jumped on the one woman who agreed with him, she was so intimidated at being yelled at that she gave up immediately and didn't say a word after that. Lynch felt strongly that you can never get justice when so many jurors just go with the flow. A passive juror is a nonjuror.

"Even when people were outside in the street yelling, 'It's your sister, do the right thing, it's your people,' " he said, "you can't look at the color of people's skin. You gotta look at what's happening. You gotta be fair. If you cannot get people on a jury that are fair, you are never going to have justice," he concluded. "Never."

The evidence convinced Lynch the guys were "guilty as sin," yet the other jurors just didn't want to hear it and he was eventually silenced. A year later he felt guilty for not hanging the jury, but he also believed that hanging the jury would have been useless because the next jury would have been just the same. Thinking about the recently concluded trial of Rodney King, he said, "I understand why people in Los Angeles went crazy. I really do. You go to a trial, you can have a videotape, you can have pictures, you can have actual evidence, which says something happened, and people will shut their eyes."

AFTERMATH

Ted Lynch was not alone in his expression of outrage. New York's mayor, David Dinkins, said to *Newsday,* "I am shocked and dismayed by the jury's not-guilty verdict. Both the evidence reported and the statements attributed to the defendants were exceedingly disturbing."[20]

Charles Rangel, Democratic congressman from Manhattan, expressed the same view. "With the testimony being what it was, with the defense admitting what they did, with the victim being so vigorously cross-examined, it's just unbelievable how people could go into a room and acquit. Where the reasonable doubt is in it I don't know."[21]

In his column for *U.S. News & World Report,* John Leo declared the verdict "a total miscarriage of justice." Leo based his conclusion on the testimony of the eyewitnesses, the evidence of physical helplessness, and on the likelihood of consent. "How likely is it that a conservative, middle-class woman, virtually allergic to alcohol, disdainful of premarital sex and facing an important exam the next morning, would voluntarily get drunk and enjoy several hours of oral sex with five or six strangers?" he asked.[22]

Dr. Loretta Devoy, Angela's theology teacher, contributed the most telling comment with respect to the jury's motivation. She had watched Angela's progressive deterioration after the incident to the point where she had to leave school. The two had talked about the theological meaning of forgiveness, and Dr. Devoy had advised Angela to go to the police. She knew how important a conviction would be to Angela's recovery.

After the verdict Dr. Devoy called *Newsday* columnist Sheryl McCarthy to express her frustration. In her opinion the outcome was definitely racial, a possibility all the jurors but Ted Lynch vehemently denied.

"I believe it was a jury that simply didn't want to stop the 'running boys.' If they had been black boys, they would not have been considered to be running anywhere because they had no future. But these were white boys, so how can we stop them from running?"[23]

Race, however, was only partly the issue. We are a nation that thirsts for male heroes and thrives on warrior dreams, stories of daring escapades, and wild sexual adventure. More than a year after the St. John's case, members of a group called the Spur Posse received a hero's welcome when they returned to school after having been accused of molesting and raping girls as young as ten. Much later, the entire nation was brought momentarily to a halt as people watched the police chase O. J. Simpson up the Los Angeles thruway.

In exchange for their allegiance to living the myth, we give our heroes sexual entitlement and excuse them when they run afoul of the law. The expression of support for O. J. Simpson far outweighed the outrage over Nicole Simpson's brutal murder. The same was true in the St. John's jury room. Angela's trauma, the wrong she alleged had been done to her, never even entered the picture. The jurors argued for acquittal as if they were protecting their own kin, and believed that Angela's charges could be dismissed as those of a woman scorned.

But we are also a nation committed to an ideal of justice for all. Ted Lynch's outrage at what took place in the jury room demonstrated that a tiny flame of justice burned as vigorously as the desire to let the defendants off the hook. The divide between the voices that acquitted the St. John's defendants and those that saw a miscarriage of justice was not new. The debate goes back as far as seventeenth-century England, if not farther. The 1990s verdict can be compared with the outcome of the case of Margery Evans in 1631. Both cases displayed a struggle between the search for truth that represents justice on the one hand, and pro-defense leanings that have continued to characterize rape trials on the other.

TWO

BIRTH OF THE FALSE ACCUSER:

The Case of Margery Evans

MOST NOTEWORTHY IN THE CASES OF ANGELA AND MARGERY EVANS IS THE fact that the alleged assaults took place in a climate of male sexual license and entitlement. Both young women were out alone on a festival night—a time of sex play and rowdiness. For Margery Evans it was a Midsummer celebration in 1631; for Angela the occasion was the celebration of the lacrosse team's first win of the year in 1990. Both were accused of "asking for it"—Margery Evans for traveling alone in the forest, Angela for going to Michael's house and accepting a drink. Both were labeled scorned women and both had their defenders. On the eve of mass migration to the New World, the case of Margery Evans is intriguing for its preview both of the pro-defense bias in America's response to acquaintance rape and its adherence to the principle of equal justice.

In her petition bringing charges, Margery Evans explained that while traveling on foot at night near the Welsh border to attend a Midsummer celebration, she was overtaken by Philbert Burghill and John Williams, both of whom were on horseback. Burghill forced her to ride behind him. Twice she jumped to the ground and was forced back on the horse. The third time Burghill made Williams hold her, whereupon Burghill, in the words of her petition, "did there most inhumanlie and unchristeanly seize upon [her] and forceablie defloured and ravished her . . . and alsoe took awaie from her a bundle of Clothes, a purse and four shillings sixpence in money."[1] Afterward Burghill left Margery at the edge of a nearby village, vowing to kill her if she reported what happened.

Ignoring their threat, Margery pursued the men to another town and accused them of their crimes. For her efforts, she was thrown into jail. This, however, did not silence her. She appealed to King Charles I and her appeal was heard. The Earl of Bridgewater, Lord President of the Council in the Marches of Wales, a man with high ideals, was chosen to investigate the case.[2]

The Earl of Bridgewater was unusual in trying to develop and promote a standard of justice that would apply equally to all. His treatment of Margery Evans offers a paradigm for the equitable handling of rape cases in any century. He dispensed compassion to Margery Evans rather than judgment. He carefully ferreted out all the facts rather than give in to his associates' dismissal of Margery as seduced and abandoned. He refused to allow sympathy for Burghill to affect his investigation.

There had been no witnesses to the alleged rape and robbery except the accomplice. However, four men testified that they had heard Margery "howleinge and cryinge" as she ran in pursuit of the two men. One of these witnesses took her into the town and another detained the two suspects. One of them was present when she was roughly handled by the bailiff who threw her in jail. There were two depositions from women who visited Evans a few days after the alleged rape in the county jail. Both women judged that Evans, a virgin, had been "ravished," for they saw that the flesh about her "secrett partes" was "bruised and torne."[3]

The earl's main associate in the investigation of the case took the side of Burghill, saying that he was incapable of the crime of rape. In his opinion Margery Evans was a scorned woman. Like many others, he wondered why the young girl was out alone at night. He found it highly improbable that a rapist would carry his victim along with him for any distance. She must have been seduced and then abandoned, he concluded. Local officials sided with Burghill, perhaps out of fear that they would be charged with the false arrest of Margery Evans. The man who had arrested Margery was either Burghill's relative or very close friend. These officials told the earl that there was "much more clamour than truth" to Margery's charges.[4]

The earl, however, pursued his investigation. The more he investigated the more he found inconsistencies as well as strong evidence corroborating her story. For example, although some early witnesses changed their story, Margery Evans's sister testified that both Burghill and Williams had confessed the rape to her, wanting to make amends, which was the way assaults on young serving maids were usually handled.[5]

Finally, in 1634, the earl concluded that Margery Evans had been denied justice as a result of Burghill's influence and tampering with the evidence. Convinced that a rape had been committed, the earl reported the case for trial. The case was tried in the same town where Burghill had used his influence to get the case dismissed. The same combination of factors that acquitted the St. John's defendants acquitted Burghill—sympathy, inconsistencies in the evidence, and questioning the complainant's motivations.

After his acquittal Burghill harassed Margery Evans with a counter-suit, a move that Angela feared from the defendants acquitted in the St. John's case. The Earl of Bridgewater was able to squash Burghill's suit and bring the parties to the table to settle the matter. After this, there were no more petitions from Margery Evans. It is likely that in the end the earl managed to achieve some measure of justice for her. The earl also served notice on the officials in the area that in the future, they were to give the same consideration to girls like Margery as they would "their own cronies and kin."[6]

TWO APPROACHES TO JUSTICE IN RAPE ACCUSATIONS

The Earl of Bridgewater's handling of the case of Margery Evans demonstrates a judicial process that searches for the truth by weighing the evidence and trying to make sense of the inconsistencies without regard to the status of the parties involved. This approach can be contrasted with the suspicion that a rape accusation is more likely to be false than true, first articulated in Matthew Hale's legal cautions in the mid-seventeenth century and casting a long shadow on Anglo-American jurisprudence.

The legacy of the Earl of Bridgewater was brought to these shores by the early Puritans, who in sexual matters tended to believe the woman as much as the man. This legacy is reflected in a short masque written by John Milton, probably at the request of the Earl of Bridgewater, and performed for the earl on the occasion of his accession to the position of Lord President of the Council of Wales. The legacy of Matthew Hale survives in his legal treatise on rape, as part of Sir William Blackstone's 1765 compilation of English common law. In time, Hale's jury instructions became the most often quoted phrase in American jurisprudence, while the ideals reflected in the actions of the Earl of Bridgewater played a more secondary role.[7] Nevertheless, the two approaches are instructive for understanding the fate of rape complainants in the history of American sexuality.

Milton's drama, entitled *Comus,* was written in the genre known as a "masque," a literary entertainment of the times created for the aristocracy and meant to celebrate the triumph of aristocratic virtue over vice. The basic plot of *Comus* concerns the attempted rape of a young woman called "the Lady." Leah Marcus, a scholar specializing in this period, believes that Milton was influenced by the Margery Evans case and suggests that *Comus* is "a paradigm for the handling of all similar cases."[8] To this I would add that *Comus* is an allegory of the meaning of sexual consent, and that this meaning is as relevant today as it was in Milton's time.

Comus was performed on Michaelmas, a holiday traditionally associated with justice and the law. In attendance at the performance on September 29, 1634, was the Earl of Bridgewater, his family, and the judicial officials under his jurisdiction, some of whom were responsible for the Evans affair. Marcus believes that the masque was an indirect criticism of their "negligence and prejudice" in the handling of the affair.[9] By way of example she cites the fact that the masque contains references to the Gospel of the day, Matthew 18, in which Jesus tells his disciples that they are to treat the "little ones" as they would treat anyone else, which could be interpreted as meaning that justice was to protect all citizens, not just the few.[10]

Comus is the name of the major male character. He is an "enchanter," who personifies the sexual license, excesses, and revels of the time. The events attributed to Comus are reminiscent of the Midsummer festival night when Margery Evans was ravished. Burghill probably saw himself merely as carrying on the time-honored traditions of Midsummer when he encountered Margery Evans on the road, just as the boys of the Trump took Angela's visit as another opportunity for their particular brand of partying.

The main female character is a young virgin, much like Margery Evans and Angela, only she is a member of the aristocracy. She is called "the Lady" and was played by the earl's fifteen-year-old daughter. She personifies innocence, purity, and strength. The masque dramatizes her predicament and escape when Comus tries to force her into sex.

At the beginning of the masque, she is traveling with her elder and younger brothers (played by her real brothers). When they become lost in the woods she is separated from them. Realizing that she is lost, the Lady recognizes that she is in jeopardy and resolves "to keep my life and honour unassailed." Hearing the noise of revellers in the forest, she moves toward them and meets Comus disguised as a gentle shepherd. Fooled by his disguise and his promise to lead her out of the maze of the forest, she goes with him. Comus concludes that she is a virgin and vows to make her his queen by casting "dazzling spells" and fooling her with "well-placed words" of friendly help.[11]

In the meantime, realizing that they have lost their sister, the two brothers worry that she might run into danger. The first brother expresses confidence that she will not be defenseless because "she has a hidden strength." That strength is her "chastity," which is "clad in complete steel." No evil can hurt "true virginity," he says, meaning that whatever might be done to her body will not sully her spirit.

As they look for their sister, convincing themselves that she is immune from danger, a spirit comes to them and explains that she has been ensnared by the great Comus, who gives "his baneful cup" to "every thirsty wanderer" by "sly enticement." Those who take the drink are transformed into the "inglorious likeness of a beast," who with "unwary sense" learns to enjoy the revelry of the forest.

Upon hearing this, the second brother bemoans the "unarmed weakness of one virgin, alone and helpless." The first brother again repeats his certainty that although her virtue "may be assailed" and "surprised by unjust force," it can never be taken from her unless she gives mental consent.

Meanwhile Comus takes the Lady to his stately palace, his place of seduction replete with soft music, comfort, and tables spread with dainties. The Lady is made to sit in an enchanted chair "smeared with gums of glutinous heat," from which she cannot rise because she is glued to the seat. The glue that imprisons the Lady has many possible meanings. It can be interpreted as a metaphor for the hold a male has over a vulnerable woman who has no way of escaping either because of sheer terror or drugged stupor. It can also be taken as a metaphor for the allure of the delights of sexual acquiescence seductively described by Comus.

Realizing that she has been trapped, the Lady tells Comus that no matter what he might do to her body, she will remain in control of her mind. This control reflects a central theme of Milton's prose, namely liberty. In *Comus,* Milton shows that neither the Lady's physical imprisonment nor her sexual restraint detracted from her inward liberty.[12]

Comus tries to break down the Lady's mental independence by describing in great detail the joy her acquiescence will bring. He states that to deny herself the pleasure he offers would be cruel to herself. To aid the seduction he offers her a magical liquor to drink.

The Lady will have none of his argument. She is angered that he has betrayed her "credulous innocence" with "falsehood and base forgery" and steadfastly refuses to take the "liquorish bait" that he offers. He presses the drink upon her, saying, "One sip of this will bathe the drooping spirits in delight beyond the bliss of dreams." As he presses the drink to her lips with the command, "Be wise and taste," the two brothers rush in with swords drawn and wrest the glass out of his hand.

The Lady, however, is fixed to the enchanted seat and cannot move. To break the "glutinous heat" that seals her, the brothers call upon the immortal Sabrina, goddess of the river Severn, who is "swift to aid a virgin." Sabrina breaks the spell over the chair, and the Lady is able to rise from her seat and liberate herself from Comus's sexual influence.

The judges watching the masque might conclude that the Lady consented because she went with Comus—as they had done in the case of Margery Evans when Burghill took her on his horse to a nearby town. The St. John's jurors had concluded the same because Angela went to Michael's house. However, the distinction Milton makes between the sex act and mental assent to that act presents a different definition of consent. The masque suggests that acts enforced upon the body of an inert or "glued" woman (or in today's terms, one who is frozen with fright or unconscious from alcohol) do not signify consent but the passivity of a young woman held against her will. Whatever the source of her passivity, it is a woman's mental assent, in today's terms her verbal consent, that determines volition. In other words, going with a man, being trapped by a man, accepting a drink, or being glued to his chair does not imply consent. Milton may have been the first to suggest that no means no; however, his message was lost because of his emphasis on what has been interpreted as puritanical sexual restraint.

The many allurements Comus offers to ensnare the Lady into acquiescence can be likened to Michael's attempts to persuade Angela to take the drink. The Lady's rejection of Comus's enticements were no doubt offered as a moral lesson for the young men and women of the earl's family. The suggestion that a greater good would come from resisting all the pleasures offered by Comus reflects Milton's definition of inward liberty. Whatever one might think of the sexual restraint suggested in this lesson, it is important not to lose sight of the fact that Milton's masque is also about sexual autonomy, a woman's right to give mental assent. One can decry the moral message of restraint without rejecting the Lady's right to decide her sexual fate.

Sabrina's freeing of the Lady from the enchanted chair speaks to the steadfast determination on the part of Angela and Margery to secure justice and to the efforts on the part of those who helped them. By going to the authorities, Angela and Margery tried to regain what they had lost in the assault on their bodies. Through appeals to authority, they distanced themselves from the sordidness of what had happened to them, just as Sabrina separates the Lady from the gum that glues her to the enchanted chair. In this sense Sabrina serves as a symbol of justice, because it is she who frees the Lady mentally as well as physically from her ordeal.[13]

BIRTH OF THE FALSE ACCUSER

The idea that women falsely accuse men of rape does not appear as such until the mid-seventeenth century. Writing in the thirteenth century on the laws and customs of England, for example, Henry de Bracton defined rape as a crime "imputed by a woman to the man by whom she says she has been forcibly ravished against the king's peace." To prove her case, De Bracton states, the woman must go immediately to the next town and report "the injury done her" to "men of good repute" and afterward acquaint responsible law enforcement officials of her "complaint."[14] Margery Evans followed this rule but was thrown in jail for her efforts. She was not the type of woman town officials deemed worthy of a hearing. More than likely, given the fear of women accusing men of rape for purposes of blackmail, Margery Evans was jailed for this offense.

It was Hale's mid-seventeenth-century concept of the false accuser that had the most influence on American law.[15] Defining rape as the "carnal knowledge of any woman above the age of ten years against her will, and of a woman-child under the age of ten with or against her will," Hale warned that

> rape is a most detestable crime, and therefore ought severely and impartially to be punished with death; but it must be remembered that it is an accusation easy to be made, hard to be proved, but harder to be defended by the party accused, though innocent.[16]

Evidence of Hale's influence on American courts is seen in the fact that this statement was read verbatim to jurors in many states until the 1970s, being removed from the California code of criminal procedure, for example, only in 1975.[17]

Criminal justice researcher Antony E. Simpson suggests that Hale's cautions were originally devised in reaction to women bringing rape charges as a form of blackmail.[18] In eighteenth-century England, the blackmail myth, as Simpson calls it, was used effectively by defense lawyers to get their clients off the hook. The conviction rate for rape was the lowest of any capital crime, a mere 17 percent in eighteenth-century London. The comparable rates for the capital crimes of burglary and robbery were 56 percent and 35 percent.[19] Based on an examination of the legal records between 1730 and 1830, Simpson was able to find few actual extortion attempts.[20]

Hale claimed that his cautions were based on two cases of malicious prosecutions for rape that he experienced as a judge in the late seventeenth century. He cites at length, for example, a case involving an accusation by a fourteen-year-old girl against a fifty-three-year-old man, which Hale believed was brought for purposes of blackmail. The man cleared himself in Hale's eyes by demonstrating that he had a physical ailment that made it impossible to commit a rape: "for all his bowels seemed to be fallen down into those parts, that they could scarce discern his privities, the rupture being full as big as the crown of a hat."[21] From this and another equally dubious case, Hale concluded that while the "heinousness of the offence" may instill "indignation" in the judge and jury, they must be careful lest they too hastily convict the accused based on "the confident testimony sometimes of malicious and false witnesses."[22]

In the seventeenth century, the very act of bringing a rape charge raised suspicions about a woman's ulterior motives. Women were not to be so bold. Woman's submission was part of the divine scheme of things, as reflected in the biblical Garden of Eden. Having been made out of Adam's rib "to be a help meet for him," woman did not participate in the superior wisdom of man. A girl's sexuality was under her father's control, and a wife's desire was subject to her husband. If either were raped it was the man to whom she was beholden, who was expected to bring charges. In return for playing according to the rules, as proper daughters of Adam, women were protected by society.

A girl like Margery Evans who pressed charges on her own conjured the image of the aggressive Eve, whose complicity with the serpent made all mortal women susceptible to the wiles of the devil: they were prone to be sexually voracious and enticing, spiritually weaker, and less rational. More likely than not, a woman bringing rape charges on her own was either a scorned woman or one out to blackmail the man who seduced her.

The oft-quoted "scorned woman," who survives into the 1990s, first took the stage in William Congreve's play *The Mourning Bride* in 1697; however, she was already a well-known figure in seventeenth-century drama.[23] In Congreve's play her name is Zara, and she is as different from Almeria, the good woman of the play, as *Z* from *A*. Zara aggressively pursues Alphonso, the man that Almeria also loves and patiently waits for. It is when Zara finds that Alphonso has rejected her that she utters the famous lines so often misquoted:

Heav'n has no Rage, like Love to Hatred turn'd,
Nor Hell a Fury, like a Woman scorn'd.

In her fury, Zara neither turns against Alphonso to kill him, as did Medea in the Greek myth, nor does she cry rape like Potiphar's wife in the biblical story. Rather, like the evil Eve, she is punished by Divine Providence. Zara's fury is turned inwardly against herself and she dies by her own hand.

The main male characters, Alphonso and Manuel, are also constructed on the model of good and evil. Alphonso stands for the good, pure hero; Manuel for the evil, tyrannical king. When Manuel discovers that he has lost his beloved Zara, he also expresses rage and fury:

Give me Rage, Rage, implacable Revenge,
And trebled Fury.

Like Medea's, Manuel's fury leads him to thoughts of murder and he vows to kill Zara and Almeria because of their love for Alphonso.

Thus, it is not Congreve's scorned woman who lashes out in fury, seeking revenge. It is the scorned *man*. Over the centuries we have imputed to women the fury of the rejected male in Congreve's play, while letting the rejected male off the hook.

Divine Providence saves and reunites Almeria and Alphonso, who epitomize the proper relationship between male and female. Almeria is truly born from Alphonso's rib, so to speak. Believing him to be dead, she thinks only of death. She is reborn when Alphonso rushes to her side to "warm her to Life, and wake her into Gladness." She awakens when he pours into her lips "the soft trickling Balm / Of cordial Sighs," which reinvigorates her bloom "with the breath of Love." Awakened by his ministrations, Almeria says: "This is my Lord, my Life, my only Husband; I have him now, and we no more will part."[24]

Like all good women, Almeria is truly a helpmeet fit for him, in other words a proper Eve.

HALE'S ANTI-FEMALE ATTITUDES

Irrespective of their personal attitudes toward women, the legal and sexual subordination of seventeenth-century women predisposed judges like Matthew Hale to protect accused males. The subordination of adult women was enforced by marriage laws. Once married, women were required to relinquish their property to their husbands. An English manual, *The Lawes Resolutions of Women's Rights,* stated in 1632, "A woman as soon as she is married, is called *covert* . . . that is 'veiled' . . . clouded and overshadowed." Like a small brook running into the Thames, which loses its track, a woman was but a "poor rivulet," who "looseth her name."[25] In short, a girl's life as she matured into womanhood turned into a flow with no track of its own and no history to speak of. A husband had entitlement to his wife's body. Interpreting a husband's sexual rights, Hale wrote that a husband "cannot be guilty of a rape committed by himself upon his lawful wife, for by their mutual matrimonial consent and contract the wife hath given up herself in this kind unto her husband, which she cannot retract."[26]

In a letter to his children, Hale warned that "an idle or expensive wife is most times an ill bargain, though she bring a great portion." In the courtroom, he ruled that in cases where a wife was "squandering away her husband's estate, or going into lewd company," it was lawful for a husband to defend his honor and his estate by restraining such a wife and confining her to the house.[27]

Hale described young gentlewomen as vain, careless creatures who thought only of painting their faces, curling their locks, dressing up, entertaining "gallants and splendid company," and going out to spend their parents' or husband's money. Twice married, Hale had little regard for his first wife, mother of his ten children, whom he believed to be far too extravagant. Following her death, he married his housekeeper. A contemporary is reputed to have said that this wife suited Hale as well as any other because in Hale's mind, women had "no wisdom below the girdle."[28]

Although Hale is frequently cited as the single greatest legal influence on American rape law, a solid argument can be made that his treatment of rape accusations was influenced less by rational legal criteria than by such anti-female attitudes. This suggestion is prompted not only by Hale's judicial treatment of rape but by his handling of one of the most notorious seventeenth-century English witchcraft trials. Contrary to Hale's well-known concern to give rape defendants the benefit of the doubt by examining the motivations of the complainant, in this case he shows no evidence of giving defendants in witchcraft trials the same benefit. Presiding over the 1662 trial, Hale specifically discounted evidence that provided a convincing demonstration of the innocence of the two accused women and sentenced them to death following the jury's guilty verdict.[29]

The evidence involved a simple experiment. Because the bewitched girls bringing the charges always acted in a certain way when they saw or were touched by the accused witches, it was decided to see whether they would have a similar reaction when blindfolded. Fooled into thinking they were being touched by the accused when they were actually being touched by strangers, the girls responded the same way. To explain their reaction, the father of the bewitched girls, hardly an objective source, argued that it was sorcery that led the girls into their mistake. Convinced by this argument, Hale did not allow the results of the experiment to come before the jury, even though other legal experts in attendance at the trial thought it provided evidence of the innocence of the accused.

In his jury instructions at this trial Hale did not caution jurors against a hasty decision as he did in rape trials. Instead, he delivered an impassioned lecture on the evils of witchcraft. Hale told the jury that there was no doubt that there were such creatures as witches. The Scriptures affirmed this as much as did the wisdom of all nations in their laws against such persons. He made particular reference to the act of Parliament that provided punishment for witchcraft proportionate to the quality of the offense. In conclusion, Hale cautioned the jurors to "observe their evidence," and asked "the great God of heaven to direct their hearts" in reaching their verdict. "For to condemn the innocent, and to let the guilty go free, were both an abomination to the Lord," he said. Since the very evidence that would have helped determine a just verdict had been discounted by a judge whose predilections in the case were all too obvious, the jury returned a guilty verdict and the two women, protesting their innocence, were hanged as witches.[30]

During the seventeenth century in England, the number of women accused and executed as witches far outnumbered the number of men accused and executed for rape. Women more than men were labeled witches because of the contemporary belief in their greater susceptibility to evil.[31] The seventeenth century was a time when demons, ghosts, and unnatural phenomena saturated people's vision of reality. Women were deemed more susceptible to witchcraft because they were "impatient," "more superstitious," more easily "displeased," and hence "more malicious" and "revengeful." It was thought that their need for power made them more prone to gossip, anxious to command, and more manipulative.[32] Because they were supposedly less rational and logical than men, it was assumed that women fell more easily under the spell of the devil.

According to researcher G. Geis, witchcraft charges were a useful method for men to keep women subordinated, "inferior and in fear" at a time when women were perceived as having too much sexual power. As long as people like Hale believed in the reality of witchcraft, it was logical that "witches" would be brought to trial. As society became more secularized, however, the requisite belief in the devil and the archetype of the wicked Eve lost their power to persuade juries. Geis suggests that anti-female attitudes in other avenues of social life, such as seen in the treatment of rape complainants, replaced witchcraft accusations as a device to keep ornery women in their place.[33]

Hale died in 1676. We don't know when he first articulated his cautions regarding rape accusations, only that they appeared in the 1678 posthumously published *History of the Pleas of the Crown*, said to be "one of

the most influential treatises on the criminal law of England ever produced."[34] Geis's likening of the motivations behind fear of false accusers
in rape cases with the fear of witches is intriguing. It suggests that smart
defense lawyers in rape cases can tap into the same fund of irrational fear
of aggressive women that once animated the fear of witchcraft. If we take
the St. John's trial as a modern example, the evidence suggests that the
fear of women asserting their independence against dominant, more re-
vered males still exists.

HALE'S CAUTIONS AT THE ST. JOHN'S TRIAL

In the 1990 St. John's courtroom, Hale's cautions could not be quoted
verbatim due to the legal reform movement of the 1970s, which changed
many of America's outmoded rape laws. However, Hale was present in
the guise of the remarks made by the defense lawyers in their opening and
closing statements. In their summations, Scaring and Silverman hammered away at Angela's character in the Hale tradition. They claimed
that Angela wanted to have sex with Michael and got drunk at the Trump
to release inhibitions. "How could decent young men be involved in such
conduct?" Silverman asked with righteous indignation. Both he and Scaring combed the testimony for evidence of initiative shown on Angela's
part to argue that she was the sexual aggressor.

The examples they found evoked a modern image of the evil Eve. The
lawyers described Angela as "aggressive" because she talked about sex
with Michael and the coach. At the Trump "she went down to the refrigerator and opened it up without asking anyone." She "picked things up"
on the desk of a St. John's administrator and "fiddled with them" while
telling her story. Citing such details, the defense lawyers implied that
because Angela was not insipid, overly delicate in her behavior, fainting
at the first sexual advance, and subservient to men at all times, her
testimony was not credible. In the jury room this portrait of Angela
intensified, giving the key female jurors ample foundation to argue for

acquittal. In that atmosphere Angela would have had to be pure as the driven snow, white as Snow White, and passive as Sleeping Beauty to pass muster as wronged and a victim.

The first evidence that Hale's cautions had reached America was in the 1760s, when Blackstone's *Commentaries on the Laws of England* became a best-seller. Blackstone's primary source on rape is Matthew Hale. Studies of sex offenses in earlier American Puritan communities show no evidence of the suspicions articulated by Hale. The egalitarian treatment of rape charges in these communities are much more reminiscent of the ideas of Milton and the Earl of Bridgewater, although these names are never actually mentioned in the records. It seems that the first period of America's response to rape was much more pro-female than it would be later in American history, when Hale's fears of the false accuser became the standard reaction to rape victims.

THREE

THE ENIGMA
OF PURITAN SEXUALITY:
Rape in Early
New England

TODAY THE WORD "PURITANISM" IS SYNONYMOUS WITH SEXUAL RESTRAINT and prudery. For example, a frequent charge heard in the backlash against the anti-rape movement in the 1990s was that feminism had become too puritanical. Camille Paglia lauded Madonna as a "true feminist" who exposed "the puritanism and suffocating ideology of American feminism." Criticizing Anita Hill for charging Clarence Thomas with sexual harassment, Harvard sociologist Orlando Patterson cited "neo-puritanism" and the "reactionary sacralization of women's bodies" as the main problem facing feminism, as if perhaps to suggest that the female body was to be offered freely at the altar of sexual license.[1]

Such remarks obscure the complexity of Puritan sexuality and misrepresent the concerns of modern feminism. Feminism of today cannot be compared with the beliefs of Puritans of yesterday because the sexual culture of today is totally different from that which dictated Puritan sexuality. In today's sexual climate, feminists seek autonomy for women by stressing the right of women to choose their sexual partners and determine the size of their families.

For Puritans there were many restraints on male sexual license, not the least of which were the fornication laws of Colonial times. For feminists the only restraint on sexuality is mutual consent and the expectation of sexual self-determination. Sex outside of marriage was forbidden by the law and by the church in all the early colonies, not just in Puritan New England. However, despite the legal constraints against "fornication," the evidence suggests that Puritan women were not prudes. It was assumed that women had a sexual appetite, which gave them sexual agency in ways that would be denied nineteenth and early twentieth-century women. The sexual agency of Puritan women meant that a man believed a woman who said no. When women charged men with rape, the authorities tended to believe them because of the assumption that women had no reason to lie.

The seventeenth-century colonists were more alike than different in their understanding of sexuality. Prior to the eighteenth century, as far back as Aristotle and Galen, Europeans believed that men and women were basically alike, sexually speaking. Women had the same genitals as men, with the difference that the male organs were outside and the female organs were inside the body. The word "vagina" entered the English language around 1700. Before that the vagina was imagined as "an interior penis, the labia as foreskin, the uterus as scrotum, and the ovaries as testicles."[2] It was routine for both sexes to experience orgasm and it was expected for both sexes. Belief that the seat of sexual pleasure for women was located in the clitoris existed centuries before Masters and Johnson rediscovered the clitoral orgasm in the 1960s. Renaldus Columbus discovered the clitoris in 1559, just a half-century after the discovery of America by the more famous explorer of the same name. He named his discovery "a female penis" and referred to it as "the seat of woman's delight."[3] Libido, which Freud attributed to masculine desire in the early twentieth century, was not gender specific in the seventeenth century.

PURITAN SEXUALITY

Scholars are of two minds about the sexual prudery of the Puritans, some arguing that they were not as "puritanical"—prudish, ascetic, and antisexual—as we make them out to be, others arguing the opposite. Historian Roger Thompson, who studied the court records in seventeenth-century Middlesex County in Massachusetts, says that it is misleading to think of the Puritans as "squeamish about sexuality." Far from being sexually repressed, the Puritans were fascinated by sexuality, and the unmarried relieved sexual tensions by various means, including intercourse.[4] Thompson finds many examples of sexual behavior suggesting that the people were not "puppets of Puritan morality." Like the peasants in many societies, they were not "passive slaves of authority" but led active sex lives, making choices, rebelling against constraints, or maneuvering within them.[5]

Historian Edmund Morgan, well known for his study of the Puritan family, concludes that Puritans showed "none of the blind zeal or narrow-minded bigotry which is too often supposed to have been characteristic of them." Puritan ministers, the most puritanical of the Puritans, expressed their horror at "that Popish conceit of the Excellency of Virginity." The ministers taught that sexual intercourse was a "human necessity." Their congregations agreed with them, as witnessed in the expulsion of a member of the First Church of Boston because he withheld conjugal "fellowship unto his wife" for two years under the pretense of "taking Revenge upon himself for his abusing of her before marryage."[6]

Analyzing Puritan sexual doctrine, historian Lyle Koehler provides a very different view. He quotes from English Puritan tracts, which are excessive in their descriptions of the body as the "fountain of Sin and wickedness" from which only evil could flow: "Evil Thoughts, Murders, Adulteries, etc." For salvation and godliness each individual was to avoid "promiscuous dancing," "card-playing, dressing in gorgeous attire," and, of course, "the 'Vomits, and Quagmires' of premarital sexual intercourse."[7]

Using apocalyptic imagery, American Puritan ministers and leaders defined sex as a cosmological force, a lust "boyling and burning" in the body, or, as Koehler describes it, "a river of fire that had to be banked and cooled by a hundred restraints if one was to preserve the individual soul."[8] Inspired by Calvinism, the Puritan view of human sexual nature was determined by the Fall, by Eve's vices and Adam's succumbing to her allure. Women were either good or evil. As proper wives and citizens they were helpmeets and breeders of sons. In their evil form they consorted with the devil, which turned them into witches or, at the least, made them more sexually voracious and enticing, spiritually weaker than men, and less rational. The Puritans were relatively egalitarian when it came to ascribing good and evil to the sexes because men, too, were subject to sexual depravity.

William Bradford, who led the first group of Puritans to Plymouth in 1620, wrote that Satan had more power "in these heathen lands." Despite the attempt to separate his flock from the surrounding enticements, Bradford was aware of their lure. Responding to an outbreak of "wickedness" in 1642, Bradford likened the frustration of sexual desire to "waters when their streams are stopped or dammed up." "When they get passage," he suggested, "they flow with more violence and make more noise and disturbance than when they are suffered to run quietly in their own channels." Bradford feared that the "strict laws" might be partially responsible for damming up the flow of desire and creating a situation whereby not letting it "run in a common road of liberty as it would and is inclined, it searches everywhere and at last breaks out where it gets vent."[9]

The Puritans gave much thought to ways to quench "the sparks of Lust's fire" and the force of the stream that seeks a vent, Koehler says. Turning one's thoughts to God was one of the more obvious diversions, along with hard work and drinking cold water (the Puritan version of the cold shower). One minister favored castration as the final solution to male sexual temptation, on the grounds that it was better "to go a cripple into heaven than to remain 'a perfect Epicure to be cast into Hell.' "[10]

The stereotype of the puritanical is promoted by such rhetoric and by the strict laws against sex outside of marriage. In seventeenth-century America, historian David Flaherty notes that sin and crime, divine and secular law, moral and criminal law were all closely intertwined.[11] Fornication was forbidden and punished by moral and criminal law. These laws, however, were not based on the notion that sex per se was sinful. The Puritans and their Colonial contemporaries were not passionless people. Indeed, as William Bradford's rhetoric shows, sex was treated as a powerful, combustible human feeling in need of a vent. Citing the apostle Paul, one advisor claimed it was better "to be lawfully coupled, than to be lustfully scorched." Marriage "was the insurance against men turning to bestiality" and women to the "temptacion of being a baud."[12]

Although outside of marriage sex was a crime against the state and God, Puritan communities had their share of errant husbands and unfaithful wives. According to Thompson, men could and did proposition women, receiving in return either a tactful "all in good time" or "in time convenient." More usually they got "tart answers" from women, "who used babies, bribes, shaming, and threats in defense." Puritan women had a definite say in sexual matters and men listened. If nothing else, men were so inhibited by Puritan teaching and the threat of eternal damnation as to be shamed out of satisfying lust by force. Popular piety and a religiously inspired collective mentality acted as a restraint on a man forcing himself on a woman. A woman threatened with sexual abuse could tell her abuser that he would have to answer to God, for God sees all, even in the dark. If men met resistance from women, "as they usually did," Thompson says, "their internalized shame inhibited them." If they went ahead anyway, they were seized with a genuine sense of guilt.[13]

The records of the Middlesex courts between the years 1649 and 1699 show that illicit sexual intercourse was fairly common, with fornication and adultery far outnumbering cases of sexual abuse and rape.[14] A particularly detailed complaint made in 1663 by nineteen-year-old Elizabeth

Holmes for infidelity and sexual abuse against forty-six-year-old Thomas Langhorn, a married man with five children and the town drummer of Cambridge, provides a picture of a sexual exchange that can hardly be called prudish. Langhorn evidently had a sexual predilection for teaching young, virginal women about sex. Elizabeth's account of their interaction suggests that she appreciated his lessons, but not his jumping on her. Langhorn introduced her to sex by teaching her all about the penis and how it worked. Part of the lesson included showing it to her.[15]

> He told me he would teach me how to lie with my husband that it should not hurt me and that I must pull up my legs, and he said that he had taught a maid so and after she was married she thanked him for it. . . . Many times he would persuade me to feel his member which was his mode for two or three years . . . and he said if I would he could teach me so that a man should never force me.

In his sex lessons Langhorn referred several times to Aristotle. His source was probably the belief, expressed by medical authorities of the time drawing on Aristotle, that although women were possessed with sexual passion in conception, the male served as "the Efficient, or Agent," and the woman as "the Matter, or Patient."[16] Langhorn instructed Elizabeth about the female anatomy as well as his own and explained all sorts of matters, including how conception took place. He explained that a man was more "suddenly taken than a woman." For this reason, "Scripture gave more liberty to married men than to married women." Elizabeth seems to have appreciated Langhorn's lessons only to a certain point. She objected strongly when he threw her down and got on top of her. In her lengthy testimony she describes some of the offenses.

> He came down when I was loading hay last year and threw me down and gat upon me . . . it was his common carriage to put his hands under my apron and would have gone further if I had not

resisted him, one time he gat his hand to my belly, and he said that most of the storys he told me he had out of Aristotle and from honest men and women.

Langhorn confessed and was sentenced to twenty-one lashes with the whip. The egalitarian aspect of Puritan justice is reflected in the fact that Elizabeth's protestations of innocence were not persuasive and she was "solemnly admonished 'for her bold familiarity with Langhorn in his wanton and wicked ways.' "[17]

RAPE IN PURITAN SOCIETY

The officials of the Massachusetts Bay colony formed their own code of laws in the 1640s based on the Bible and legal tracts they imported from England. With respect to rape, their guide was Sir Edward Coke's 1642 treatise on the law, not Matthew Hale, whose treatise would be published later in the seventeenth century. Using the common law definition of rape, Coke defined rape as consensual or forcible copulation with a female under ten and nonconsensual intercourse with a female over ten.[18] Beyond this basic definition, the Massachusetts legal code did not speculate about false accusers.

At first the Massachusetts colonists did not make rape a capital crime, as it was in England, because there was no biblical precedent for doing so. This changed after a case of child abuse shocked the people of Boston in 1641. This case involved a man who "carried on 'sexual dalliance' " with three young girls under the age of ten, sometimes joined by two male servants. According to Governor Winthrop, the girls consented to this activity. As he recorded it in his diary, they had "grown capable of man's fellowship, and took pleasure in it."[19] The idea that "she wanted it," so commonly heard today, could only originate in a society that believed in female as well as male lust.

The Puritan populace, however, felt that male sexual license with young girls was unlawful. Upon hearing about this case they expressed the opinion that only the gallows would be sufficient atonement for this crime. Since there was no published law at the time, nor any biblical precedent, hanging was not possible. Community consensus and discussion in the general court decided that a rape had been committed, even though the girls were said to have consented. In the absence of a law either in the Bible or in the published criminal code authorizing a death sentence, the man in question was severely whipped and sentenced "to wear an halter about his neck visibly all his life." After this sentence was passed, the general court enacted laws providing death for rape of a child under ten years of age, irrespective of her consent, but this law was not incorporated into the compiled laws until much later. The court did enact a law making rape of any maiden or single woman above the age of ten punishable by death or, at the court's discretion, by some other "grievous punishment."[20] Making rape a capital offense conformed with seventeenth-century English common law on rape.

All the evidence suggests that there was a relatively low rate of rape in Puritan society. Thompson found an average of one case of sexual abuse every four years in Middlesex County, a population that ranged from three thousand to twelve thousand during the second half of the seventeenth century.[21] Historian Lyle Koehler's study of rape in seventeenth-century New England yielded similar results.

Koehler's study covered Calvinist New England in the seventeenth century. He found that seventy-two men were brought before the authorities for taking forcible sexual liberties with seventy-eight nonconsenting females. Most (85 percent) of the rape cases involved people who knew each other, the perpetrator being a neighbor or a member of the household. Almost all of the victims waited two months to a year before reporting rapes, suggesting that Puritan officials did not fear "malicious" accusations. Most of the cases ended in convictions.[22]

Koehler describes the Puritan response to rape in some detail. Almost half of the men accused of trying to forcibly seduce women stopped using force when the women called out or objected vociferously. According to testimony from the women, the rape was completed in only twenty-eight of the cases. Quoting from a case in 1670 in which the male said about a maidservant who struggled against him, "[A]re not woo[men] made for the lives of men," Koehler suggests that the males who didn't take no for an answer assumed that "women existed to serve their needs."[23] Thus, at least some Puritan men believed in male sexual entitlement.

The victims included thirty-five wives, twenty-six unwed servants, nine single women, and eight children between the ages of three and thirteen. There was a disproportionate number of servants among the victims (one third), considering they represented no more than 10 percent of the adult female population. Several authors suggest that servants were more likely to be victimized by men who believed that woman was made for man's use.[24]

The defendants were also mostly from the lower social classes of Puritan life: servants, yeomen farmers, or single members of farm households, as well as a few Indian men and black servants or slaves. Only four of the accused men were designated as "Mr.," the title for a gentleman.[25] Typically, the men accused of rape defended themselves by asserting that the devil or lust overcame them.

The victim's testimony alone could convict a man of rape. If an examination by midwives revealed injuries or bruises in the genital area, this was grounds for conviction of rape. According to Koehler, Puritans assumed that rape would so immobilize the victim with fear she would be unable to actively resist. Puritans rarely accused the woman of attracting the assailant. In only eight cases did the defendant maintain that the woman enticed him. Rape was such a serious offense, no one thought a woman would lie about it. Even in those cases where there might be evidence of a woman inviting an advance, the man who made the advance was punished.[26]

Koehler describes such a case that took place in New Haven in 1653. A serving maid charged that the defendant forcibly "discouered her nakedness," pulled down his breeches, and would have raped her had she not cried out. The defendant declared that the complainant had flirted with him by pulling provocatively on his sleeve. He placed her on the bed and kissed her until she told him to leave her alone. There was some debate over the complainant's veracity because she was known to have lied previously. The defendant, on the other hand, had not been known to lie. However, the court decided "that doth not prove that she tells untruth in this case; nor is it likely that such a young girle should bee so impudent as to charge such a carriage upon a young man when it was not so." Despite his unblemished reputation, the court decided that the defendant might lie in an attempted rape case, and he was punished with a whipping to keep children "safe from temptations and defylement."[27]

Eight defendants were acquitted and the final disposition of fifteen cases is unknown.[28] The majority of the convicted defendants received severe whippings and fines. At least six were hanged. Lighter penalties were exacted by avoiding the label "rape" in favor of other terms such as "ravishing," "carnal knowledge of a female without her consent," "indecent assault," "shameful abuse offered," "indecent actions," or "assault."[29]

Based on information collected on rape in Massachusetts cases from 1698–1797, historian Barbara Lindemann concludes that Puritan society was relatively free of rape. She suggests that customs regulating sexual behavior "probably minimized the occurrence of rape." Extramarital sexual activity was condemned and punished. Sexual license was not encouraged in Puritan communities, either for women to enhance their sexual attractiveness or for men to assert their manhood. Women were seen as being as interested in sex as men were, which meant that it was unlikely that a man would interpret a woman's no to mean a yes. Furthermore, the small, face-to-face communities meant that most women who cried out would be heard. Lindemann's conclusions, although suggestive, must be evaluated in light of the fact that she also found class prejudice operating. According to Lindemann, "the only cases that would be reported and prosecuted were those in which the community acknowledged that the attacker had no right to the woman sexually," which would have been men of a lower social order than the victim.[30]

In his study of the enforcement of morals in early America, historian David Flaherty describes patterns similar to those of Puritan New England. In Virginia, he notes that "sins of the flesh" were excused when committed by gentlemen "so long as one was not gross, did not seduce the innocent, and provided for one's illegitimate offspring." It was more unlikely that victims of gentlemen would choose to prosecute, because of their dependence on the gentlemen in question either for employment or other favors.[31] Flaherty states that in general free persons were not as likely as servants to be prosecuted for fornication or adultery.[32] He concludes that sexual license was not as widespread in the colonies as in England, particularly in comparison with London.

WITCHCRAFT IN PURITAN NEW ENGLAND

Like all English women, Puritan women were inferior in the eyes of religion and the law. The subjection of women to man paralleled man's subjection to God. The legal status of women under English common law carried over to the colonies. A married woman had no independent legal status. She could own no property or sign contracts. Only widows and single women over the age of twenty-one had legal rights.[33]

Nevertheless, historians recognize that Colonial women exercised considerable power through informal channels. As long as they stayed within the confines of their appointed roles, women found power in their mutual work groups, gossip, and economic transactions. According to historian Sara Evans, the formal power of the male-dominated government and religion would sometimes pale "before the informal powers of female voluntary association and gossip."[34]

The rigidity of the Colonial Puritan code is seen in its punitiveness against women who challenged or broke with religious or social expectations. Rebellious women were either hauled into the courtroom and charged with contempt or branded as witches and executed or banished from the community.

Anne Hutchinson was the first of many famous American women to say what she thought and pay for it. She came to Puritan Boston in 1634, a few years after the first settlement. Her heresy was to challenge the Puritan theocracy of Boston on matters having to do with religious dogma and the exclusion of women from having a voice in church affairs. She wanted to be permitted to think for herself about God. In maintaining that an individual could commune directly with God and by drawing to her a large female following, she threatened the Puritan religious and state hierarchy.[35]

The first significant backlash against American women was seen in the reaction of the male hierarchy of Massachusetts Bay to Anne Hutchinson's influence. The Synod of 1637, a meeting of the Puritan civic and religious hierarchy, banned Hutchinson's practice of meeting with groups of sixty or more women, declaring it "disorderly, and without rule." At her trial, when she defended herself brilliantly, Governor John Winthrop was mortified to find himself debating with a woman. "We do not mean to discourse with those of your sex," he admonished her. Another interrogator accused her of stepping out of the proper role for one of her sex: "You have stept out of your place, you have rather bine a Husband than a Wife and a preacher than a Hearer; and a Magistrate than a Subject."[36] Finally, the general court charged Mrs. Hutchinson with "divers matters," such as making public lectures every week in her house, and banished her.[37] She left Boston and went to Rhode Island and then to a Dutch colony near Long Island Sound, where she and five of her children were killed in an Indian raid in 1643.[38]

The accusations of witchcraft that occurred throughout the seventeenth century were a way of controlling independent women. Virtually everyone knew the signs proving allegiance to the devil. The most intense witchcraft mania came at the end of the century in Salem village, a time when New England women seemed to be stepping more and more out of their appointed place. The problems confronting Salem villagers in 1692 reflected the uncertain quality of life in an unsettled age. There were commercial conflict between rural and urban centers, break up of communities, difficulties between ministers and their congregations, and crowding of sons on family land, to mention just a few of the most obvious tensions. In the year of 1692–93 alone, 204 witchcraft accusations were made in Massachusetts—56 males and 148 women.[39]

In Salem, as elsewhere, most of the accusations were made by females against females. Koehler's discussion of the reasons why women turned against women provides another source of insight into the irrational antagonism shown by the female jurors against Angela. According to Koehler, most of the accusations were made by powerless adolescent girls and conservative Puritan wives against "independent-spirited women" in an "unconscious search for power."[40] Witchcraft accusations provided the means for subjugated women to manipulate husbands and male relatives and relieve the oppressive force of Puritan restrictions. Jealousy of women with the courage to adopt nontraditional roles also played a part.

Some of the accusers used their newfound power to criticize the ministers in church, which violated the biblical injunction against women speaking in church. Where once such individuals would have been chastised, it was now assumed that witches were to blame. Not only did accusers claim the power to speak in church, they also claimed the ability to vanquish supernatural creatures.[41] In so doing, the accusers more nearly approximated the supposed behavior of witches than the alleged witches themselves.

The women accused of witchcraft were either innocent victims of circumstances or community eccentrics, women whose defiance of the ideal feminine sex role reflected the unconscious desires of their accusers.[42] Fear of repressed sexual aggression is suggested by the fact that juries of midwives who examined the accused saw "a witch's teat" in the unusually large clitoris of one of them.[43] Many of the accused were guilty of rebellion against their superiors (parents, husbands, or magistrates) or of adultery. The first "witch" to be hanged in Salem village would not be dominated by her three husbands. She operated an unlicensed tavern and dressed provocatively. Another lived in a common law relationship with her "wild" Irish servant and another gave birth to a mulatto child.[44] Witches threatened the established order in other ways. They inherited money directly, thus upsetting the transmission of property through the male line. Others were simply newcomers who had not yet learned to keep to their proper place. In a study of witchcraft in New England between 1620 and 1699, Koehler identified 315 individuals who were accused, the overwhelming majority of whom were females. Thirty-three people were executed, twenty-five women and eight males.[45] It is a striking commentary on Anglo-American jurisprudence that, as was true in England, many more women were executed for witchcraft than men for rape.

After the Salem witchcraft trials of 1692–93, no more Puritan women were accused of witchcraft. The last hanging took place on September 22, 1692. Juries lost heart for the task of sending more victims to the gallows. In May 1693, Governor Phips refused to allow the grim business to continue. A sense of guilt lay heavily on the hearts of many who had participated in the proceedings. Five years after the 1692 witchcraft prosecutions at Salem village, one of the judges publicly begged forgiveness for finding accused witches guilty.[46]

The same forces that brought about the mania—growing commercialism and increasing secularization—weakened Puritan religious and political control. As the century closed, the numbers of professional women in New England increased and more women became literate as educational opportunities for middle-class girls expanded. In the 1690s, women comprised 45 percent of the innkeepers in Boston. More women became lawyers and achieved the same success rates as men. In 1711, Sam Sewall remarked after two decades of experience with female attorneys that "Many Women are . . . good Lawyers, & of . . . quick understanding in the Fear of the Lord." In 1699 a Boston church decided that women should have the right to vote in electing a minister.[47] All of these developments demonstrated that a public domain was opening in America's cities in which women played an important role. In the growing urban centers, as the numbers of independent women increased and popular piety diminished, more accusations of sexual abuse and rape began to come to the courts.

The Puritan heritage was a major factor in shaping the American spirit. In many ways, the Puritan impulse to reform and their dedication to self-determination fueled the American Revolution. Many scholars have noted the contribution of Puritanism to the development of democracy and the demand for independence. The dualism of the American sexual culture is also archetypically Puritan. Although Puritans conceived of lust as evil, its lure was always more powerful than the rewards of godliness. In this respect they were as dedicated to sexual excess, albeit to restrain it, as the libertines they condemned.

If Anne Hutchinson's experience demonstrated the informal power and influence women could develop, her fate demonstrated the opposing power of male domination. The Salem witch trials illustrated the two sides of women's informal power: the civic power granted the accusers and the negative power projected on the accused. Women were central to this major social upheaval as accusers, accused, and witnesses. Yet, as Sara Evans notes, "they remained outsiders to the formal power of male political and religious elites."[48]

The divided Puritan conscience—straining toward purity but beset with guilt—would be transformed in the eighteenth and nineteenth centuries to the division between passionlessness and licentiousness. As the American experiment developed and women began to enter the public sphere, passionlessness became the new vision for female sexuality and moral righteousness the basis for women to widen their influence. In denying a sexual appetite to women and turning restraint into a moral virtue, the new approach was in some respects more puritanical than the Puritans.

The old ideas about female lust, however, were not lost. In the eighteenth century, socially respectable women were untouchable, whereas women deemed lusty, independent, or otherwise outside polite society were sexual prey. Women who challenged the system of male sexual and social prerogatives too aggressively were branded as false accusers if they charged a man with rape and unwomanly if they were too outspoken. Where the Puritan courts took a woman's word that she said no, in the early national courts she had to prove that she didn't say yes either with her body or her eyes. The rigid sex-role stereotyping reflected in this approach to rape complaints checked women's progress and kept them locked in the role of the weaker sex.

FOUR

THE NO-MEANS-YES DEFENSE:

Rape at the Birth of the Nation

We hold these truths to be self-evident: that all men are created equal; that they are endowed by their creator with inherent and inalienable rights; that among these are life, liberty and the pursuit of happiness.

—THE DECLARATION OF INDEPENDENCE, 1776

FROM ITS BEGINNINGS, AMERICA WAS MARKED BY VIOLENCE ON THE frontier, individualism in its growing communities, and subordination of its women. The founding fathers were not just those eighteenth-century gentlemen who "composed a nation at Philadelphia," as Richard Slotkin writes, they were the men who carved a nation "from the implacable and opulent wilderness—the rogues, adventurers, and land-boomers; the Indian fighters, traders, missionaries, explorers, and hunters who killed and were killed until they mastered the wilderness."[1] The rationale for violence lay in the belief that life is a "war of all against all," a concept that guided the framers of the Constitution. Like Hobbes, the founding fathers believed that "men are selfish and contentious," and that "the natural state of mankind was a state of war." Like the Puritans they also believed "that the carnal mind is at enmity with God."[2]

Where violence is a way of life, rape is easily confused with "amiable seduction." For some classes of women rape has always played a role in the history of American sexuality, but through the centuries other women had less to fear. Popular piety, social controls, and the enforcement of rape laws protected women in the seventeenth- and early eighteenth-century colonies. The idea that women lacked sexual passion helped to protect "ladies" in the late eighteenth century, the "angel in the house" in the nineteenth century, and the "good girl" in the twentieth century. Women who played their appointed roles as reflected in these images were part of the dominant European culture, which the colonists strove to emulate on these shores. In return for playing according to the rules, as proper daughters and wives, they were protected by society. If they were raped by men of lower station, they received instant sympathy. Even if raped by men of the same station, if they came to court with protectors and showed a proper sense of helplessness, their case had merit.

Outsiders and socially marginal women—Indians, slaves, rebellious women, indentured servants, and, in later centuries, white working-class women, freed slaves, and housemaids—were either fair game or outright sexual prey. Indian and African women were especially vulnerable. As they were not considered fully human, the early rape laws did not apply to them. Southern legislators inserted the word "white" in front of the word "woman" in their states' rape statutes as the abolition movement grew.[3] Sexual liaisons between white men and black females were accepted because female slaves did not exist legally independently of their status as property. European males rationalized sexual abuse of slaves by defining them as less than human, at the animal pole of the chain of being. Those men who showed compassion and love for women of the wilderness or for slaves of the plantations were themselves turned into outcasts.

In the eighteenth century, prosecutions for rape and fornication diminished considerably. The number of morals cases heard in the Virginia courts peaked in the 1720s and declined thereafter. In New England, the courts convicted fewer attempted rapists after 1775 and tended to convict on the lesser charge of assault rather than rape.[4] The relaxation of laws enforcing sexual morality in eighteenth-century America was inspired by the realization that there were practical limits to what the law could accomplish in the enforcement of morals. The founding fathers understood that self-interest and personal liberty provided the fuel that fired the train of progress. In 1778, John Adams argued that "the foundation of national Morality must be laid in private Families." Gradually, in all the colonies there was an almost total collapse of prosecutions for immorality, and the law shifted from "the preservation of morality to the protection of property."[5]

The decline in the influence of Puritanism and the spread of libertinism meant that the courts no longer tended to believe the victim. In the Hale tradition, popular stereotypes of good and evil women determined the outcome of rape allegations. Hale's influence is seen in the popularity of Blackstone's compilation of English common law in the American courtroom, which relied primarily on Hale as a source. In this new climate, fears of false accusers permeated rape trials. Generally speaking there were three types of false accusers: the blackmailer, the scorned woman, and the woman who was pure on the outside but all passion within; in other words, a woman whose no meant yes.

EVOLUTION OF NO MEANS YES

To understand the development of the defense, still common in rape trials, that a woman's no really meant yes, it is necessary to examine the interplay between male libertinism and female passionlessness in the eighteenth century.

In his autobiography, John Adams mentions his preoccupation with young women before his marriage but reassures his children "that no illegitimate Brother or Sister exists or ever existed." To this "blessing," he claims a debt to his parents, who "held every Species of Libertinage in such Contempt and horror" and to a "natural temperament that was always overawed by . . . Principles and Sense of decorum." Besides, he added, he had "seen enough of the Effects of a different practice."[6]

Not all of our illustrious forefathers were so virtuous. In many other ways, cultural attitudes encouraged sexual license. In 1738 a writer in a South Carolina newspaper complained that even those professing religion and virtue welcomed in their homes "an abandon'd Fellow, who has been often over-run with a polite Disorder, debauched two or three innocent Virgins or kept half a dozen Negro Wenches in the Face of the Sun."[7] The "Negro Wenches" had no defense against white men. Often they were sold as "breeders." By 1860, the census listed 588,000 mulattoes.[8]

Benjamin Franklin was one of those afflicted by "that hard-to-be-governed passion of youth," which led him into sexual adventures in Philadelphia and London. In eighteenth-century Philadelphia, Franklin wrote bemusedly about the throngs of streetwalkers and joked about their contribution to the city's shoe leather economy, recognizing that the growing commercialism of the American economy was transforming everything, even a woman's body, into a salable item. William Byrd of Virginia wrote about his sexual exploits in his diary from 1709 to 1712.[9] Byrd admitted to keeping mistresses in London and being on intimate terms with streetwalkers. Eighteenth-century London was well known for its licentiousness and corruption. Roger Thompson suggests that "the staggering change in the behaviour of William Byrd on his return to Virginia from the carnalities of London is eloquent witness to a less arrogantly immoral society."[10] Yet by the end of the eighteenth century in New York City, commercial prostitution linked with the city's waterfront commerce was well entrenched, albeit confined to a small area.[11]

According to historian Lynn Hunt, aristocratic libertinism and pornography as a "sex aid" developed in seventeenth-century Europe among upper-class males in "revolt against conventional morality and religious orthodoxy." In the eighteenth century the libertine ideal spread into the artisan and lower-middle-class circles of England and France. Libertines were both the propagators and consumers of pornography. They were "imagined to be free-thinkers who were open to sexual, and literary, experimentation."[12]

Randolph Trumbach traces the interconnection between pornography and libertinism in his study of John Cleland's 1748 novel, *Memoirs of a Woman of Pleasure*. Published in England, this two-volume novel was neither satire nor political tract, like some earlier pornography. *Fanny Hill* (as it was popularly known) was devoted primarily to the sexual arousal of the reader. "With that purpose and by those means," Trumbach suggests, "Cleland established in England the modern pornographic genre." The novel was part of a broader genre of English erotic writing, which became part of a new religion of libertinism in the eighteenth century.[13] As Trumbach writes:

> This religion can be defined as believing, in contradistinction to orthodox Christianity, that sexual experience was central to human life and that sexual desire and pleasure were good and natural things. The sexual organs and acts of sexual intercourse were, therefore, symbols of a great life-giving force and were as worthy of human worship as the symbols of the Christian sacraments and the grace that was the life of the soul.[14]

Women's bodies were offered as the glue for male bonding in this new religion. Men wrote for the sexual arousal of male readers, and gathered together in libertine fraternities for sexual celebrations that included homoerotic rituals.[15]

In the late eighteenth century, libertinism was an important part of masculine popular culture in England and America. Rakes prided themselves on seducing women. As one English gentleman wrote, "Who would keep a cow of their own that can have a quart of milk for a penny?" Eighteenth-century England was a time when the demand for virginity in the brothels culminated in "a mania of defloration which contemporary observers agreed was without parallel in Europe."[16]

The role of seducer and rake attracted men more than the role of husband. Rape was glorified, a source of amusement, a demonstration of masculine sexual prowess. Men talked about sex as a conquest, in which the woman was "taken," as if she were a piece of property. Such "military metaphors," historian Anna Clark points out, "blurred the distinction between rape and seduction."[17]

American women were not silent about the sexual and political freedoms granted men. Some of them recognized that as men gained, women lost. A few unusual women saw themselves as doubly disadvantaged, first by their exclusion from the new political freedom and second by the fact that the liberty and justice promised men did not protect them from dangers posed by men.

Writing in 1776 to her husband, John Adams, Abigail Adams put in her famous plea for the ladies:

> . . . I desire you would Remember the Ladies, and be more gener-
> ous and favourable to them than your ancestors. Do not put such
> unlimited power into the hands of the Husbands. Remember all
> Men would be tyrants if they could. If perticular care and attention
> is not paid to the Laidies we are determined to foment a Rebelion,
> and will not hold ourselves bound by any Laws in which we have no
> voice, or Representation.[18]

Abigail suggested that men were "Naturally tyrannical," and asked her husband "to put it out of the power of the vicious and the Lawless to use us with cruelty and indignity with impunity." In a 1771 letter to a male friend, she described her desire to travel and roam the world as a man, to "explore the amaizing varity of distant Lands," but despaired of ever having that opportunity. Accepting the prevailing notions about feminine weakness, she wrote that she was handicapped by "the Natural tenderness and Delicacy" of a lady's constitution. She also referred to the "many Dangers" to which "we are subject too from your Sex." Although she didn't list these dangers, they were clearly of a sexual nature, for she mentions it is "almost impossible for a Single Lady to travel without injury to her character."[19]

John Adams's response illustrated the role women were to play in the new nation. "We know better than to repeal our Masculine systems," he wrote to his wife, because to do so would subject men to the "Despotism of the Peticoat." Writing to a male friend, he was more forthright. Giving women the vote would open the floodgates to all the dispossessed: "every man who has not a farthing, will demand an equal voice with any other, in all acts of state." This could only bring disaster by destroying all distinctions and prostrating "all ranks to one common level."[20] In other words, the democratic ideal of revolutionary rhetoric was a sham.

PASSIONLESSNESS AS POWER

Nevertheless, the "Peticoats" were not without power. In addition to their alleged despotism within the home, the founding fathers granted women symbolic power based on sexual virtue. "Virtue, Virtue alone . . . is the basis of a republic," Benjamin Rush declared in 1778. "To be destitute of virtue, is to cease to be a citizen," a Harvard student asserted in 1785, echoing the contemporary view. Virtue was to be adopted as "a national characteristic," the regulator of all conduct. If too many families strayed from the virtues of "industry, frugality, temperance, moderation, and the whole lovely train of republican virtues," the Harvard student noted, the nation would be placed in jeopardy.[21]

According to historian Nancy Cott, "there was vast potential for sexual exploitation in a society in which women's sexual nature was considered primary and their social autonomy slight." She coined the term "passionlessness" to describe the ideology of virtue that became synonymous with American womanhood in the late eighteenth and nineteenth centuries. The initial source of the new ideal was eighteenth-century opposition to the aristocratic pretension and libertinism threatening middle-class virtue and domestic security in England. Cott defines passionlessness as an ideology that stressed "sexual self-control," was marked by "verbal prudery," called for an end to the "double standard of sexual morality," and redefined virtue "in primarily sexual terms." By elevating sexual control to the highest of human virtues, female chastity became the symbol of human morality.[22] In their passionlessness, women were thought to possess "to an extraordinary degree, far more than men, the capacity to control the bestial, irrational, and potentially destructive fury of sexual pleasure."[23]

In America, Cott points out, British social ideals became increasingly relevant in the eighteenth century "with the decline in Puritanism, the diffusion of Protestant energies, and the growth of an affluent urban class." In her best-selling book, first published in the late eighteenth century (1799), Hannah More, an English religious writer, described the power women could command as a moral, rather than a sexual, being. Cott likens More to her more famous contemporary, Mary Wollstonecraft, who criticized "libertine notions of beauty" in women and emphasized "women's moral and intellectual powers rather than their 'mere animal' capacities." These two critiques, according to Cott, "rose from shared indignation that women were degraded by their sexual characterization."[24]

In America the ideology of female passionlessness gave churchgoing women a new status and protected them from male sexual predators. Being considered more virtuous than men created a sphere of control and social respect for the sex that had been denied rights as citizens in the new republic.[25] The ideology spread in conjunction with evangelical religion between the 1790s and the 1830s in the Protestant churches, where women became the numerical majority. Evangelical works of the 1790s claimed that libertine ways corrupted women's potential. By placing the solitary burden of moral agency on women, which in Puritan society had been borne more equally by both sexes, women found power in their submission and superiority in their righteousness. Passionlessness wedged a tiny opening for women in the male public sphere and created grounds for female solidarity in the name of "Christian duty."[26] This opening would be widened by the formation of the first female moral reform society in 1834, in New York City, the goal of which was to eradicate prostitution by targeting the licentious men who sustained prostitution. In 1848 it would give women the fortitude to hold the first women's rights convention.

In making women the gatekeepers of an explosive, uncontrollable male sexuality, the creators of female passionlessness ensured the continued reality of male libertinism just as the Puritans ensured the existence of explosive sexual energy by erecting so many taboos against it. Parenthetically, one can also note that the emergence of this approach to sexuality, which Thomas Laqueur calls the two-sex model, effectively excised female sexual pleasure from public sexual discourse until the twentieth century, when Havelock Ellis and later Masters and Johnson resurrected it once again.[27]

The idea of passionlessness, however, did not do away with the old notion of women's inherent lustfulness; it simply stressed the corresponding biblical ideal that "women who embodied God's grace were more spiritual, hence less susceptible to carnal passion." The old idea of "women's inherent licentiousness persisted," Cott says, "to be wielded against women manifesting any form of deviance under the reign of passionlessness."[28] The Calvinist idea that the daughters of Eve were more prone to excess of passion persisted in the courtroom and in the culture of prostitution that evolved in the cities.

EIGHTEENTH-CENTURY RAPE CASES IN EARLY
NATIONAL NEW YORK

The ideology of passionlessness did not protect women of the lower classes to the degree that it protected churchgoing women of the middle and upper classes. Destined to be the virgin brides of the rakes who roamed the streets, the girls of privileged backgrounds were insulated from male sexual whims by families preparing them for the right marriage, where they would go unsullied to breed the sons who would carry on the family name and fortune. Because they knew their place and kept to it, they were less likely to be preyed upon.

Women who were found in male-controlled public spaces in the burgeoning urban centers after working hours were fair game. Historian Christine Stansell describes several cases of women raped by a single man or by groups of men in early national New York.[29] It was a time when women were "taking new territory for themselves" in a city where gender roles were rapidly changing. No doubt the libertine men felt it was their right to mark off a male space where anything was possible sexually. In such spaces women's intentions were probably deliberately misinterpreted by men used to sexual license and who believed that a no meant yes.

In the courtroom, belief in female sexual voracity remained the dominant view of female sexuality. A study by Marybeth Arnold of forty-eight cases brought before the New York County Court of General Sessions between 1790 and 1820 shows that most of the cases involved acquaintances, as was true of the seventeenth-century Puritan communities.[30] Many cases involved girls under the age of ten. Arnold's study, together with court records of the seventeenth century, suggest that rape in early America was a charge leveled against an acquaintance, not a stranger. Additionally, rape was a crime whose victims more often than not were either young or very young.

The cases described by Arnold are permeated with fears of the false accuser, suggesting the influence of the Hale tradition. As mentioned earlier, Hale's approach to rape entered America through Sir William Blackstone's compilation of English common law, *Commentaries on the Laws of England,* which reached the American colonies in the late 1760s and became a best-seller. Like Hale and Sir Edward Coke, Blackstone defined rape as "the carnal knowledge of a woman forcibly and against her will" with any person above the age of ten. Under the age of ten, consent or nonconsent was immaterial, due to the fact that "by reason of her tender years she is incapable of judgment and discretion."[31]

Blackstone quoted Hale's cautions that rape was "a most detestable crime," which ought "severely and impartially to be punished with death." To decide whether a complainant's testimony was "false or feigned," Blackstone offered Hale's jury guidelines. Jurors were to ask whether the "witness be of good fame." Other questions of importance had to do with how quickly the crime was reported; whether the complainant searched for the offender; and whether the accused had attempted to flee. Negative evidence was also to be considered. Was the complainant "of evil fame"? In addition, Hale advised that consideration be given to whether the complainant's testimony was supported by others and whether she had cried out so that she could be heard at the time of the rape.[32]

Marybeth Arnold's study demonstrates that rape was "overwhelmingly a crime of the poor." The complainants were largely "wives of shopkeepers, day laborers, and craftsmen; single women, working as domestic servants and seamstresses; and children as young as six years of age . . ." With a few notable exceptions, most of the assailants came from the same station of life, often from the same neighborhood. Living in crowded quarters, two or three families together in subdivided buildings hastily erected, women and girls were fair game. Arnold is concerned not just with females as victims, whose movements were curtailed and their freedom limited by the threat of rape. She sees women also as "historical agents" and rape "as a battle between neighbors; in the tenements and on the streets [where] working-class women and men fought out conflicting understandings of sex, courtship, and female autonomy."[33]

In all the rape cases she examined, Arnold found that the men accepted "violent pursuit as entirely compatible with amiable seduction." Although they might have asked the woman's consent, they did not consider it essential to their sexual activity, "perhaps in the belief," Arnold suggests, "that every sexual encounter required a bit of a struggle to overcome most women's veneer of reluctance." In these cases, the men "assumed the women involved to be, at heart, as willing as they."[34]

The no-means-yes defense was common in the cases Arnold describes.

In the 1793 case of Henry Bedlow, discussed below, the defense argued that while a woman might "carry a fair outside . . . all was foul within." In 1800, a defense lawyer said that whatever happened to the thirteen-year-old who accused his client of rape must have been with her consent. Speaking in a philosophical vein, he opined, "the passions may be as warm in a girl of her age as in one of more advanced years, and with very little enticement she may have consented to become his mistress." In a case tried in 1813, the defendant argued that when his seven-year-old employee didn't cry out or protest, he assumed that she must have desired and welcomed his attentions when he "operated on her private parts," despite the injuries she sustained.[35]

Guilty verdicts were handed down in at least eighteen of the cases Arnold examined, a higher rate of conviction than Antony Simpson found for eighteenth-century London, but far lower than that reported for seventeenth-century New England by Lyle Koehler.[36] Until 1796, those convicted of rape in New York were executed or given life imprisonment thereafter, which would have made jurors more reluctant to convict.[37] Analyzing the convictions, Arnold finds a common pattern. The most successful cases painted a picture of "male villainy and female helplessness." Men had to be despicable cads, unfit for citizenship, and women had to demonstrate their extreme helplessness and dependence on upstanding male citizens. Women who appeared too assertive or self-reliant did not display the requirements of a good woman—dependence and innocence.[38]

If the defendant was of higher station than the alleged victim, the case had no chance at all. Arnold describes a 1793 case, which involved a seventeen-year-old sewing girl and "a notorious rake," son of a prominent New York City family.[39] The arguments presented in this case as well as the conduct of the defense team provide an eighteenth-century parallel to the 1991 William Kennedy Smith case.

The defendant was the aristocrat Harry Bedlow, who was accused by Lanah Sawyer of rape in September 1793. Sawyer was a seventeen-year-old sewing girl who lived with her parents in the city. Her father was a well-known seaman. She met Bedlow while taking a stroll on Broadway, where she was harassed by a group of Frenchmen. Bedlow presented himself as a chivalrous gentleman who came to her rescue, escorting her home after silencing the Frenchmen.[40]

Introducing himself as "Lawyer Smith," probably to hide his real identity, the two met again by prearrangement in front of Sawyer's home for a stroll in the company of another couple. When the other couple didn't show up, the two continued with their walk. Strolling past a brothel, Bedlow dragged Sawyer into a room, where he raped her after she refused to consent to his advances.[41]

At the trial the prosecution portrayed the incident as a "perfect instance of villainous ravishment." The defense team, which included some of the city's most prominent lawyers, used a number of arguments. The girl should have known better. One defense lawyer pointed out that a man takes a poor girl out for only one reason.

> Considering the difference of their situations, to what motives could she attribute his assiduities? Could she imagine that a man of his situation would pay her any attention . . . unless with a view of promoting illicit commerce? Was it probable that Lawyer Smith had any honorable designs in his connection with a sewing girl?[42]

Accepting the possibility that intercourse had taken place and that Sawyer might even have put up a struggle, the defense justified Bedlow's actions with the no-means-yes defense.

> Some degree of force possibly might have been used by the Prisoner at the Bar; but it was a force only to save the delicacy and feelings of the Prosecutrix. Any woman who is not an abandoned Prostitute will appear to be averse to what she inwardly desires; a virtuous girl on the point of yielding will not appear to give a willing consent, though her manner sufficiently evinces her wishes.[43]

According to Arnold's criteria for a successful case, Lanah Sawyer's chances of winning a conviction were slight. By strolling the streets alone, Sawyer appeared too self-reliant and assertive. Obviously she was up to no good. Indeed, Sawyer's independent movement was all the evidence needed for the defense to claim that she was out to gratify her passions. In the words of the 1990s, "She wanted it." Expressed in the more verbose style of the times, one of the defense lawyers put it as follows: "The manner of her acquaintance with the Prisoner, her indiscretion throughout the whole of her behavior to him, affords a strong presumption of her consent." The jury agreed and acquitted Bedlow after only fifteen minutes' deliberation.[44]

In addition to everything else working in Bedlow's favor, there was his status as "citizen," an identity that was unavailable to Lanah Sawyer and all women in early national New York. At the opening of the trial, one of the defense attorneys referred to him as a "fellow citizen." Raising the specter of a false accusation, he warned the jury that rape "is an offense . . . so easily charged by the woman . . . putting the life of *a citizen* in the hands of a woman, to be disposed of almost at her will and pleasure." This statement transformed the case "into a dispute between a citizen and an outsider," which Arnold notes was "potent rhetoric in a post-revolutionary climate in which the glories of citizenship had been so recently hardwon."[45]

This rhetoric also demonstrates that the notion of the false accuser was well entrenched by the end of the eighteenth century. The defense claim that rape "is an offense . . . so easily charged by the woman" echoed the cautions of Matthew Hale. This defense had appeal for several reasons. It effectively countered the prosecution's portraits of Bedlow as a "vicious aristocratic libertine" who violated "the honor of a young girl of common but honest background" by raising the spectacle of a woman accusing a prominent man to reap financial gain.

The popular uproar in the aftermath of the trial showed that women like Lanah Sawyer were not without their defenders. According to Christine Stansell, Bedlow's acquittal touched off a riot staged by a crowd of six hundred, who were probably mostly men. The target of their ire was the bawdy house where Bedlow took Sawyer. The mob caused some damage to this and other houses, including the houses of Bedlow's attorneys, before they were turned back by mounted militia. Stansell believes that the crowd was not acting on behalf of Lanah Sawyer but against aristocratic sexual license. The riot was a male class war over women, she suggests, with men of lower classes lashing out at the privileged men who came into their communities and used their women. The mob, comprised of "Boys, Apprentices, Negroes and Sailors," seems to have been motivated primarily by loyalty to Lanah's father and the desire to take revenge on his behalf.[46]

One lone woman took up the pen to protest Bedlow's acquittal. Using the pen name "Justitia," in letters to the newspaper she denounced Bedlow, calling him "a wretch . . . whose character is too vile to be portrayed." She also took some well-targeted shots at the bawdy houses, mentioning the "comfortable hours" men passed "in these peaceful abodes far from the complaints of a neglected wife." Displaying a most unusual boldness, she complained that the authorities were less than effective in policing the bawdy houses because they themselves used them. According to Stansell, the response was a verbal war in which Justitia's honor was put on trial, one writer complaining about the "weakness of her misunderstanding and the indelicacy of her pen."[47] The antipathy shown Justitia by males responding to her letters served notice that rape and prostitution were considered male, not female, matters. The tone of the letters suggested that men thought of themselves as the guardians of sexuality, including "the public discourse of sexuality."[48] At the end of the eighteenth century, when Justitia wrote, the male backlash was quick to rail against women who stepped out of line verbally, even if they were ladies.

SEXUAL POLITICS IN THE EIGHTEENTH CENTURY

Although Justitia's concerns would be taken up in the nineteenth century by the thousands of women who joined the female moral reform societies, at the time she penned her letters her protest was most unusual. Abigail Adams, who preceded Justitia by nearly twenty years, was perhaps the first American woman to raise the question of social equality for women and express an understanding of the connection between female political subordination and male tyranny. Justitia may have seen the same connection. Most unusual was the fact that she made her sentiments public.

Only a few women at the time dared to speak out in so public a manner. Those that did adopted a gentle, virtuous tone. The boldest woman of the times was Judith Sargent Murray, who published essays under the pen name Constantia. She is best known for an essay entitled "The Equality of the Sexes," published in *Massachusetts Magazine* in 1790, the same year that Mary Wollstonecraft published her *Vindication of the Rights of Women* in England.[49] The American reaction to these two women previewed the course of women's rights in the nineteenth century, a movement marked by a split between virtuous, moral reformers and more pragmatic women seeking equal rights.

Although Wollstonecraft's message was very similar to Murray's, the forthrightness of her style and her out-of-wedlock pregnancies made Wollstonecraft the subject of controversy and ridicule. She wrote too much like a man, with none of the daintiness and apologetic consciousness of her sex that infected the writing of so many women. American women feared that if they adopted her principles, they would fall into her "corruption." Men called her "unchaste," a "vulgar, impudent Hussy," and a "strumpet." Her husband wrote that people expected to find that she was "a sturdy, muscular, raw-bone virago." She fit all too easily into the American category of a woman of "evil fame."[50] Yet, in time, the reaction to her work would be credited with initiating the American women's rights movement.

By contrast, Judith Sargent Murray wrote like a woman, more indirect in her meaning and gentle in her rhetoric. In her essay on the equality of the sexes she proclaimed that "minds are not alike," suggesting that male and female were different. Yet, like Wollstonecraft, she argued that education would help a woman to become a "rational being," less inferior, weak, and servile, and able to develop "a reverence of self." Through education she dreamed that young women could become qualified to lead an independent life if they chose so that "the term, *helpless widow,* might be rendered as unfrequent and inapplicable as that of *helpless widower.*"[51]

Murray and Wollstonecraft both stressed the conservative view of the times that better education would prepare girls to become "affectionate wives and rational mothers." The goal of improving female education in the United States succeeded because so many thought it would produce wives who could both make their husbands "virtuous and happy" and "instruct their sons in the principles of liberty and government."[52] This view is nowhere better expressed than in a Columbia College commencement oration in 1795. "Liberty is never sure, 'till Virtue reigns triumphant,'" the orator told the assembled female students in a paternalistic tone. Their education would make them the generation responsible for protecting liberty and the future of their country:

> Already may we see the lovely daughters of Columbia asserting the importance and the honor of their sex. It rests with you to make this retreat [from the corruptions of Europe] doubly peaceful, doubly happy, by banishing from it those crimes and corruptions which have never yet failed of giving rise to tyranny, or anarchy. While you thus keep our country virtuous, you maintain its independence . . .[53]

Three years later, in 1798, Murray gloated over the fact that female academies were everywhere. "I may be accused of enthusiasm," she added, "but such is my confidence in THE SEX that I expect to see our young women forming a new era in female history."[54]

She turned out to be right. The Columbia students and those who read in their end-of-the-century schoolbooks that "the modest virgin, the prudent wife, or the careful matron are much more serviceable in life than petticoated philosophers, blustering heroines, or *virago* queens" became the mothers and leaders of the cult of true womanhood in the nineteenth century. Not so well known is the other face of Victorian prudery and passionless womanhood—the culture of prostitution that expanded as the nineteenth century progressed, to nurture the other side of republican manhood.

The dualism of American womanhood had a dramatic impact on the American sexual culture. In the courtroom the images conjured by the cult of true womanhood constituted the standard by which rape cases were judged. The long shadow cast by the archetype of the passionless, virtuous woman obscured the relevance of a woman's verbal sexual consent for nearly two centuries. To this day in many circles of American life, no still means yes.

FIVE

RAPE AND SEXUAL POLITICS IN THE NINETEENTH CENTURY

We hold these truths to be self-evident: that all men and women are created equal . . . in view of this entire disfranchisement of one-half the people of this country, their social and religious degradation—in view of the unjust laws . . . and because women do feel themselves aggrieved, oppressed, and fraudulently deprived of their most sacred rights, we insist that they have immediate admission to all the rights and privileges which belong to them as citizens of the United States.

—"Declaration of Sentiments and Resolutions," Seneca Falls Convention, Seneca Falls, New York, July 19–20, 1848.

Godliness and carnality, female sexual restraint and male sexual freedom marked the moral climate of nineteenth-century America just as commercialism and consumerism increasingly marked the economic order. In the early part of the century, the phrase "true womanhood" was found almost as frequently in religious writing as was a reference to God. The true woman was defined by four "cardinal virtues—piety, purity, submissiveness, and domesticity." She symbolized virtue and reinstated the values of the "temple of the chosen people" in an increasingly materialistic and lustful society. She preferred death to loss of innocence. As one man advised women in 1807, being by nature "stronger and purer," the true woman never gave in to let man "take liberties incompatible with her delicacy."[1]

The other side of the sexual restraint of true womanhood was the sexual excess of prostitution, which played an increasingly important role. Although the laws no longer punished fornication, a Puritan approach to morals was still evident and Eve's vices lingered on in the courtroom. Any woman found to be engaging in premarital intercourse was in danger of being labeled a prostitute regardless of whether money was exchanged or not. The contrast between the lustful and the true woman played an important role in the nineteenth-century approach to rape. Cases were decided either by evidence of the use of force or of the complainant's prior sexual behavior. A sampling of the opinions rendered by nineteenth-century appellate judges suggests that justice in rape was predicated on two major goals: protect chastity if the complainant was deserving; otherwise, as the frequent reference to Matthew Hale in cases where the complainant was unchaste implies, the goal was to protect men from false accusers.

The legacy of Puritanism and its underpinnings of Calvinist orthodoxy is seen in the interpretation many judges gave to the word "will." Usually criminal law defined the word "will" as the "power of the mind" to direct actions. In rape cases, however, judges tended to argue that "will" referred to sexual desire lurking in a woman's body, which responds to seduction irrespective of the woman's mental assent, especially if the woman was already launched on a career of promiscuity. The emphasis on the carnal body encouraged the "she wanted it" defense, just as passionlessness was responsible for the idea that no means yes. Although most rape cases began with the assumption that guilt was to be determined by evidence of the use of force, the presumed duplicity of woman's nature created confusion as to how much force was necessary for the act to be considered rape. In some courts a resistance standard developed that required a woman to resist not just a little to protect her reputation but to the utmost to prove her chastity.

In addition to the element "against her will," "incapacity to consent" became part of the legal definition of rape. This element was predicated on the notion that "against her will" required a woman to have the capacity to consent. "Incapacity to consent" was generally applied to underage, mentally incompetent, or unconscious women. One court argued that because mentally incompetent women had no "will," they couldn't be raped! In the case of underage females, it was argued that regardless of the appearance of consent or bodily desire, real consent was impossible due to immaturity and therefore any sexual acts were automatically rape. The legal argumentation over incapacity to consent was often confused and there was no legal consensus. Yet, the issue showed that the courts were not unanimous about the location of consent, whether it be primarily in the body or a capacity of the mind.

The decisions rendered by appellate judges in nineteenth-century rape cases reflect the social trends and gender relations of the times. Often decisions were delivered in rhetoric that could have been heard from the pulpits of the moral reformers. Less frequently, judges spoke in voices reminiscent of the Earl of Bridgewater and the egalitarian goals of the nineteenth-century women's rights movement. Taken as a whole, they provide a fascinating record of nineteenth-century gender ideology and sexual politics.

GENDER IDEOLOGY AND NINETEENTH-CENTURY SEXUAL POLITICS

According to historian Timothy J. Gilfoyle, before 1820 "prostitution functioned on the fringes of urban society." At the end of the eighteenth century, as we have seen, commercial prostitution in New York was concentrated in a small area, mostly linked to the city's waterfront commerce. In 1818, a visitor from England commented on the relative absence of crime and visible prostitution in New York.[2]

At mid-century a Norwegian visitor called New York the "Gommorha [sic] of the New World." Prostitution was a visible public activity, with streetwalkers strolling the most celebrated avenues and courtesans in attendance at the theaters, concert halls, and hotels. For the first time in American life, Gilfoyle says, "sex became an objective consumer commodity." Dr. William Sanger, a physician at New York's women's prison, remarked in 1858: "Every day makes the system of New York more like that of the most depraved capitals of continental Europe."[3] Interviewing two thousand prostitutes, he found that most had either been servants or had come to the streets directly from their home. Many were seduced and abandoned by lovers and husbands.[4]

The culture of prostitution was supported by a "sporting-male culture," which expanded on the tradition of eighteenth-century libertinism. "Sporting-male sexuality," as Gilfoyle calls it, rested on the same ethic of sensual pleasure and absence of emotional attachments to women that characterized the European libertine religion of the eighteenth century. Organized around gaming and "blood" sports such as cockfighting, Gilfoyle says that "sporting-male culture defended and promoted male sexual aggressiveness and promiscuity." The spread of pornography after 1840, "with its glorification of 'rough' masculinity and sexual promiscuity, also defined New York's sporting-male subculture." Male heterosexual freedom and the delights of bachelorhood were not limited to New York or the cities, but permeated much of America, Gilfoyle observes. The rationale for the culture was escape from the middle-class ideal of male sexual discipline and female passionlessness.[5] If true womanhood lay in reproductive heterosexuality and family life for privileged females, the cult of virility lay in the excitement of prostitution, erotic entertainment, pornography, and unregulated sex for their male counterparts.

Male urban culture also included gangs of rampaging drunks who moved from one saloon or brothel to another, laying waste and raping the women they encountered. Such group intoxication, known as the "spree" or the "row," was commonplace after 1820. Gilfoyle suggests that the spree "endowed the participants with feelings of liberty and independence while inducing a sense of equality." Sprees often included men from the middle- as well as those of the working-class.[6]

Prostitution, pornography, and the sporting-male culture were part of capitalistic progress in the cities. The nation had long since seen the end of the seventeenth- and eighteenth-century face-to-face, agrarian communities based primarily on subsistence agriculture that included the labor input of women. In the eighteenth century the economic networks reaching from small American towns to European capitals linked farms and plantations to the urban economic system and had opened up opportunities for "she-merchants." Either through their own enterprise or jointly with that of their husbands, women, by the late eighteenth century, were separated into rudimentary economic classes designated by such labels as the "better," "middling," and "lower sort."[7]

Women's central contribution to the productive sphere, so important to the agrarian household and the early urban communities, dwindled in the nineteenth century as men took over the economic order. On either side of the divide between the carnal, "lower" woman of the streets and the "better," true woman of the middle-classes, a separate and distinct "woman's sphere" developed. Poor women worked for bare wages or sought more lucrative gain by servicing the carnal side of the husbands whose wives promoted the moral order. Both groups of women were peripheral yet necessary to the male-dominated economic order.

Mainstream women were guided by the books and magazines circulated to a large female readership by a thriving publishing industry. The editor of the most important purveyor of mainstream woman's culture, Sarah Joseph Hale, offered Queen Victoria as the archetype of femininity. According to Hale, the queen represented "the moral and intellectual influence which woman by her nature is formed to exercise."[8]

By looking to such an exemplary model, it was clear that Hale conceived of womanhood as being more than merely subservient to Victorian manhood. However, she had specific ideas about the scope of female power and how it was to be exercised.

Authority over the men must . . . never be usurped; but still, women may, if they will, exert their talents, and [by] the opportunities nature has furnished, obtain an influence in society that will be paramount to authority. They may enjoy the luxuries of wealth, without enduring the labors to acquire it; and the honors of office, without feeling its cares, and the glory of victory, without suffering the dangers of the battle.[9]

In her historical analysis of nineteenth-century popular culture, Ann Douglas calls this "a crucial passage for the history of middle-class northern women." According to Douglas, Sarah Hale rationalized for women "the joys of vicarious livers, of parasites." The lady's role was not that of helpmate, but of conspicuous consumption and display. She was the jewel in the march of capitalistic progress, parading her husband's wealth in the clothes she wore and in the objects adorning her parlor and dining room. She contributed to American culture through the sentimental novels and magazine articles she wrote and consumed. She, along with her companion the minister, Douglas says, "were appointed by their society as the champions of sensibility."[10]

These middle-class ladies gained positions of influence by promoting themselves as proper helpmates and virtuous leaders. Neither feminist nor radical, they comprised the bulk of educated churchgoers and the vast majority of the reading public. They studied language, sewing, music, literature, and history in the "female academies" and displayed their knowledge in polite conversation while males discussed more weighty, practical topics.

In the churches, in an increasingly secular era, Douglas notes, clergyman and lady formed a social partnership, each giving the other a reason for being and an outlet for influence. According to Douglas, "in the name of various holy causes," women could speak out, become aggressive, even angry; while ministers "could become gentle, even nurturing, for the sake of moral overseeing." Together their activities propagated the "feminization" of America, which Douglas suggests intensified "sentimental rather than matriarchal values" and "provided the inevitable rationalization of the economic order."[11] Those women of the nineteenth century who posed a significant challenge to the male sphere by initiating a women's rights movement did so at the risk of losing status in this mainstream woman's culture and incurring a backlash from powerful men. Yet even these women stayed within the sphere of the proper Victorian lady.

THE EVOLUTION OF THE WOMEN'S RIGHTS MOVEMENT

Early in the nineteenth century, women let the clergymen speak and act on their behalf. Then they struck out on their own, campaigning for their own version of moral reform. Anti-prostitution was one of their causes. In 1830s New York, a report was issued by the New York Magdalen Society claiming that ten thousand prostitutes who lived and worked in the city were regularly visited by men from all social ranks. In 1834 a group of women affiliated with this cause founded the New York Moral Reform Society to "extirpate sexual license and the double standard from American society." These women resolved "that the licentious man is no less guilty than his victim, and ought, therefore, to be excluded from all virtuous female society." They also agreed that it was "the imperious duty of ladies everywhere, and of every religious denomination, to cooperate in the great work of moral reform."[12]

Although they did not champion women's rights per se, their concern, as an all-women's organization, with male sexual abuse and with the power asserted by husbands over wives and children would today be labeled feminist. They were "among the very first American women to challenge their completely passive, home-oriented images," historian Carroll Smith-Rosenberg suggests. They refused male leadership of their society when it was offered, traveling throughout the country on their own, publishing a paper with female editors, and defying "a bitter and longstanding male opposition to their cause." Such activities helped to broaden female identity beyond the confining restrictions of the home, parlor, and the church. The movement spread to some 445 chapters throughout the country. Some of their members would later become the founding members of the American "woman movement."[13]

The "Declaration of Sentiments" read at the first women's rights convention in 1848 at Seneca Falls, New York, was the first organized call for women's rights. The tone of the statement was boldly critical of men in power. The grievances of women against men listed in the declaration made it clear that women wanted equal rights as citizens, wives, and employees. At first the movement was called the "woman movement." The term feminism did not appear until the 1910s, imported from France and England. Before that the woman movement consisted primarily of women fighting for different causes, such as temperance, abolition, suffrage, and moral reform. The importance of this movement is that it gave women a female-dominated forum for debate. They turned the woman's sphere into a significant social movement that brought women the vote in 1920 and provided the model for the anti-rape movement in the 1970s.

As the century progressed, a few of the more radical women broke completely with the doctrine of passionlessness. In 1870, for example, Victoria Woodhull and her sister Tennessee Claflin started publishing a radical feminist newspaper in which prostitution, venereal disease, abortion, and female sexuality were discussed. The sisters publicly expressed their commitment to "free love," and they led uninhibited sex lives, which they made no attempt to conceal. Victoria Woodhull labeled wives "sexual slaves," and talked about the central importance of "sexual love" in her own life and the harmful effects of intercourse without pleasure or without orgasm, which she referred to as "consummation."[14]

Between 1868 and 1896, activists working within the social purity framework of the female moral reformers decried "crimes against women." They took up the cause of battered wives and denounced pornography and male sadomasochism. Women provided local support services for victims, lobbied for legislative reform, and wrote about the social origins of women's oppression. Chicago feminists "provided legal aid for victims of incest, rape, and wife beating; appeared in court along with rape victims to encourage them to testify; and lobbied the state legislature to pass stiffer criminal penalties against rapists and perpetrators of incest."[15]

For all their reform efforts on behalf of women's rights, the nineteenth-century women's rights activists still tended to maintain a belief in the moral superiority of women, and they did not go very far in challenging conventional sex roles. Even the more activist women accepted the idea of a "maternal instinct," which would benefit society once women were granted more equality.[16]

The attack against them illustrated more than anything else the belief that women were supposed to serve men. An editorial from the New York *Herald* in 1852 commented on the women's rights convention, calling the women leaders unattractive old maids who had been "sadly slighted by the masculine gender in general." Those who were married were accused of having made such a bad marriage as to therefore be "down upon the whole of the opposite sex." Others were said to "have made so much of the virago in their disposition" as to be "mannish women, like hens that crow." The men who attended their conventions were "hen-pecked husbands," who would be better off wearing petticoats. All of this was against nature, the editorial writer opined. Comparing the position of women with that of the "negro," he said that Woman would always be inferior "to the end of time . . . and therefore doomed to subjection." The difference between Woman and the negro was that Woman was happier subjugated because it was "the law of her nature." While the Negro might rebel, Woman embraced her subjugation.[17]

RAPE IN THE NINETEENTH CENTURY:
THE RELEVANCE OF CHARACTER

The unique character of American rape law continued to take shape in the nineteenth century. Although each state developed its own laws, in general rape was defined as "sexual intercourse with a female without her consent, or where her consent is extorted by fear or obtained by fraud, or with a female who either is in fact or is deemed in law incapable of such consent."[18] This definition drew from English common law and added the new element of "incapacity to consent," which usually referred to statutory rape but sometimes to the rape of either mentally incompetent or unconscious women.

Once again, many cases examined by historians and scholars involved the young and very young. Historian Christine Stansell found that close to one fifth of the cases she examined from the New York Court of General Session between 1820 and 1860 involved complainants who were under twelve years of age. Timothy Gilfoyle found that although the majority of rape victims appear to have been single women over age nineteen, one third of all the rape and attempted rape cases prosecuted by the New York district attorney from 1810 to 1876 involved female victims age twelve or less. He explains the emphasis on young victims by noting that their immature bodies provided a " 'built-in' form of birth control" and provided some protection against venereal disease. Further, males may have been guided by the nineteenth-century theory that intercourse with a virgin could cure venereal disease.[19]

Given the cultural assumptions about women's passivity and the necessity of women protecting their virtue to the death, if necessary, the main question in rape trials focused on whether the sexual activity was forced and against her will or was with her consent, however reluctant. Mary R. Block, who provides an important analysis of rape cases in the nineteenth century, remarks that although the question of the woman's consent was central to rape trials, there was no legal consensus as to what constituted consent.[20] A sampling of appellate court decisions demonstrates that often a woman's will did not refer to mental assent, as it did in Milton's *Comus,* but to alleged sexual desire. Thus, a woman could withhold consent with her mind but give it with her body, a splitting of body and mind that to this day creates ambiguity over the line between rape and seduction.

Because nineteenth-century law did not permit defendants to take the stand on their own behalf in criminal cases, rape trials were often decided on the basis of the complainant's testimony. English common law did not permit delving into a woman's prior sexual history except as it pertained to previous conduct with the defendant. Testimony on the character or reputation of a witness was admissible but only as to the truth or veracity of her testimony. This rule was followed in American courts, and at the turn of the nineteenth century, New York courts were fairly consistent in its application.[21] This rule would change as courts increasingly concluded that a woman's will resided in the body rather than in the mind.

The key case was *People* v. *Abbot* (New York), decided in 1838 and cited frequently thereafter. The case involved "a married man and preacher of the gospel," who was charged with the crime of rape and with an assault with the attempt to commit a rape. The jury found him guilty of assault and battery only. At trial, following the common law rule that acts of prior sexual behavior with people other than the defendant are not admissible, the defense lawyer was prohibited from asking about the complainant's prior sexual behavior.[22] The defendant appealed, arguing that the trial judge should have allowed him to investigate this issue.

Judge Cowen, who heard the case in the New York Court of Appeals, agreed with the defense argument. According to the judge, due to the private nature of the act, to which there were no witnesses but the two in question, certain criteria were necessary to determine her "willingness or reluctance." Along these lines, he uttered a phrase that would go down in the history of rape law: "Any fact tending to the inference that there was not the *utmost reluctance and the utmost resistance,* is always received" (emphasis added). According to Judge Cowen, a woman's prior sexual history could be a fact that spoke to the issue of reluctance.

In his decision, Judge Cowen referred to Hale's guidelines for determining the kinds of circumstances that the jury could take as supporting a complainant's testimony. For example, he said there had to be immediate disclosure, and outcry by the complainant. To these circumstances he added that indications of violence to her person should also be present.

The absence of any of these criteria, Cowen said, yielded a "mixed case," which would not do, because any sexual activity that occurred had to "be absolutely against the will."[23] The complainant had to show lack of consent with both body and mind.

Judge Cowen found that the complainant in question was deficient in all these criteria. According to Cowen, she had not reported the case immediately, and there had been no outcry or indications of violence to her person. Because she was also a "common prostitute," Judge Cowen expressed surprise that the case was even brought to trial. "Are we to be told that previous prostitution shall not make one among those circumstances which raise a doubt of assent?" he asks. Should not the triers, he continued

. . . be advised to make no distinction in their minds between the virgin and a tenant of the stew? Between one who would prefer death to pollution, and another who, incited by lust and lucre, daily offers her person to the indiscriminate embraces of the other sex? And how is the latter case to be made out? How more directly and satisfactorily than by an examination of the prosecutrix herself?[24]

"Will you not more readily infer assent in the practised Messalina, in loose attire, than in the reserved and virtuous Lucretia?" he asked. It was important to understand the difference between one who "submitted herself to the lewd embraces of another, and the coy and modest female, severely chaste and instinctively shuddering at the thought of impurity," he opined. Although both might be equally worthy of protection by the law, he said, there was one important distinction to be made between the cases of a Messalina and a Lucretia. At trial the "proof is quite different," he claimed. "Stronger evidence" was required in the first than in the second. In support of his conclusion, Judge Cowen cited "the law of human nature." One who has "started on the road of prostitution, would be less reluctant to pursue her way, than another who yet remains at her home of innocence, and looks upon such a career with horror."[25] A prostitute was more likely to yield a "mixed case" than a virgin, saying no with her mind but assenting with her body. Thus, it was necessary to know about the past sexual history of all rape complainants. Predictably, Judge Cowen discharged the defendant and expressed doubt (although it was not his province to do so) as to whether the defendant was guilty even of a simple assault and battery.[26]

Judge Cowen's ruling would be the first time an appellate court held that character evidence could be introduced not just to impeach a woman's testimony, but for showing that the woman had probably consented.[27] Once character became relevant to consent, the next step was to bring in a woman's prior sexual history to argue that once introduced to sexual intercourse, a woman was more likely to consent thereafter. This approach is reminiscent of the "She wanted it" defense heard in modern times. It is a logical supposition by those whose view of female sexuality is based on the Puritan assumption that the carnal appetite rules the mind and is essentially addictive, which was Judge Cowen's view. To explain his departure from the usual legal procedure regarding the admissibility of character evidence, Judge Cowen stated that if greater latitude be allowed anywhere, it was "emphatically proper in a case of rape."[28]

During the nineteenth century, a number of cases around the country referred to the *Abbot* decision in terms of either agreement or of disagreement. In 1857, the New York appellate court overturned *Abbot* in the case of *People* v. *Jackson.* The case involved an immigrant from Liverpool, England, who had been in the United States only three days before two men allegedly attacked her on August 23, 1856. The defense tried to enter into evidence the fact that she had sexual intercourse with a passenger on the ship, a fact she denied. The prosecution objected on the grounds that no "proof of particular acts of illicit intercourse between the prosecutrix and other persons, or any other person than the defendant" was admissible. The judge agreed, but the defendant appealed his conviction on the grounds that the evidence should have been allowed. The appeals judge followed common law, not *Abbot,* saying that the testimony of a woman charging rape "should be subjected to the strictest scrutiny compatible with due administration of justice." Drawing a distinction between stranger and acquaintance rape, the judge expressed the opinion that because she yielded to someone she knew provided no grounds for assuming that she then yielded to comparative strangers. The judge offered another reason against admitting acts of unchastity. The accused might find potential witnesses to perjure themselves, which would sacrifice the character of an "innocent and greatly abused female" and defeat the ends of public justice.[29]

Another appellate case, heard in 1868, reaffirmed Judge Cowen's ruling on *Abbot,* with a notable statement from a dissenting judge.[30] This was a civil action for assault and battery with "intent to have carnal connection." The majority allowed the introduction of evidence of the complainant's prior acts of "lascivious" conduct, which might be construed as her inviting the defendant "to take liberties . . . with her person." The rationale was that evidence of previous intercourse between complainant and defendant "is competent, not to excuse the prisoner guilty of the force alleged, but because such evidence renders the assent of the prosecutrix probable, although she testifies to the contrary."[31]

Dissenting from this opinion, Justice Johnson compared men with women as they stood before the law and suggested that the law should apply to both equally. He argued that if a woman's prior sexual history became an issue at a rape trial, the man's prior sexual history should also be an issue, on the theory that the "same rule must be 'sauce' for the male as well as the female when they are before the court as parties." Displaying logic that would give parity to accused and accuser, he said:

> But suppose the same evidence should be offered against the accused, that he was in the habit of assaulting other females with intent to ravish, for the purpose not only of proving the assault, but the criminal intent. All *men* would see its injustice at once and exclaim against it.[32]

According to Justice Johnson, "The law has no prejudices, and does not yield to vulgar clamor. . . . [Women] are not beyond the pale of the law and do not become the lawful prey of a licentious man, even if they are prostitutes."[33] According to criminal justice researcher Charles Nemeth, this argument expressed "a sense of outrage which was rarely heard in that era."[34]

Nemeth believes that the pivotal case to change the common law rule of admissibility of character evidence in rape prosecutions was *Woods* v. *People* in 1874. This case made Justice Cowen's ruling in *Abbot* standard legal doctrine. Basing its argument on *Abbot,* the defense counsel had tried to prove with seven or eight witnesses that the complainant was in the habit of receiving men for intercourse and drinking. The court sustained the prosecution's objection that specific instances of conduct with others were irrelevant to the case.[35]

When the defendant was found guilty, the conviction was appealed. In the appellate division, the prosecution referred to the *Jackson* ruling to argue that evidence of illicit sexual intercourse between the complainant and other persons cannot be admitted. The appellate judge ruled in favor of the prosecution. But the defense appealed to the New York Court of Appeals.

According to Nemeth, the defense counsel argued before the court of appeals that evidence of specific acts of intercourse with other men showed "a propensity or tendency to consent to sexual activity, to imply a desire for sex, and to negate the charge of rape." This argument fashioned a loophole for getting around the common law restriction against admitting prior acts of sexual intercourse by the claim that because such acts went to the issue of consent, they were admissible.[36]

Writing for the majority of the New York Court of Appeals, Justice Grover agreed. Evidence from witnesses who had had sex with the complainant or who testified about her relationships with other men was admissible. Grover's opinion, however, did not strike down the traditional rules. He stated that evidence of specific acts was inadmissible for impeachment purposes, yet he held that such evidence could be admissible if it bore on the issue of consent. In the case before him, he reasoned that the testimony was admissible because, in his judgment, it would show that the woman was a common prostitute.[37] With this circuitous reasoning, Judge Grover transformed the common law notion that evidence of "evil fame" could be presented to speak only to the veracity of a witness into evidence that would speak to the issue of consent.

According to Nemeth, the *Woods* ruling brought "a drastic change in the tenor of rape trials." Two years after the decision in this case, the admission of a complainant's prior sexual behavior was treated as a doctrine and *Woods* was characterized as "landmark law by legal scholars."[38] The ruling initiated the practice of regularly putting the complainant on trial for her past sexual history. Two years later it was cited as "doctrine" in another case, in which a homeless woman's allegations failed on the grounds that although by sleeping in public places she may not have "consented" to sexual intercourse or to rape, "[s]uch conduct is not consistent with a virtuous life, and marks the existence and progress of moral depravity." From then on, Nemeth says, *"Woods* became the source of a doctrine of considerable impact,"* supplying the legal rationale for arguing consent on the basis of the complainant's "bad character for want of chastity, common decency and the like."[39] This approach to consent in the courtroom would plague rape victims for nearly a century.

THE RELEVANCE OF INCAPACITY TO CONSENT
AND FRAUD

The distinction between "will" and "consent" is nowhere better represented than in nineteenth-century rape cases discussed by Block involving mental retardation, insanity, drugs, or fraud in which the prosecution argued that the victim was incapable of consent.[40] Around midcentury some states began to amend rape laws to make special provisions for "idiot" and "insane" women. In these cases the law treated these women either like infant or underage females, presuming them incapable of consenting to sexual intercourse or that such women had a will, though "weakened and impaired." An 1853 Ohio case, for example, concluded that because insane persons possessed a will, it could be "legally and metaphysically said, that a carnal knowledge may be had of their persons *forcibly* and against their will." In Ohio any male who had sexual relations with such a woman knowing her to be "idiotic or lunatic" could be tried not for the crime of rape but the offense of carnally knowing and abusing an insane woman.[41]

In an 1865 case in Michigan involving a woman declared "insane," the appellate judge's Puritanism is transparent in his conclusion that "will" did not imply "the faculty of mind by which an intelligent choice is made," but was to be treated as "synonymous with *inclination* or *desire.*" The judge based this conclusion on the fact that there were no cases in which "against the will" had been construed as "equivalent in meaning" to "without her intelligent assent." The judge concluded that the woman in question, who was said to have a "predisposition to be with men," had a will, albeit one that was "active, though perverted." This meant that the normal definition of rape applied. Because the defendant had used neither force nor fraud, the court concluded that he had not raped the woman.[42]

Block describes another case, tried in Iowa in 1869, in which the dissenting judge tried to make a legal distinction between nonconsent and "against her will." According to the judge it was possible to do something to an individual without her consent but which could not be said to be against the will. For example, a female could passively submit to intercourse with a man without consenting, "although it was not *against her will.*" "In other words," the judge reasoned, "the law requires that the jury must find that the act was against the will—a positive overriding of it, not simply a negative or non-resistant condition, expressed by the words, 'that she did not consent.' "[43] This kind of double-talk adds up to the conclusion that no matter what women want consciously, the interpretation that their bodies want sex will be there. According to Block, making a legal distinction between consent and will effectively means that a woman diagnosed as suffering from nymphomañia could never be the subject of a rape, no matter how impaired her mental capacity, because desire, will, or animal inclination could always be said to be present.[44]

Such judicial conclusions suggest that the interpretation of "incapacity to consent" did not depart from the standard notion that without force there can be no rape. Block describes a case involving a woman who was raped while unconscious from alcohol, tried in New York in 1867, which suggests the same conclusion. The case involved three men and a woman who went to a liquor store, where they drank heavily. When the woman became "stupid from intoxication" the men carried her outside of the store to a farm, where at least two of them had sexual relations with her. The defense claimed that there was no evidence of nonconsent on the part of the woman and that the defendants should not have been indicted for rape but for carnal knowledge of an insensate woman, a lesser offense.

The appeals judge concluded that the defendants had been wrongly indicted. He claimed that it had not yet been established that merely having carnal knowledge of an intoxicated woman without her consent was a rape. Reiterating the standard definition, the judge held that rape required sexual connection that was "absolutely against the will of the female, and that there should be the utmost reluctance and the utmost resistance by her." He agreed that the men should have been charged with the lesser offense and ordered a new trial.[45]

Whether or not a woman could be raped by the use of fraud or other deception was also debated in the nineteenth century. Fraud was the issue in cases where sexual intercourse took place with someone impersonating a husband, for example, or with a medical practitioner who took advantage of the victim's vulnerability. Usually, the outcome was again determined by application of the force rule. For example, an 1853 Arkansas decision declared that "if a man accomplishes his purpose by fraud, or by surprise, without intending to use force, it is not rape, because one essential ingredient of the offense (force) is wanting." The lack of legal consensus in such cases is seen in the outcome of an Indiana decision of 1883 that declared the defendant guilty of rape. This case involved a physician who declared that a girl of nineteen was suffering from a womb disease and under pretense of making further examination had "connection with her without her making any outcry." Most of the cases raising the issue of fraud, however, concluded that fraud was not enough to negate consent and that force had to be present.[46]

By the end of the nineteenth century the archetype of the false accuser was firmly implanted in the American legal procedure and collective imagination, where it would remain. "For almost one hundred years," Nemeth says about the aftermath of the *Woods* ruling, "women were deterred from bringing rape prosecutions because of the operation of the character evidence rules."[47] The accumulation of bias against the complainant is dramatically evident in instructional material developed by W. Robinson for Yale University law students in 1882. Robinson paraphrases Blackstone's section on rape law and Judge Cowan's conclusion about the necessity of "utmost resistance." Summarizing Hale's cautions, he stresses that rape is a "heinous crime," one meriting "severe punishment." But whereas Hale stated that rape "is an accusation easy to be made, hard to be proved, but harder to be defended," Robinson goes one step further and claims that rape accusations "are always to be regarded with suspicion, being often, if not generally, made either under sexual hallucination, or for purposes of extortion or revenge."[48]

Today the distinction between the true and the lustful woman has not been entirely lost. On college campuses one still hears gossip about the slut, the girl who will do anything. She is distinguished from the "good girl," who always shows reluctance, and whose no means yes. For example, in 1983, on the college campus where I teach, fraternity brothers argued that it was acceptable to use alcohol to "work a yes out."[49] They readily admitted that they gave alcohol to women to "get them good and drunk" so as to "loosen up inhibitions." One frat brother, who called in on a TV talk program where I appeared in 1990 with a young woman who alleged she had been raped at a fraternity party, volunteered that the goal of all parties at his fraternity was "to get 'em drunk and go for it."

The idea of the man awakening the woman to sexuality through seduction with alcohol is the modern blend of the eighteenth- and nineteenth-century stereotypes of the passionless woman and the common prostitute. The sexual female of the modern era is both prostitute and true woman. Like Sleeping Beauty, her sexuality lies within her, waiting to be awakened by the touch of a male, just as Almeria of Congreve's play was awakened by Alphonso. She has no agency of her own, sexual or otherwise. She does not initiate a conversation with males, as Angela was condemned by the defense lawyers for doing; she does not look for food in a refrigerator, a point the defense also dwelled upon; and she does not fiddle with things on an administrator's desk, additional evidence offered that Angela was aggressive. The implication at the St. John's trial was that all women are to sit quietly, with legs crossed, and speak only when spoken to. Like a prostitute she is assumed to be ready for sex at all times; however, as a true woman she must say no to instill a sense of conquest, but mean yes.

If a woman charges a man with raping her, the fact that she took the drink or went to the man's house—as Patricia Bowman, Angela, and Desiree Washington all did—is material to consent, just as a woman's character once was and, indeed, still is. The certainty with which the phrase "she wanted it" is uttered today, even though she is drugged or forced, betrays many of the same assumptions about female sexuality that plagued rape trials during the nineteenth century.

Today women continue to contend also with the belief in the ungovernability of male sexuality. A woman who doesn't protect herself—who goes to the man's quarters for whatever reason—is now said to be "asking for it." However, we no longer associate the alleged uncontrollable nature of male sexuality with Puritanism. Instead, we accord it the status of biological and evolutionary necessity, thanks to the science of sexology, which developed early in the twentieth century. The new sci-ence legitimized libertinism for all men and liberated female sexuality from its former passionlessness, only to confine it to a new form of passiv-ity. This would have a dramatic impact on the American response to rape in the twentieth century.

SIX

CONSTRUCTION OF MODERN SEXUAL STEREOTYPES

The sexual restraint that marked polite nineteenth-century society was replaced by the cult of sexual freedom in the twentieth century. The change was slow and not as revolutionary as many have supposed. The major ideas of nineteenth-century sexuality were carried over into the early twentieth century. Only now, female passionlessness was transformed into a biologically based sexual passivity, while the license of the sporting-male culture was recast as sexual aggression governed by man's evolutionary affinity with the animals. Women were given back their sexual appetite but only in so far as they did not display an overly aggressive desire.

Feminist historians designate 1880 to 1930 as the period during which a distinctly modern sexual ethos developed in America.[1] In the nineteenth century, independent working-class women ignored the restrictions of Victorian prudery as did middle-class "New Women" such as Victoria Woodhull and Elizabeth Cady Stanton, who spoke out in behalf of the naturalness of female sexual desire. According to Nancy Cott, by 1912 the "right of women to a frank enjoyment of the sensuous side of the sex-relation" was a "staple of sophisticated urban discourse."[2] In 1913 an anonymous author wrote that "a wave of sex hysteria" had invaded the country and the former "reticence on matters of sex" was giving way to a "frankness that would even startle Paris."[3]

There were several forces favoring a woman's sexual revolution. Religion exercised less control over women's daily lives. An influx of thirteen million immigrants reached America in the first decade of the twentieth century, and by 1920 more Americans lived in cities than in the country. But it was urbanization that broke the moral hold of family and community, and as America moved from an economy of deficit and saving to one of surplus, the American character became considerably less austere and decidedly more fun loving. Expanded opportunities for work allowed young women to leave home and live alone or with other women in boardinghouses, giving them many more opportunities to experiment sexually away from the prying eyes of family and community.

In 1909 the social worker Jane Addams lamented that "never before in civilization have such numbers of young girls been suddenly released from the protection of the home and permitted to walk unattended upon city streets and to work under alien roofs." As women moved to the cities, the older system of courtship where couples visited in family parlors was supplanted by the dating system. The shift from visiting to dating, in which men "treated," created a sense of obligation which sometimes led to arrangements that could be interpreted as close to prostitution.[4] In New York, adventurous working women frequented the dance halls looking for a good time, picking up men, and moving their bodies in the "pivoting," "tough," highly sexualized dances of the day. Couples hugged and kissed in public and carried on "like a mob of lunatics let lo[o]se," to use the words of a 1917 vice investigator.[5]

Among middle-class women, the drive for sexual freedom and independence was first evident among a group of them living in Greenwich Village. These women called themselves "feminists" to disassociate themselves from the social purity advocacy of the woman movement.[6] Declaring "that sexual drives were as constitutive of women's nature as of men," they argued for female "sex rights," "heterosexual freedom for women," and a single standard for both sexes.[7]

Feminists embraced the theories of sexuality coming from Europe, established by the new science of sexology. Couching his notions in the evolutionary framework of Charles Darwin, Havelock Ellis gave male sexual aggression and female sexual passivity the status of inherent biological fact, imperative for man's evolutionary progress. The new field of psychoanalysis, developed by Freud and his colleagues, took the added step of charting sexuality's place in the human psyche.

On balance, the ideas of Ellis and Freud were more detrimental to women than encouraging of their sexual freedom. Although Ellis spoke out against the idea that women were "cold" or "sexually frigid," he expressed concern that women might "rebound to an equally unnatural facility or even promiscuity."[8] In the courtroom, this concern was translated into a new version of "she wanted it," named the "hypersexual" female.

Freud's theory of hysteria provided a new explanation for the false accuser, renamed in psychiatric jargon the "pathological liar." In the courtroom, the female hysteric, the "pathological liar," and the "hypersexual" female joined the vindictive, scorned woman and the temptress Eve. The new stereotypes were introduced into modern legal practice by the noted law professor and legal treatise writer John Henry Wigmore. In his ten-volume work on evidence, heralded by enthusiasts as the greatest legal treatise of Anglo-American jurisprudence, Wigmore updated Hale's guidelines and added some of his own based on modern psychiatry.

SEXUAL DARWINISM

Havelock Ellis and Krafft-Ebing are credited with founding the science of sexology. The scientific basis for the new science drew heavily on Darwin's theory of evolution, particularly his idea that evolution depends on the free play of aggression and competition. Another important source came from Darwin's theory of "sexual selection." In *The Descent of Man,* published in 1871, Darwin described the mechanism of sexual selection to explain the evolution of human sex differences. Like natural selection in evolution, Darwin's notion of sexual selection was based on the idea of strife. Sexual selection referred to competition for mates and choice. Those characteristics that made men more successful in attracting females and women more attractive to males would eventually become standardized in the species through heredity, thus accounting for the observable sex differences at a particular point in time.

Building his argument by analogy with animals, Darwin claimed there could be no dispute "that the bull differs in disposition from the cow, the wild-boar from the sow, the stallion from the mare." He found similar differences in humans. Males differed from females "in size, bodily strength, hairiness, etc., as well as in mind in the same manner as do the two sexes of many mammals." "There can be no doubt," he said, "that the greater size and strength of man, in comparison with woman . . . are due in chief part to inheritance from his half-human male ancestors." Darwin believed that such characteristics "would have been preserved or even augmented during the long ages of man's savagery, by the success of the strongest and boldest men, both in the general struggle for life, and in their contests for wives." The success of such bold men was to be measured in "their leaving a more numerous progeny than their less favoured brethren."[9]

Darwin's theories were applied by the sexologists to human sexuality and by social scientists and politicians to social affairs. The latter followed Herbert Spencer's dictum that since struggle was not only natural but necessary for progress, men had to face up to the inherent hardship and battle of life. Progress would lead men slowly to a glorious future only if it unfolded naturally, like a biological organism, in the absence of state interference. Spencer, the founder of what is called social Darwinism but is more rightly labeled social Spencerism, objected to social reformers who wanted to make things easy for the poor. This went against nature's law, he argued, which always implied struggle. American businessmen hailed Spencer's views, and as one of them put it, "You can't make the world all planned and soft. . . . The strongest and best survive—that's the law of nature after all—always has been and always will be."[10] According to historian Peter Gay, of great appeal in particular to American businessmen was "what they called Darwin's conclusive demonstration that progress results from a ruthless struggle of all against all."[11]

Applied to the sexual arena, these ideas can be seen in the argument that because male sexual aggression is instinctive, it is best left alone in the interest of progress. Darwinian conceptions applied to a theory of sexuality are most apparent in the work of Havelock Ellis. However, there are some glimmers of this approach also in the first classic of sexology, Krafft-Ebing's magnum opus, *Psychopathia Sexualis.* Published in German in 1886, this book is hailed as the most comprehensive collection of case histories of sexual deviation ever published. It was enormously successful, reaching its twelfth edition in 1902, from which the English edition was adapted. Both Havelock Ellis and Freud were inspired by this work in their treatises on the nature of the human sexual impulse. Krafft-Ebing introduced the notion that sex is at the base of most behavior and that religion and art are fueled by a redirection of the sexual impulse, predating Freud's concept of religion and art as sublimation of the sex instinct.

Krafft-Ebing's work is important because it provides the bridge between passionlessness and the sexual freedom argued by Ellis and Freud. Krafft-Ebing calls "gratification of the sexual instinct . . . the primary motive in man as well as in beast." Echoing the Puritan notion that sex is an explosive drive in need of an outlet, he describes the unbridled sex instinct as "a volcano that burns down and lays waste all around it . . . an abyss that devours all—honor, substance and health." Males had the "stronger sexual appetite." "A mighty impulse of nature makes him aggressive and impetuous in his courtship," Krafft-Ebing wrote. However, once the male won his prize, he was not immune to the social interests of reproductive sex. For this, men looked to women.

Krafft-Ebing held on to the general conception of female sexual purity by arguing that female passionlessness was the safety valve for society.

He claimed that properly educated, physically and mentally normal women have "little sensual desire." Like Rousseau, he believed women's passionlessness was necessary for social life, otherwise "marriage and family life would be empty words."[12] Krafft-Ebing explained that the exalted position granted the wife by civilization reflected the fact that she "sexually furthers the moral interests of society." On the other hand, it was the man's job to bring his natural-born qualities to social life: "physical strength, courage, nobility of mind, chivalry, self-confidence, even self-assertion, insolence, bravado, and a conscious show of mastery over the weaker sex."[13]

Krafft-Ebing can be called a sexual Darwinist primarily in his analysis of human male sexual nature as being instinctual and aggressive, like that of other animals. His attribution of passionlessness to women was a holdover from the Victorian cult of true womanhood. However, Krafft-Ebing's interest in sadomasochism also led him to propose a different, more modern view of female sexual nature. In his pioneer study, he suggested that sadomasochism was an extreme extension of normal male and female sexuality, attributing sadism primarily to men and masochism to women.[14]

Havelock Ellis and Sigmund Freud also assumed sex differences in sexual desire. However, rather than assuming that passionlessness was necessary for the control of male sexual aggressiveness, they granted women a sexual appetite. Both encouraged the expression of the female sex drive by speaking out against the "civilized" morality of the nineteenth century and the evils of sexual repression. Ellis held that female desire was inherently masochistic, while Freud viewed female desire as passive and in service to male desire. Both stressed the important role of male aggressiveness in sexual arousal for both sexes. Both argued for modern versions of no means yes.

HAVELOCK ELLIS: WOMEN'S LOVE OF PAIN

At first, Havelock Ellis was far more popular in America than in his home country, England. His magnum opus, *Studies in the Psychology of Sex,* was a multivolume work, published in Philadelphia between 1897 and 1910. In the third volume, Ellis created the sexual version of the sex differences Darwin postulated—the aggressive, competitive male and the placid, accepting female. Where Darwin had made the use of force by men in competition for mates necessary to sexual selection, Ellis made women's love of force a primary ingredient of sexual excitement for both sexes. He resurrected female lust by suggesting that all women were primarily sexual. As he put it, without apparent conscious intent to sound disparaging or anti-female, women's "brains are in their wombs," suggesting that in addition to their sexual desire women were focused mainly on their childbearing function.[15]

In the third volume of his *Studies,* Ellis asserts that the "sexual impulse" is part of the "sexual instinct," which has four component parts. The most important for human sexuality are the first two: the "internal messages" that give rise to the sexual impulse and the "external stimuli which cooperate with the impulse to affect the nervous centers."[16] This process of sexual arousal is called "tumescence." In females it can be compared with the mammalian "pro-estrum" in producing the "vascular congestion" that is "an essential preliminary to acute sexual desire" or "estrus," which is the period of desire.[17]

According to Ellis, tumescence is achieved primarily through combat. He suggested that Darwin did not take enough into account the "coexistence of combat and courtship." The object of courtship is "not sexual selection by the female, but the sexual excitement of both male and female," he says.[18] Courtship relies on external stimuli to initiate the physiological aspects of tumescence in both sexes.[19] The modest, coy female plays the role of hunted animal in a game in which the goal is to be caught. The male exerts energy to capture the female or to lead her to a state where surrender is her only desire. Female modesty renders the male more ardent and forceful. The hunt becomes more sexually charged for all parties, introducing "an element of real violence, of undisguised cruelty" if the male has to compete with another male for the female. "Here," Ellis concludes, "we are brought close to the zoological root of the connection between love and pain."[20]

Ellis accepts the Darwinian theory of natural selection when he states that it is through sexual aggressiveness that a man displays his virility and courage to the female. "In the struggle for life," he says, "violence is the first virtue." A woman who resisted "the assaults of the male" aided natural selection "by putting to the test man's most important quality, force."[21] Modesty in women was thus as important as force in men.

As evidence of the legacy passed to humans from their animal fore-bears, Ellis describes the rape fantasy of a woman that he says demonstrates "the ancient biological character of animal courtship, the desire of the female to be violently subjugated by the male."

> When her lover asked her why at the moment of coitus she would vigorously repel him, she replied: "Because I want to be possessed by force, to be hurt, suffocated, to be thrown down in a struggle." At another time she said: "I want a man with all his vitality, so that he can torture and kill my body."[22]

Aware that his claims might be interpreted as supporting the "subjection of women," Ellis appealed to science for support, saying that this tendency in women was too well established "by the experience of normal and typical women—however numerous the exceptions may be—to be called into question."[23]

FREUD'S CONTRIBUTION TO MAN-THE-SEXUAL-HUNTER

Freud's contribution to sexual Darwinism comes in one of his most famous books, *Three Essays on the Theory of Sexuality,* first published in German in 1905, two years after Havelock Ellis published his study on love and pain. Freud acknowledges his debt to Krafft-Ebing and Havelock Ellis in the first essay. In the opening sentences, he claims that sexual needs are similar in animals and humans. Both possess a "sexual instinct," or libido, which like hunger can be thought of as a basic drive.[24]

According to Freud, libido is always masculine and occurs in both men and women. The word "masculine" here refers to the active as opposed to the passive nature of the sex drive. Although all human beings, male and female, display a combination of masculine and feminine traits, in general biological males are more aggressive and females more passive.[25]

"The sexuality of most male human beings," Freud says, "contains an element of *aggressiveness*—a desire to subjugate; the biological significance of it seems to lie in the need for overcoming the resistance of the sexual object by means other than the process of wooing."[26] Freud theorized that all humans start out as basically masculine, hence aggressive, in their sexuality. In the female, masculine sexuality is associated with the clitoris. At puberty females must repress clitoral, masculine sexuality to become heterosexually active as mature women because male libido is stimulated by female resistance or passivity.[27] Thus, Freud seems to be suggesting that women must say no not to protect their reputation but to enable male desire and the development of true femininity.

Most startling and pertinent to American thought with respect to rape in Freud's thinking is the underlying proposition that renders women responsible both for male arousal and aggression on the one hand and her own subordination on the other. To become a true woman, it seems, a woman must conspire in her own rape. The more passive she is, the more feminine she becomes, and the more likely she is to attract male aggression. As she draws the aggressive male to her through modesty—by saying no with her words—she becomes a woman through the yes that lurks deep within her body, in response to the aggressive thrusting of the male. Femininity, in other words, is based on submission and sexual service.

THE PSYCHOANALYTIC VERSION OF THE FALSE ACCUSER

Freud's theories were responsible for a new breed of false accuser unknown to Matthew Hale: the female hysteric, who made sexual accusations to cover up her own desire. Freud's thought on this subject was influenced by two opposing nineteenth-century medico-legal views of accusations of incest and childhood sexual abuse. The first view, which tended to validate the reality of abuse, was one that Freud held at the beginning of his career and then abandoned. In his original study of hysteria, Freud presented what he called his theory of seduction. Based on some eighteen cases he had personally treated, Freud claimed that childhood sexual abuse caused the obsessional neuroses of these patients.[28] In some cases, he suggested, early sexual experiences could be regarded as "severe traumas—an attempted rape," for example, "which reveals to the immature girl at a blow all the brutality of sexual desire . . ."[29] Freud even went so far as to say that he was able to discover the connection between childhood sexual abuse and hysteria "in every single symptom," and confirm it by therapeutic success.[30]

It was none other than Krafft-Ebing who responded by calling Freud's theory of seduction "a scientific fairy tale" after Freud presented his original study formally to his colleagues of the Society for Psychiatry and Neurology in Vienna in 1896.[31] The response from his other colleagues was also overwhelmingly negative. According to author and psychiatrist Jeffrey Masson, "in accepting the reality of seduction" and in believing his patients, "Freud was at odds with the entire climate of German medical thinking."[32]

Freud gave up this theory in 1897, slightly more than a year after the fateful address in Vienna. The reasons he gave for his change of mind were very similar to the critiques of his colleagues, suggesting Freud's desire to effect a reconciliation.[33] Freud now proposed that the culprit was not sexual abuse, but the girl's "sexual constitution."[34] According to Freud, in line with his theory of aggressive female sexuality, a girl covers up feelings of sexual desire by inventing tales of seduction from her early childhood, which are nothing more than her own desire projected onto others. Thus, for example, a girl's desire for her father or for a male relative might lead her to fantasize or "remember" sexual incidents as a means to fulfill her dreams while denying her desire.

In the famous case of Dora, Freud argued that her hysterical symptoms, which included difficulty in breathing, loss of voice, migraine headaches, depression, and vaginal discharge were all caused by repression of sexual desire first for her father and then for Herr K, her father's friend.[35] Dora claimed that Herr K had twice tried to seduce her. The first time she told no one; the second time she told her father, Philip Bauer. Herr K assured Bauer that she "fancied the whole scene" because she was overexcited by the erotic books she was in the habit of reading. Bauer agreed with Herr K, and brought her to Freud hoping that he would "bring her to reason." He told Freud that he believed her tale to be a "phantasy."[36]

Freud's analysis of the case expressed his revised view of hysteria. Sexuality was still the key to the problem of the psychoneuroses, he said, but the culprit was now the *patient's* sexual activity, not sexual abuse. In Dora's case, the sexual activity was repressed desire. Although Dora said no to Herr K twice, indeed slapped his face and beat a hasty retreat, Freud claimed that in reality Dora was in love with Herr K, having displaced her Oedipal love for her father onto him. The slap "by no means signified a final 'No' on her part," Freud said. It was not a slap of rejection. Her no meant yes, Freud implied. As he put it: "If he had disre-

garded that first 'No,' and had continued to press his suit with a passion
which left room for no doubts, the result might very well have been a
triumph of the girl's affection for him over all her internal difficulties."[37]

Freud acknowledged, however, that had Herr K persisted with his
seduction (Freud's term for sexual abuse), he might have encountered a
quite different result. Due to her unacknowledged love for Herr K, Freud
opined that Dora was just as likely to turn into a vindictive, revengeful
woman as she was to submit to Herr K's affections and acknowledge her
love for him, which Freud was quite convinced of.[38] In other words, the
energy of repressed desire is expressed as hate and revenge. Were that to
be the case, in the face of his persistence Dora's imagination could lead
her to making even more fantastic charges against Herr K.

According to Freud's analysis of Dora's charges, a woman is always
subject to a man's advances. What Freud's patients described as unwanted
sex, he viewed as acceptable seduction. A patient's accusation can only be
false because in her unconscious she really wants the man. Freud thought
that the appropriate response to the advances of acceptable men like Herr
K was to yield, to suffer and be still. According to Freud, since libido is
the heart of the unconscious, "there is no such thing at all as an unconscious 'No.' "[39]

THE IMPACT OF ELLIS AND FREUD DURING
THE PROGRESSIVE ERA

As the grip of Victorian morality and the cult of true womanhood began
to loosen on American sexual behavior in the first decades of the twentieth century, rates of premarital pregnancy and intercourse rose for women
born after 1900. By 1916, the ideas of Ellis and Freud were widely
known. Freud made his one and only visit to the United States in 1909,
to give a series of lectures on psychoanalysis, in which his sexual theories
played a prominent role, at Clark University in Massachusetts. Freud
offered something to both sides of the struggle between the reformers and

the "free lovers" of the Progressive Era. In his fifth Clark lecture Freud stated that sublimation and the repression of sexual desire were necessary for the development of civilization. Yet, he also cautioned that humans ought not to completely neglect "what was originally animal in our nature . . . the satisfaction of the individual's happiness cannot be erased from among the aims of our civilization."[40]

Women calling themselves feminists started organizing in New York in 1914. One of their early "feminist mass meeting(s)" presented a program entitled "Breaking into the Human Race." Women spoke on a variety of avowedly feminist topics: women's right to work, to keep their names, to have their own convictions, to organize, and to ignore fashion. The meeting was organized by a group of women who called themselves the Heterodoxy Club. "Beginning with twenty-five women in 1912," historian Nancy Cott notes, "Heterodoxy epitomized the feminism of the time." According to Elizabeth Gurley Flynn, one of their members, Heterodoxy provided "a glimpse of the woman of the future, big spirited, intellectually alert, devoid of the old 'femininity.' "[41] Not afraid to display their radicalism, members of the club called themselves the "little band of willful women, the most unruly and individualistic you ever fell upon."[42]

Abandoning the repressive stance of moral superiority of many suffragettes, the early feminists argued explicitly for female "sex rights." Cott points out, however, that feminists "did not make very clear what were meant by women's sex rights beyond the basic acknowledgement of erotic drives" and the demand that sexual relations in or out of marriage be based on "egalitarian companionability and mutual desire."[43] Many of these women accepted the prevailing assumption that men like Ellis and Freud had greater knowledge and sexual experience. Margaret Sanger, the noted advocate of birth control, sought out Ellis in 1913 when she traveled to England to escape prosecution in the United States for her advocacy of birth control. Sanger was concerned that women not be sexually coerced and urged couples to discuss sex openly, yet she urged "male sexual mastery." On the wedding night, she argued, the bridegroom must "dominate the whole situation."[44] Freud's ideas about sexuality, especially his call for lifting the restraints of "civilized sexual morality," were considered revolutionary by the Greenwich Village feminists.[45] Emma Goldman, the famous anarchist, socialist, and feminist who called herself a "free lover," adopted Freud's ideas enthusiastically. She and other feminists saw the new ideas as a means for escaping the straitjacket of Victorian morality.[46]

THE PROGRESSIVE REFORM MOVEMENT

The social purity advocates and moral reformers of the Progressive Era responded to the sexual revolution with a sustained government-supported campaign that included anti-prostitution efforts, widespread sex education to combat venereal disease, and efforts to control female sexuality by punishing sexually precocious girls.[47] American psychiatrists played an important role in this campaign by curtailing the freedom of women who were too independent and sexually assertive. Many more females than males were confined to the psychiatric institutions built at the turn of the century, such as the Boston Psychopathic Hospital, founded in 1912; the University of Michigan's Psychopathic Institute of 1906; and the Pathological Institute of the New York State Hospitals, organized in 1895. The women were usually prostitutes, promiscuous working-class women, or juvenile delinquents.[48] Between 1912 and 1921, for example, three quarters of the patients diagnosed as psychopathic at the Boston Psychopathic Hospital were women.[49]

There were two psychopathic illnesses of a sexual nature: one was called "pathological lying," the other "hypersexuality." In their book entitled *Pathological Lying, Accusation, and Swindling*, published in 1915, William Healy and his wife, Mary, defined pathological lying as "falsification entirely disproportionate to any discernible end in view" by children who, although they might appear normal, were depraved, insane, hysterics, epileptics, or feebleminded. The book was based on one thousand case histories of juvenile delinquents committed to the Juvenile Psychopathic Institute headed by the Healys. They identified 1 percent (ten cases) as false accusations of sexual abuse.[50]

In another well-known text of the time, entitled *The Individual Delinquent,* Healy lists "hypersexualism" as one of several diagnostic categories for "abnormal sexualism," which also warranted institutionalization. He defined hypersexualism as an "organic over-development, or over-energizing of related nerve centers" leading to "delinquencies of girls, which are so frequently along sex lines."[51] Prostitution was only one such delinquency. Obsessive sexual behavior was another. Typical symptoms describing one young woman, aged fifteen, were as follows: she was "crazy about sex matters," sought "illicit sex relations," talked about the facts of these relations "without shame," was "diseased," and pregnant. In this case, Healy dismisses the girl's story that she had been raped, saying "even had it occurred it would not have explained the intense inclinations which she had shown over a long period." He suggested instead that the cause was "bad environment" and "very definite innate hypersexualistic tendencies."[52]

SOCIAL PURITY IDEAS IN THE MODERN COURTROOM

The ideology behind the warehousing of openly sexual young women and alleged pathological liars reaches down to the present through the work of John Henry Wigmore. In section 924a of his ten-volume 1940 edition of the *Law of Evidence,* Wigmore warns that because of the possible mental instability of rape complainants, they should be examined by a psychiatrist. Wigmore begins by advising judges to forget their chivalrous concept of womanhood and recognize "that there exist occasionally female types of excessive or perverted sexuality, just as there are such male types." According to Wigmore, since these women look like ordinary people on the surface it is essential to inquire into their "social and mental history" to determine their "degree of credibility."[53]

Wigmore cautions that a judge who was unacquainted with modern psychiatry might too readily believe "a plausible tale by an attractive, innocent-looking girl" because the rules of evidence permitted "no adequate probing of the witness' veracity."[54] According to Wigmore, judges would do well to turn to modern psychiatrists because they understood the behavior of "errant young girls and women." The females coming before the courts, Wigmore warned, were likely to be possessed of distorted "psychic complexes" due to "inherent defects," "diseased derangements or abnormal instincts," "bad social environment," or "temporary physiological or emotional conditions."

> One form taken by these complexes is that of contriving false charges of sexual offenses by men. The unchaste (let us call it) mentality finds incidental but direct expression in the narration of imaginary sex incidents of which the narrator is the heroine or the victim. On the surface the narration is straightforward and convincing. The real victim, however, too often in such cases is the innocent man; for the respect and sympathy naturally felt by any tribunal for a wronged female helps to give easy credit to such a plausible tale.[55]

To guard against the nefarious female accuser, Wigmore concludes that all complainants should be examined by a psychiatrist: "No judge should ever let a sex offense charge go to the jury unless the female complainant's social history and mental makeup have been examined and testified to by a qualified physician," he wrote.[56] In support of this conclusion Wigmore published three letters written in 1933 by prominent psychiatrists confirming the necessity of a psychiatric examination on the grounds, as one wrote, that "fantasies of being raped are exceedingly common in women, indeed . . . they are probably universal."[57]

Wigmore garners further support for the necessity of a psychiatric exam from a report issued by the American Bar Association recommending "that in all charges of sex offenses, the complaining witness be required to be examined before trial by competent psychiatrists for the purpose of ascertaining her probable credibility, the report to be presented in evidence." Wigmore does not mention that he himself chaired this committee and was the author of the report.[58]

But the most dramatic evidence of Wigmore's bias comes in his inclusion in section 924a of excerpts from cases cited by the Healys as examples of false accusations of sexual abuse. In some of these cases the Healys provide striking evidence of actual sexual assault or incest even as they claim the accusation to be false and diagnose the individual as a pathological liar. Wigmore, however, selectively edits out such details.

For example, there is the case of the nine-year-old "B," called Bessie by the Healys, who is diagnosed as a pathological liar for accusing her father and brother of incest. Wigmore notes that "B" had vulvitis, a physical symptom of sexual contact. However, he neglects to include the additional fact that her genitals were so swollen a physician was unable to make a gynecological examination to determine whether her hymen was intact. The Healys suggest that the vulvitis was caused by masturbation with foreign objects, which the girl had admitted using; however, they also admit that the infection could just as well have been the result of sexual abuse.

The Healys list some "causative factors" of Bessie's "false accusations" that by today's standards would be suggestive of sexual abuse. For example, they note "her local irritation for which her father had treated her," crowded living conditions with her father and brother, and "early and intimate acquaintance with atrocious sex knowledge and sex habits." As further evidence that Bessie was lying they note the "vileness of family conditions," which made her "the center of interest in a group of friends."[59] Wigmore notes all these causative factors and concludes with the Healys' remark: "The case illustrated well the fallibility of a young girl's accusations coming even from the lips of a normally bright and affectionate daughter or sister."[60]

The legal response to Wigmore's concerns was to devise even more protection for men against false accusers. Wigmore's request that "the female complainant's social history and mental makeup [be] examined and testified to by a qualified physician" made it standard to use the victim's past sexual history as a defense. A parade of witnesses could be called to testify to the victim's reputation for unchastity, mental derangement, or other reasons for bringing charges. Wigmore's rationale for such evidence was bolstered by the stereotype of the unchaste woman as liar. As one court put it in a 1949 decision: "wherein a woman charges a man with a sex offense, immorality has a direct connection with veracity."[61]

A prompt complaint was also evidence of the veracity of the charge. The necessity for a prompt-complaint restriction was based on the old common law notion of "hue and cry," namely, that when a woman was assaulted against her will, it was natural that she "cry out." Failure to do this was taken as evidence that an assault had not occurred. Finally, the victim's testimony had to be corroborated by other witnesses or by circumstantial evidence. In the absence of corroboration, the judge was forced to tell the jury that it could presume reasonable doubt regarding the veracity of the victim's testimony.[62]

The ideas of Krafft-Ebing, Ellis, Freud, and Wigmore shaped the way Americans thought about rape in the twentieth century. In the courtroom, the leeway granted male sexual aggression and the assumption of female sexual desire hidden under a passive, modest, or masochistic outer demeanor provided the newest and perhaps most intransigent rationale for no meant yes. As Ellis wrote in an essay on "The Art of Love," first published in 1933, although there was now a larger body of women who definitely knew what they wanted, they definitely knew also "that to make that clear would cause misunderstanding, if not repulsion, in the very men . . . in need of that knowledge."[63]

The assumption of the naturalness of male sexual aggression meant also that women brave enough to venture into the public spaces of the sporting-male culture—dance halls, saloons, city streets after dark—contributed to their own sexual abuse. They "asked for it" and showed that they "wanted it" by the way they looked, danced, dressed, or comported themselves in general, if not by their presence alone. By midcentury, the cumulative impact of the anti-female stereotypes promulgated by the sexual Darwinists and passed on to legal argument by Wigmore gave rape involving acquaintances one of the highest acquittal rates of any major crime.

SEVEN

THE

GREAT AMERICAN

SEX BUSINESS

SURVEYS OF AMERICAN MAGAZINES SHOWED THAT APPROVAL OF "SEX freedom," divorce, and birth control reached a peak in the 1920s.[1] The telephone and the automobile made it possible for couples to carry on clandestine affairs. Social purity advocacy fell off and Miss America became the new, sexualized symbol of the True Woman, on whom the "hope of the country lay." The Miss America pageant was born in 1921, the year after women won the vote. According to Samuel Gompers of the American Federation of Labor, the Miss America beauty queen represented "the type of womanhood America needs—strong, red-blooded, able to shoulder the responsibilities of home-making and motherhood."[2] She also became the focus of a growing commercial industry of home and beauty products targeted for the twentieth-century female consumer.

The second most important female symbol of the twenties was the flapper. She was embraced equally by pleasure-seeking working women, looking to escape from the suffocating restrictions of the middle-class moral code, and their male compatriots. If Miss America was a man's dream wife, the flapper was his dream playgirl. She posed little threat to men because it was assumed that she was more interested in having a good time and finding a husband than a career. She was the precursor to the *Playboy* bunny, an ideal sexual partner for the new male, a woman who "stayed out late, danced close, and necked and petted without feeling imposed upon."[3]

The call to "liberate the libido" heard in popularized psychoanalysis meant that men and women had to find an acceptable bridge between the sexuality of the brothel and that of the marriage bed. How was the man to treat the woman he didn't pay, whom he found studying or working alongside of him in daily life? How was the woman to respond to his entreaties? Men had to learn seduction and women needed to overcome the residue of guilt left by the mores of social purity.

On the male side, as historian Estelle Freedman points out, the sexual liberation of young women required men to jettison Victorian habits of chivalry and respect in order to retain a dominant role over the newly sexual female. Freedman quotes Victorian scholar Carol Christ: "If women in fact should be a sexual creature, what kind of beast should man himself become?" Accepting open female sexuality as normal instead of patholog- ical "called for a more vigorous male sexuality in response."[4] Male sexual energy was redefined as a positive life force and source of creativity, as compared with the Victorian view of sexual energy as draining physical power. The sexual male was the " 'healthy animal,' responsive to women yet unafraid of his natural drives." This image was contrasted with the sexuality of the " 'poor worm,' a repressed and fearful man unable to muster the sexual energy to master women."[5]

Males developed a sexual politics designed for seduction. Hearing that Freud had warned that too much sexual repression was bad, they used psychoanalysis to argue that sex would prevent neurosis.[6] Women who didn't submit to male sexual demands or who didn't fit the male definition of the appropriate female character were rejected as prudes, lesbians, gold-diggers, controlling, neglectful, or exploitative. Such nega- tive images were meant to teach women how to be both sexual and responsive to male needs.[7]

Male sexual assertiveness was glorified by macho novelists from Law- rence to Mailer, who filled their pages with fantasies of dominant male sexuality. The hunt-pursuit-capture scenes of sexual intercourse in D. H. Lawrence's *Lady Chatterley's Lover* (published in 1928) provided the first novelistic portrayal of the new sexuality. It is remarkable how faithful this novel is to the evolutionary fantasies of Havelock Ellis. The male hero does not indulge in foreplay and the heroine swoons at his touch, enjoying an orgasm in the few short seconds that he is managing his own. This book shows how, as Kate Millett remarks, the " 'new woman' could, if correctly dominated, be mastered in bed as everywhere else." Whatever satisfaction Lady Chatterley's hunter-lover deigns to provide converts her to a "wonderfully cowering female" whose flashing haunches he perceives as prey. Sex between them is literally a hunt. In one scene, having pursued and caught her, "he tipped her up and fell with her on the path, in the roaring silence of the rain, short and sharp, he took her, short and sharp and finished, like an animal."[8]

This model of intercourse was suggested by American sex researchers and sex manuals of the 1920s. Two researchers in the Ellis tradition wrote: "The physical relation between a man and a woman should end in an explosive sort of climax for the woman quite as much as for the man." Having studied the orgasmic experience of one hundred women, Dr. G. V. Hamilton and Mr. Kenneth Macgowan were at a loss to explain why nearly half had never felt such a climax.[9] The idea that female sexual agency might have been blocked or constrained by Ellis's animal model of sexuality or by Freud's doctrinal excision of the clitoris from adult female sexuality did not occur to them, given the certainties of the new sexual science.

The well-known "Bible" of sex manuals, Van de Velde's *Ideal Marriage,* was first published in 1928 and remained popular up through the 1950s. One might say confidently that this book taught generations of men and women how to copulate. Van de Velde's thesis was simple:

What both man and woman, driven by obscure primitive urges, wish to feel in the sexual act, is the essential force of *maleness,* which expresses itself in a sort of violent and absolute *possession* of the woman. And so both of them can and do exult in a certain degree of male aggression and dominance—whether actual or apparent— which proclaims this essential force.[10]

Not all Americans, even among the more liberal, totally abandoned social purity and the idea of the moral mother. As strong as he was on liberating the libido, Freud also talked about the benefits of sublimation. The ambivalence was reflected in much of the liberal commentary of the 1920s. For example, in a long, rambling discourse on Freud and the sexual revolution, published in 1929, Samuel D. Schmalhausen, trained in philosophy at Columbia University, straddles both sides of the fence. He seeks to find a new, nonmarital set of sexual mores at the same time that he decries the loss of the old family ways.

For the first time "in the history of life," Schmalhausen says, human beings could accept as "axiomatic" the notion that "the sex relation is not to be dedicated primarily to procreation but quite naturally to recreation."[11] Love and romance are subordinate to the "primacy of the genitals."[12] Though highly ambivalent about such tendencies, Schmalhausen concludes that they were inevitable. He refers to the new sexual freedom as the "terminal phase" of the scientific revolution, in which "God was reconceived as Matter" by such notables as Newton, Copernicus, Galileo, Descartes, and Leibniz.[13] As man tampered with nature in his quest for scientific understanding and technological innovation, he became more mechanical in his pursuit of sexual fulfillment.

Schmalhausen's ambivalence about all this emerges when he first credits the "feminist revolution" with the new sexual revolution and then expresses fear that the result will be the erasure of sex differences all together, making women into "she-males." His fear of the mannish woman and the womanish man betrays his ambivalence and his problems with masculine identity. As much as he promotes the new sexual order, he displays nostalgia for the old. The flood of women into the workplace was bringing an end to the old family values, the "final emotional extinction of 'home, sweet home.' "[14] Such fears recall other periods in our history. During times of rapid change, over and over again a return to the old order is sought by attacking the alleged agents of the new, as is evident in the current call for a return to family values.

THE THIRTIES

In the 1930s, calls for a return to the old order increased in response to a wave of brutal, seemingly sexually motivated child murders. Although there was no evidence that violent sex crimes were actually on the increase, the public panicked. A 1937 article in *The Nation* conveyed the hysteria attached to the subject of sex. According to the author, "pathological sex offenses and sexually motivated homicides" showed that abnormal sexual expression was at work in the land, caused by feeblemindedness, epilepsy, alcoholism, premature senility, and the new emphasis on sex. Likening the new sexual morality to a revolution comparable to the American and French revolutions, the author claimed that the pendulum in America was swinging "from sex repression to sex obsession."[15]

Institutionalization of the male sexual psychopath became the reform movement of the thirties. Politicians, law enforcement officials, and psychiatrists all got into the act. J. Edgar Hoover used the panic to gain support for stronger law enforcement. With the fervor of the old moral reformers, in 1937 Hoover called for a "war on the sex criminal" and charged that "the sex fiend, most loathsome of all the vast army of crime, has become a sinister threat to the safety of American childhood and womanhood." In 1947, he suggested that "degenerate sex offenders," "depraved human beings more savage than beasts are permitted to rove America almost at will."[16]

The legal and psychiatric professions worked to pass "sex psychopath laws," which required offenders to be given psychiatric examinations and, if need be, committed to mental institutions. The definition of the male sexual psychopath was similar to that of the "hypersexual" female, in that he was someone with "utter lack of power to control his sexual impulses."[17] In the male, however, uncontrolled desire led him to attack, not passively await the desired object as did the female hypersexual, who drew the male to her like a moth to the candle's flame. Even in their sexual pathology and uncontrolled desire, male and female represented active and passive principles.

Historian Estelle Freedman notes that between 1935 and 1939 five states passed sexual psychopath laws. After World War II, twenty-one additional states and the District of Columbia enacted such laws between 1947 and 1955. Freedman suggests that the panic and the laws came at a time when the disruption of traditional family life during the Depression put record numbers of men out of work, and the new ethic of sexual freedom made women and children more vulnerable to risks once experienced primarily by prostitutes. In the absence of the symbolic power of female purity to regulate sexual behavior, she suggests that the sexual psychopath reflected popular fears about the consequences of the new sexual values. The sexual psychopath helped define the outer range of normal sexual aggression. The boundaries were drawn such that adult women were defined as "suitable objects for 'normal' male sexual desire, even normal male aggression." The forbidden zones were acts of extreme violence, sex with children, and sex with other men.[18] This kind of thinking created jump-from-the-bushes stranger rape as America's standard in defining rape, leaving all other forms of male sexual imposition to be suffered by women and overlooked by the law on the grounds that "aggression is a normal component of the sexual impulse in all males."[19]

The sex crimes panic did not mean that fears of the female false accuser abated. The thirties was the time when Wigmore wrote section 924a, warning judges about the nefarious complexes of false accusers and advising that all complainants be examined by psychiatrists. The sexual psychopath laws also provided provisions for defendants to be examined by psychiatrists and committed to psychopathic hospitals. Thus, the thirties achieved a degree of sexual parity in the medical treatment of complainant and defendant. However, Wigmore's suggested protection against false accusers weighted the balance of the scales of justice toward the defendant.

THE NECESSITY FOR SEXUAL RELEASE: WILHELM REICH AND ALFRED KINSEY

In 1945 Wilhelm Reich published the English translation of his book *The Sexual Revolution.* In this book the trend of turning the sexual into the purely mechanical continued to evolve. As God was degraded to matter by the scientists, Reich turned love into orgasm as an outlet for sexual energy. Reich made the Puritan concern with venting sexual energy into a matter of social survival. Sex couldn't and shouldn't wait for marriage; it had to be released or society would crumble. Any holding back of sexual desire was sure to result in "sex-negative" activities such as warfare, social oppression, and widespread human anxiety leading to other sex-negative social expressions. In other words, the free expression of sexual energy was necessary for the peaceful operation of society.[20]

Building on Ellis, Freud, and Reich, Alfred Kinsey's massive study of male sexual behavior, published in 1948, dispenses with love and relationship altogether in favor of the outlet for achieving orgasm.[21] Of the great sexual scientists, Kinsey was the first American and the first entrepreneur of sex. Like the tycoons of American business, Kinsey focused on the production end—the more orgasms the better—to the exclusion of social responsibility. Kinsey's emphasis on orgasm helped to give scientific legitimacy to the behavior of future generations of young males, who rather than regulating their sexual activity, as Reich suggested would happen in an atmosphere of sexual freedom, would mindlessly sow their seed like animals without concern for pregnancy, their partner's consent, or her pleasure.

Kinsey's "scientific objectivity" gave America a new sexual hero to contemplate along with the fictional heroes in the novels of D. H. Lawrence and Henry Miller—the man who, out of the 5,300 white men Kinsey interviewed, reported he had thirty orgasms a week for thirty years.[22]

Like Havelock Ellis, Kinsey relied on analogies with animal behavior. This was perhaps not surprising given that he was a biologist (zoologist) and had conducted a massive study of insects (the gall wasp especially). Kinsey defined sex as "a normal biologic function acceptable in whatever form it is manifested."[23] He described the human sexual drive as conforming to a "picture of an animal who, however civilized or cultured, continues to respond to the constantly present sexual stimuli, albeit with some social and physical restraints."[24] Kinsey advised his readers that the position most humans adopted for sexual intercourse was not natural. The only position, he said, "which might be defended as natural because it is usual throughout the Class Mammalia," involves rear entrance "with the female more or less prone, face down, with her legs flexed under her body, while the male is above or to the rear."[25] For Kinsey human sexual fulfillment lies in following the practices of our mammalian forebears.[26] Fulfillment might even lead humans to use animals as a sexual outlet, underscoring Kinsey's basic message: sexual release is the key, however it happens.

For all of Kinsey's idealism regarding the biological nature of human sexuality, his research established the importance of social conditioning. One of the most widely cited of Kinsey's results concerns the effect of social class on male sexual behavior. Kinsey found that a man's sexual history is conditioned by peers, social mores, and previous experiences. Kinsey calls social mores "prime forces which produce variation in the sources of sexual outlet in different groups." "In an astonishingly high percentage of cases," he says, patterns of male sexual behavior merely reflect "the patterns of the particular social level to which an individual belongs."[27] He also notes that male sexual behavior is shaped mostly by other males. Other studies confirm this finding. For example, a study conducted of 948 U.S. college males in the early part of the century (published in 1915) found that 85 percent learned most of what they knew about sex from their friends, usually an older boy. The same finding would hold later in the century in studies of male sexual behavior on college campuses.[28]

PLAYBOY AND THE NEW MALE

As a self-described former virginal college student, Hugh Hefner's life was irrevocably changed by reading Alfred Kinsey's study of male sexual behavior. In a short period of time Hefner went from a struggling husband and father to a divorced libertine, the millionaire publisher of *Playboy*. Hefner's success came from marketing a new sexual outlet for men: orgasm by means of the *Playboy* centerfold.

Hefner designed his magazine to reach young men of the middle to upper classes. His target reader was "a sharp-minded young business executive, a worker in the arts, a university professor, an architect or engineer." Above all, Hefner wanted his reader to have "a certain *point of view.*" The sort of man he had in mind when he used the word "playboy" was one who was never sad. He took joy in his work, but was not a workaholic. He was "an aware man, a man of taste, a man sensitive to pleasure, a man who—without acquiring the stigma of the voluptuary or dilettante—can live life to the hilt."[29]

Hefner's view of his mission strikingly recalls the libertine aristocrats of the eighteenth-century. Sex was a male privilege, but it was not to be a man's only obsession. Men might bond through pornography, but they were also expected to appreciate good literature. According to Hefner, "a good men's magazine should include *both* fine fiction and pictures of beautiful girls with 'plunging necklines or no necklines at all' . . . because most normal men will *enjoy* both, and both fit into the concept of a sophisticated urban men's magazine."[30]

Hefner offered the nude female as the glue for male bonding. Where men once resorted to paying prostitutes, they now bought *Playboy* and got sophistication in the bargain. Through a variety of means—the *"Play-boy* Interview," the "Forum," the *"Playboy* Philosophy," not to mention the widely advertised delights of the *Playboy* clubs and the underwater bar at the Playboy Mansion—Hefner made sex a new frontier and middle-class males its gunslinging heroes. Burying themselves in the pages of the magazine, men could imagine themselves in a male world safe from dom-inating women.

Like the Puritans, Hefner defined sex in terms of the separation of body and mind, as part of man's animal nature. Unaware that the Puri-tans affirmed sex as good and necessary in the marital context, he mistak-enly portrays Puritanism as associating sex with sin. Hefner stressed the fact that *Playboy* was different from the older men's magazines that associ-ated sex with "sickness, sin or sensationalism." "In *Playboy,"* Hefner ex-plained, "sex is offered in the form of pretty girls and humor." "It seems obvious to us," he claimed, resorting to the papal "we," that this was the "healthy, the natural, the right" approach.[31]

The sexual zeal of Hefner's new religion predictably displays a de-cided anti-female impulse. The early pages of *Playboy* are filled with pronouncements on the good and bad woman. The good woman is the curvaceous, soft, pliant, always passively posed body in the centerfold picture. During its first decade she has the hour-glass figure of the un-clothed Victorian nymphet; later she becomes more angular, but only below the waist. She exists solely for male sexual pleasure—the sexual helpmeet fit for the post-Kinsey Adam. She comes with no price attached. Neither prostitute nor gold-digger, her sexuality is a free commodity.

The bad woman appears often in *Playboy*'s pages. The very first issue, published in December 1953, starts off with a scathing denunciation of "Miss Gold-Digger." The article begins by extolling "the frivolous flap-per days of blackmarket booze and short skirted women," when "a man knew where he stood."[32] Bob Norman, the author of the article, laments the loss of a time when it was a "man's world, and a nice young woman without a husband had a difficult time making her own way." In those days working girls "were uninhibited, wives were faithful, and alimony was reserved for the little floosies who periodically married and divorced millionaire playboys."[33]

Nowadays, Norman continues, "even the simplest wench can make a handsome living." You'd think that they would have abolished alimony, the author complains. Instead, "alimony has gone democratic," and any man can get hit. Addressing his male reader directly, he says, "It can happen to you too, brother." Hinting at a lingering fear of female carnality, even in this most liberated of magazines, Norman states that even if the wife is a "trollop," who crawls in and out of bed with her husband's friends, or "a spendthrift" with tastes her husband cannot afford, the judge still grants "the little missus a healthy stipend for future escapades and extravagances." The conclusion is simple: the alimony laws of the nation must be overhauled. "Till then," the *Playboy* reader is warned, "it's important to remember that the modern gold digger comes in a variety of shapes and sizes. She's after the wealthy playboys, but she may also be after you."[34]

Playboy's fear of independent women was also evident in a series of articles spanning the fifties and sixties promoting masculine sexual assertiveness to combat the trend toward matriarchy allegedly sweeping America. Hefner saw himself and his magazine as solving the fifties version of "the womanization of America" by reinstating sex differences and "decontaminating sex," his term for "taking the sin out of sex." Like Schmalhausen, Hefner interpreted the gain in female sexual and social autonomy as a threat to masculinity. The trend, as described in the pages of *Playboy*, was enough to convert any anxious male to the *Playboy* religion.

Writing in the September 1958 issue, Philip Wylie declares men to have "abnegated" and women to have "won dominance." Striking the same note of gloom characteristic of Schmalhausen's commentary in the 1920s on the consequences of more women in the labor force, Wylie finds American national life (especially as reflected in middle-class marriage) in "sad condition." There had been "a deadly distaff encroachment of what started as feminism and matured into wanton womanization."[35] All of this was not new, coming from Wylie. In his 1942 book, *The Generation of Vipers,* he had coined the term "momism" to describe the destructive influence of the mother on her son.[36]

Wanton womanization, it turns out, does not refer to greater female power in the political and work arenas of American public life, but to the feminization of food, alcoholic drinks, and interior decorating meant to entice female consumers. With a barely concealed nostalgia for the high-class brothel, Wylie mourns the fact that the "large and candid nude" no longer hung over the bar to satisfy the "male esthetic requirements for drinking establishments." Also under siege were the all-male clubs (reminiscent of the sporting clubs of old), which Wylie calls "places where the hunted, haunted masculine sex can actually be sure that no woman can get nearer than a phone call." Wylie bemoans such trends, saying that "reality is so softened and maleness so subdued that the only inanimate object" that "still has masculine integrity is the freight car and even some of these are being glamorized."[37]

MOMISM AND MALE SEXUAL AGGRESSION IN THE FIFTIES

In the mid-fifties male sexual aggression was considered a natural reaction to momism as men took out their hostility toward allegedly suffocating mothers on the women in their lives. According to Lester Kirkendall, professor of Family Life at Oregon State University, whose study of the sexual behavior of two hundred college males in the 1950s was published in 1961, the male was to be the hunter, the woman the pursued. Anything else threatened a man's masculine identity, which he needed to assert due to the damaging influence of momism. Like other social commentators of the fifties, Kirkendall believed that male aggression, if not due to biology alone, could be traced to a "matriarchal" upbringing in a "mother-dominated home." Tired of being "supervised, directed, and . . . 'bossed' by women," Kirkendall explained, the male directs his hostility to "the girls he dates, the woman he marries, or the daughter he begets."[38]

Kirkendall described two sexual subcultures. One is the culture of relationship sex; the other is the culture of exploitative, casual sex, which he found was typical of about half of the males in his sample. The latter is reminiscent of the sporting-male culture of the nineteenth century, where the sex partners of choice were women perceived merely as sex objects.

The stories Kirkendall heard about their casual affairs suggests that for the college men the fun was not in the sex but in the chase. The hunt metaphor was frequently used to describe the pursuit of women. Sex was a game of "stalk," "set-up," "catch," and "score" or "gore." The students admitted to mistreating females, but thought they "wanted it." One of them said: "We boys have an expression to describe this. We say, 'No matter how much you gore 'em, they still come back for more.' "[39]

The adventure of the hunt was often a group effort, a source of amusement and hilarity. The students would share with their friends all the details—"every parry and thrust," as one put it. Many described participating in gang bangs, but expressed mixed feelings. Although most went into the experience with a sense of excitement, many came away chastened. One student remarked that by the end of the evening the thirteen-year-old girl he shared with five of his friends seemed "so beat up . . . that she couldn't react."[40]

Less than half of the males involved in casual liaisons used a condom. Casual sex with dates was not much different. Contraceptives might be used the first few times and then ignored. Whether a man used a "rubber" was the woman's responsibility. If she got pregnant it was her fault because she didn't insist that her partner wear one.

Few of the male students describing casual affairs showed any interest in or even knowledge about their partner's satisfaction. In reply to the question, "Did your partner have an orgasm?" one indicated that he didn't know there was such a thing as a female orgasm. Another admitted that his partner probably didn't and he did nothing to help her. Another never bothered to ask.[41]

Sex for women, as seen through the eyes of these males, was mostly for marriage. Women wanted love and were willing to accept any risk on the chance that a relationship would develop. Because marriage was so important, the male students could promise anything and get anything in return. Women were "stupid," "dumb," or "suckers," many told Kirkendall. If a woman showed that she enjoyed the sex, she was dumped in favor of a nice girl. The shotgun wedding was something that the male students feared so much that the casual sexual relationship often became a hostile battleground.[42]

Some of the students admitted to sexual coercion. On the assumption that women needed an excuse, alcohol aided seduction. One student said he bought liquor for a pick-up he hoped to "make," because he had heard of guys using liquor on women to impair their judgment and release inhibition.[43]

Verbal coercion, called "pouring on a big line," was common. "I told her she was just the kind of girl I liked: I would surely be back and I thought a great deal of her." "It was terrible, the line I gave her," another said.[44]

Force was also used. A woman's no was almost always interpreted as yes or maybe. Women were expected to resist for show, which only encouraged the males to move ahead. It was assumed that a woman wanted to be forced so that she could do what she liked and preserve her reputation.[45]

Neither the students nor Kirkendall thought of the use of force as rape. Kirkendall, however, was not blind to the exploitative nature of the culture of casual sex he was describing. He said this culture "makes participation in sex a game," which "demeans and debases" the female participants by treating them "only as sexual objects." However, he excused the behavior as part of the double standard that condones sexual exploitation by encouraging men to regard women as the guardian of moral values, which they feel gives them the right to go for whatever the woman will permit.[46]

According to Kirkendall, a healthy dose of "the aggressive exercise of sexual powers is definitely a masculine characteristic." The female is the passive party, the one whose role is to "receive and accept." This is a "simple fact of biology which can never be altered," and which makes the male in our culture "generally the overt sexual aggressor." Because the "youth sub-culture" is especially prone to place "a high value on sexual prowess as evidence of masculine achievement," he concludes that "the line between aggressiveness and exploitation becomes very thin, indeed."[47]

Kirkendall has some interesting things to say about women who take the initiative in sexual relationships. Although most of the males in his study were the aggressors, he often heard tales from them about aggressive females who were looking for a relationship or marriage. Out for sex alone, the male students expressed anger toward women who wanted a relationship. According to Kirkendall, such "marked aggressiveness" from females justified "masculine counter-aggression" in the minds of Kirkendall's subjects. Women who exploited them for a relationship could be exploited in turn for sex.[48]

Several studies in the 1940s and 1950s showed the same lopsidedness in male and female premarital sexual experience found by Kirkendall. Kinsey's studies of the sexual behavior of males and females, published in 1948 and 1953 respectively, reported that 44 percent of the males and 20 percent of the females in the sixteen to twenty college-age group had experienced premarital intercourse. Of those women engaging in premarital intercourse, half did so with their fiancé or with one partner only.[49] Winston Ehrmann, who studied sexual behavior on a college campus in the late 1940s, reported that only 14 percent of the women had experienced intercourse, as compared with 68 percent of the males. Ehrmann also stated that 50 percent of the women interviewed said they had been forced by their companions. Although Ehrmann did not explain what he meant by force, one can assume he was referring to forced petting or attempted intercourse, because most of the college women he interviewed were virgins.[50]

The first study of acquaintance rape was conducted in 1957 by sociologist Eugene Kanin. He stops short, however, of applying the word "rape" to the use of force. This study of a college campus reported that 55 percent of the 291 college women interviewed said they had experienced offensive episodes "at some level of erotic intimacy." Twenty-one percent said they were offended "by forceful attempts at intercourse and 6.2 percent by 'aggressively forceful attempts at sex intercourse in the course of which menacing threats or coercive infliction of physical pain were employed.' " Of the latter group 48 percent told no one. None reported to anyone in authority.[51]

SEX IN THE 1950S

Playboy took the evil out of sex by sexualizing the nice girl next door. College boys no longer needed to rely solely on prostitutes or travel to the other side of town to find their partners. The girls on campus were ready to be liberated and so was the secretary in the office. Hefner made an example out of himself by picking playmates from the women around him, usually women whose delights he had already tasted. One of the first came from his office staff. To show his male readers what they might look forward to from the women in their everyday lives, Hefner appeared as a shadowy, fully dressed figure in the background of the photograph of his newfound office Playmate. In the accompanying story, he told his male readers that potential Playmates were everywhere: the new secretary at the office, the beauty sitting opposite him at lunch, or the girl selling shirts and ties in his favorite department store.[52]

Hefner spread his message on college campuses through *Playboy* wardrobes for "the well-clad undergrad" and *Playboy* formal parties, which became an institution on campuses across the country. In 1958, for example, more than 25,000 students and faculty members attended *Playboy* parties from coast to coast. At these events the *Playboy* rabbit was the mascot, *Playboy* covers and cartoons served as decorations, and the highlight of the evening was often the selection of a campus girl as university or fraternity Playmate. Sometimes she later appeared as a *Playboy* centerfold.[53]

If the sin was taken out of sex through shindigs on college campuses, the thrill was definitely left in the chase. The chase made men feel masculine and women feminine. The chase was kept for seduction and for finding and persuading a Playmate to pose in the nude. Though she might undress for the camera, however, the cult of purity still obtained, at least publicly for legal reasons. Hefner didn't want anyone associated with his organization being arrested for prostitution. The monthly Playmate was presented as the unattainable nice girl—touched only on paper, never in the flesh.

By the 1950s the growing sexualization of America, galvanized in large part by Kinsey's and Hefner's popularity, produced a sexual culture where young men were convinced of the naturalness, indeed the expectedness, of male sexual aggression. The messages from literature, science, and popular culture defined masculinity primarily in sexual terms. Literary classics of the hunt-pursuit-capture genre represented the potent, virile male as an animal in bed, vigorous and notably nonverbal. The man imagines the woman's response as sparked by his overpowering manhood. Only he has the power to stoke her inner fire; she feels no desire on her own.

Lionized in *Playboy*, Henry Miller's books provided the literary model as did the work of D. H. Lawrence. In his autobiographical *Sexus*, published in Paris in 1949, Miller's alter ego describes the power of his sexual charm with the wife of a friend.

> As she stooped over the tub to put the towels on the rack her bathrobe slid open. I slid to my knees and buried my head in her muff. It happened so quickly that she didn't have time to rebel or

even to pretend to rebel. In a moment I had her in the tub, stockings and all. I slipped the bathrobe off and threw it on the floor. I left the stockings on—it made her more lascivious looking, more the Cranach type. I lay back and pulled her on top of me. She was just like a bitch in heat, biting me all over, panting, gasping, wriggling like a worm on the hook . . . After a while I made her stand up, bend over; then I let her have it from the rear. . . . I bit the nape of her neck, the lobes of her ears, the sensitive spot on her shoulder, and as I pulled away I left the mark of my teeth on her beautiful white ass. Not a word spoken.[54]

THE MEANING OF CONSENT IN THE FIFTIES

In the fifties no one would have called forced sex such as described by Miller rape. The woman in the bathroom was behaving according to the Ellis-Freud mode. Like an animal she was in heat; she wanted it but would never ask for it, lest the asking dampen his aggressive ardor.[55] This approach to consent was represented in a 1952 article published by the *Yale Law Journal,* which provides a mid-century demonstration of the accumulation of biases from Hale to Wigmore on the subject of sexual consent.

The *Journal* commentary opens with a definition of rape as "ranging from brutal attacks familiar to tabloid readers to half won arguments of couples in parked cars or intercourse with willing girls who lack the legal capacity to grant consent."[56] The sexual nature of the crime, according to the *Journal,* "is conducive to false accusation." Quoting Hale, the *Journal* suggests that sympathy for a " 'wronged' girl on the witness stand, may lead to conviction of a defendant, 'though never so innocent.' "[57]

A substantial portion of this commentary is devoted to the problems entailed in proving rape in cases involving acquaintances. The major issue is to show that the woman was in opposition to the act. In a case of stranger rape—"a sudden sexual demand on a dark and isolated street by one or more unknown men, perhaps intoxicated and armed"—the circumstances alone are conducive to the assumption of nonconsent. In the first nod to the subject of "date rape," the *Journal* states that where the parties are acquainted, "perhaps to the extent of a 'dating' relationship," one cannot "so easily assume the woman's attitude of opposition."[58]

Referring to Freud and the work of American social psychologists and psychoanalysts, the *Journal* provides a detailed analysis of the reasons why we can never assume that a woman's no actually means no.

> When her behavior looks like resistance although her attitude was one of consent, injustice may be done the man by the woman's subsequent accusation. Many women, for example, require as a part of preliminary "love play" aggressive overtures by the man. Often their erotic pleasure may be enhanced by, or even depend upon, an accompanying physical struggle. The 'love bite' is a common, if mild, sign of the aggressive component in the sex act.[59]

When the parties know one another, consent is always ambivalent and unclear, because the woman's need for sexual satisfaction "may lead to the unconscious desire for forceful penetration, the coercion serving neatly to avoid the guilt feeling which might arise after willing participation." In such cases there may be physical evidence of resistance due to the woman's ambivalence. The woman may have alternately approached and then rejected the man, "first scratching and pushing him, at the next moment soliciting his caress." Such behavior may constitute "compelling evidence of non-consent," but a conclusion "of rape in this situation may be inconsistent with the meaning of the consent standard and unjust to the man."[60]

In addition to "the distorted recall of the 'normal' girl," there are other reasons why women might falsely accuse a man of rape. The woman may be looking for "money, marriage, or revenge." She may be "psychopathic," fabricating "a forceful sexual act yet . . . unaware of the fanciful origin of her complaint." Referring to Wigmore's section 924a, the *Journal* advises that accusers be examined by psychiatrists because their accounts are "often highly convincing and immune to the lie detector." The "psychopathic origin of the accusation" can be detected only by "highly trained medical men."[61]

Between 1935 and 1956 arrest rates for rape nearly doubled, as did the rates for other sexual offenses, while those for prostitution fell by two thirds.[62] While the data on acquittal rates are hard to come by, a national study of more than three thousand trials held during the fifties found that in cases of "simple" as opposed to "aggravated rape," where the victim knew her alleged assailant or no significant force was used, the acquittal rate was the highest of any other major crime.[63] Other studies came to the same conclusion. In California, for example, the acquittal rate for rape was higher than for any other felony. Regional studies elsewhere showed that only a small percentage of those charged with rape went to prison.[64]

As America entered the 1960s, the decade in which the sexualization of everyday life accelerated at an ever-increasing pace, there was very little to protect the legions of young women who thought the sex game was one they could play as equal partners. Although the cultural image of the "sex fiend" warned them about sexual violence, the sexual psychopath was as removed from their lives as Jack the Ripper. Thus, they were not prepared for male sexual aggression when they encountered it from males they knew. If raped or sexually abused, they had nowhere to turn. Had they sought help they would have been lectured about boys being boys and advised to be more careful the next time. Thus, they had few guide-posts as they embraced in large numbers the supposedly sex-affirming sexual revolution.

The consequences of many young women embracing sexual freedom only to find themselves face to face with the twentieth-century version of sporting males proved to be revolutionary, however not in the way most people think. Rather than leading to greater sexual freedom and peaceful relations as Reich theorized, the sexual revolution of the 1960s saw an even sharper increase in the reported incidence of rape. The sexual abuse of women during the 1960s, which stood in sharp contrast to the civil rights rhetoric of the times, gave birth to a nationwide anti-rape movement as part of the resurgence of radical feminism.

EIGHT

FEMINISM IN THE SIXTIES AND THE ANTI-RAPE MOVEMENT

THE ACCELERATING SEXUALIZATION OF AMERICA DURING THE 1950s WAS first popularly hailed a "sexual revolution" in *Esquire*'s July issue of 1961. After the *Esquire* article was published, all the major magazines weighed in with their own, decidedly male accounts of the new sexual trends. There was general agreement with *Esquire*'s position: that the sexual revolution brought to life "the efforts of a long line of sex libertarians— from William Reich through Henry Miller to Norman Mailer and the Beats."[1] As was true of the commentators of the 1920s, sexual revolution was made synonymous with unrestrained sexual freedom. *Time* defined the basic message of the day as Reich once had: "sex will save you and libido make you free."[2] As before, however, it was clear from the masculine emphasis of the commentary that sexual freedom was synonymous with male control of female sexuality.

The sexuality of the 1960s was less a revolution and more another step—albeit a giant one—along a familiar trail. The symbolic and actual importance attached to female chastity was finally put to rest, at least in theory, even on college campuses. An increasing number of young women liberated themselves from the idea that they had to save themselves for their husbands. They traded in passionlessness for passion and rediscovered the female orgasm along with the role of the clitoris. The advice manuals with their maps of how to have an orgasm made sex ever more mechanical. Women who did not rush into a man's bedroom were once again in danger of being labeled frigid or lesbian, subject to being coerced and cajoled either by verbal pressure or physical force.

The experience reported by Jane Meredith was not atypical. In 1969 she was a virginal college student and not even dating the guy who raped her. Years later she would tell Stephanie Mansfield of *The Washington Post* about her experience, which she had never talked about with anyone. She described how she had met the young man for study sessions in the library and talked homework over coffee. She was certain that she never gave him any indication that she was interested in sex. Yet, one night he knocked on her dormitory door and pushed his way inside. Placing his hands around her neck he said, "I'm going to take you."

Maybe the fantasy of "taking a woman" was this young man's idea of sexual freedom. Like the man who accosted Emma Goldman thinking that she was dispensing sex for free, maybe he thought Jane was a "thing" to be had for the taking.

"I panicked," Jane told Mansfield. "My life passed before me. I was so afraid he would kill me. He spent the night raping me and then passed out. I lay there petrified. Then I ran out, past a policeman, and didn't get help."

She didn't get help, she said, because she didn't think people could be raped by someone they knew.

Stephanie Mansfield's article in 1979 was one of the first journalistic accounts to use the terms acquaintance and date rape. At that time, Jane was working as a counselor for a northern Virginia rape crisis center. She was part of a recently designed acquaintance-rape prevention program aimed at teenagers. The program made use of films commissioned by the Department of Justice and the Department of Health, Education and Welfare in response to a recently released study estimating that 20 to 30 percent of girls then twelve years old would suffer a violent sexual attack during the course of their lifetime. The goal of the films, Jane said, was to expose "the kids and the law enforcement people to a form of rape they may not have labeled as rape before."[3]

In the 1960s, no one would have called Jane's experience rape any more than they would have in the 1950s. A study of sex offenders conducted by members of the original Kinsey research team, published in 1965, argued that male sexual aggression was normal and men should not necessarily be jailed for forcing women. The team defined rape in terms of the degree to which the complainant resisted. To protect her reputation a girl had to say no, the authors explained. Men were "expected to overcome maidenly modesty or even mild disinclination, but not to overpower an active aversion." Since society "expects the male to be the aggressor in heterosexual relationships," they concluded, "a certain amount of physical force and duress is consequently acceptable and perhaps even socially necessary."[4] The amount of leeway allowed men for aggression is expressed a little less academically by a college student in Shere Hite's study of female sexuality who said that the sixties revolution liberated "a vast amount of masculine bestiality and hostility and exploitiveness."[5]

The increase in the incidence of women experiencing rape beginning in the 1930s suggests that not all women agreed that the masculine use of force was normal. A survey conducted by Mills College professor Diana Russell in San Francisco in the mid-seventies, for example, found that the rates for rape and attempted rape for women over age fifteen increased dramatically between 1931 and 1976. The sharpest increase took place between 1956 and 1971.[6] A similar trend can be seen in government statistics. According to FBI *Uniform Crime Reports,* the rate of reported rapes increased more than a hundredfold between 1956 and 1970, as did all other categories of crime. Between 1970 and 1980 there was another 100 percent increase.[7] Contrary to Reich's prediction that more sex would mean less crime, all the evidence of the sixties suggested that more sex was strongly associated with more crime. In 1969 the rape rate surged ahead of all other crimes against the person, and in the early 1970s it again increased markedly.[8]

If by revolution we mean significant resistance and change, then the true revolutionaries of the sixties were the women who resisted the sexual and social dominance of men not by becoming like men or seeking to master or manipulate men but by organizing to change American sex roles and sexuality. The feminists of the 1960s differed from the early feminists in seeing Ellis and Freud as part of the problem, not the solution. In a world where womanhood had long been defined by others—psychiatrists, medical specialists, dress designers—they stressed the importance of "self-definition." Out of their self-study a significant critique of the American social order emerged.

An important element of this critique was recognition of the interconnection between sex, society, and what it means to be female. Feminists saw their goal as nothing short of changing women's lives by lifting them body and soul from the feminine mystique and fighting for the rights still denied women. They sided with the view that society, not biology, determines sexual practices, a position which grew out of opposition to social Darwinism by some of the country's first sociologists and anthropologists. Sexual liberation was very much a part of the feminist program for change; however, liberation did not necessarily mean more sex or sex as usual in its active-passive definition.

Feminists were not interested in teaching women to manipulate men through sex, as Helen Gurley Brown preached in her 1962 best-seller, *Sex and the Single Girl*.[9] Although Brown stressed a woman's sexual freedom, she left the indelible impression that women were to use sex to bag a man. Written for working women, her book sets female against female in a cat fight for the boss. The witch is the boss's wife; the saint is the single woman who manages to make herself the boss's obsession. Whether she sleeps with him or not, she is told to go for him, snare him, accept his gifts, or just string him along. The ultimate goal of all this conniving turns out not to be sexual liberation, but finding a rich husband. The manipulation Brown encouraged is hardly different from the misogyny

that fills the pages of *Playboy*. The only thing new in Brown's approach, it seems, was in showing women how to play the sex game the male way.

Feminists sought sexual freedom by struggling for female sexual choice and control over their bodies. In time their ideas fractured the homophobic, masculine nature of America's sexual culture, making it more diverse and creating an unprecedented arena of public debate about sex roles and sexuality. Feminists coined the term acquaintance rape and spearheaded lobbying efforts in state legislatures to change the rape laws. These efforts initiated the campus anti-rape movement and brought to an end Matthew Hale's official influence in the courtroom.

THE REVOLUTION FOR SEXUAL EQUALITY

Betty Friedan was the first American popular writer to tell large numbers of American women that it was their right, indeed their destiny, to choose a human identity, that anatomy was definitely not destiny.[10] Friedan's book *The Feminine Mystique* helped women break the shackles of the momism complex, which left them feeling guilty and paralyzed by timidity and politeness. She introduced American women to feminism by reminding them that in 1848 a group of well-known American women had protested the conditions that held them in bondage. Friedan quotes at length from the "Declaration of Sentiments" presented at Seneca Falls. She ends her discussion of the declaration by saying that at the time "feminism was not a dirty joke." "The feminist revolution had to be fought because women quite simply were stopped at a stage of evolution far short of their human capacity."[11]

The magnitude of the social change necessary for achieving sexual equality became evident even before Friedan and a group of like-minded women established NOW in 1966. As early as 1964, women working for "freedom," "participatory democracy," and "justice" in the civil rights movement, the anti-war movement, various student movements, and the New Left learned that they were expected to take a backseat, get the coffee, and serve men sexually. Those who refused these roles found themselves desexed and isolated. Their male colleagues protested on behalf of equality for others and yet expected service from the women sitting next to them. Few men protested when Stokely Carmichael cut off all debate on the issue of women's rights when it was broached by two women at the Student Non-violent Coordinating Committee conference in 1964. In response to their protest that they were not given equal say-so in day-to-day decision-making, he is reputed to have said, "The only position for women in SNCC is prone."[12]

When the idea of women's liberation was raised at a Students for a Democratic Society convention in 1965, it was "laughed off the floor by the male radicals."[13] Countless similar incidents all over the country led women to start their own movement. The first group is said to have organized after one of its members, Shulamith Firestone, was patted on the head when she tried to introduce a women's resolution at a national meeting of New Left groups in August 1967. Firestone was told, "Move on little girl; we have more important issues to talk about here than women's liberation."[14] In outrage the women who drafted the resolution met with others in Chicago the following week, where they promised themselves that never again would they allow others, namely men, to define their issues, methods, and goals. "Only we can and must define the terms of our struggle," they wrote. They decided that it was incumbent on them, and them alone, "as women, to organize a movement for women's liberation."[15] In a short period of time, groups were organized in New York, Washington, D.C., Boston, Florida, and cities in California such as Berkeley and San Francisco.

That it was a national movement organized for common goals became evident in the first mass demonstration of the new wave of feminism, in 1968. The occasion was the Miss America pageant in Atlantic City. About two hundred women, including the organizers from New York Radical Women and feminists from groups in other cities, staged an all-day demonstration, singing, chanting, and performing guerrilla theater nonstop on the boardwalk outside the convention hall where the pageant was taking place. By refusing to speak to male reporters, they highlighted the feminist goal of getting more women reporters into the media. In a document that was both call to arms and a press release, the organizers also served notice that if they were to be busted for demonstrating they wanted policewomen. They protested the image of Miss America by listing ten ways the pageant oppressed women. One was "the unbeatable madonna-whore combination" of Miss America and *Playboy's* centerfold. Calling this duo "sisters over the skin," the document would be the first strike by the new wave of feminism against the sexual oppression of women.[16]

By 1970, feminist groups were organized in cities throughout the country. As Robin Morgan, one of the organizers of the Miss America protest, writes in the introduction to *Sisterhood Is Powerful,* the first anthology of contemporary feminist writing, there was something "contagious about demanding freedom, especially where women, who comprise the oldest oppressed group on the face of the planet, are concerned." Morgan explains why she broke away from the radical movement she was involved with to join one of the early New York groups.

> Thinking we were involved in the struggle to build a new society, it was a slowly dawning and depressing realization that we were doing the same work and playing the same roles *in* the Movement as out of it: typing the speeches that men delivered, making coffee but not policy, being accessories to the men whose politics would supposedly replace the Old Order. But whose New Order? Not ours, certainly . . . Suffice it to say that women, who had been struggling on a one-to-one basis with their men, began to see that some sort of solidarity was necessary, or insanity would result.[17]

Out of this solidarity would come organizational efforts that would spread throughout the United States, inspiring the anti-rape movement and many other activities. The women who initiated these activities were known as "radical feminists." Betty Friedan often referred to their rhetoric and strategies as "man-hating," the same reception given feminism earlier in the century. Yet, one would have to call them the true revolutionaries of the 1960s because they were willing to critique and resist the old order to pave the way for radical change. They were not man-haters any more than they were women-haters. They wanted to change the basic themes and attitudes that guided the public and private lives of both sexes.

THE PERSONAL IS POLITICAL AND SO IS THE SEXUAL: THE DEVELOPMENT OF RAPE AS AN ISSUE

While the anti-rape movement took root in the ferment of radical feminist activities of the early 1970s, it was eventually embraced by NOW and ultimately reached far beyond feminism into the mainstream of American life. Yet, the development of rape as an issue was not immediate. Throughout most of the sixties, male sexual aggression and female passivity were still considered natural. In line with the sexual ethic of the times, most women did not name forced, nonconsensual sex involving acquaintances rape. Nor did they call marital sexual abuse or abuse in institutional settings rape.

Testimony of the narrowness of the definition of rape was evident in a 1965 public protest against what we would now call rape but was then euphemistically described in the news as a "humility" and an "indignity." The protest was made by Andrea Dworkin before the radical feminist movement was formed. Like so many women who would later affiliate with feminism, she was then a member of the New Left. Her story is a case study of the personal tragedies that brought many women to feminism and anti-rape activism either as survivors themselves or secondary survivors (those who knew women who had been abused).

In February 1965 Dworkin was arrested in an anti-war demonstration and sent to the New York Women's House of Detention for four days. In jail she was raped, but no one, even she, called it rape. Dworkin tells the story as follows:

> While in jail, in addition to the many strip-searches by hand that police and nurses made into my vagina and anus, I was brutalized by two male doctors who gave me an internal examination, the first one I ever had. They pretty much tore me up inside with a steel speculum and had themselves a fine old time verbally tormenting me as well. I saw them enjoy it. I witnessed their pleasure in doing it. I couldn't understand why they would like to hurt me. I began to bleed right after. When I came out of jail I was mute from the trauma.[18]

Dworkin hemorrhaged for days after. She found refuge with writer Grace Paley, who called a woman reporter to protest. The response was: "So what?" Dworkin, however, did not drop the matter.

> . . . that night I went to the Student Peace Union Office and typed letters to newspapers to tell what had happened to me in the jail: blunt letters. The antiwar boys, whose letters I typed during the day, whose leaflets I mimeographed, laughed at me; but I mounted a protest against the prison. *The New York Times,* the *Daily News,* and the *New York Post* carried the story. The city was forced to conduct a grand jury investigation. . . . Television news shows did documentaries on the prison, which had a long history of brutalizing women, some of whom had died. Eventually, the grand jury vindicated the prison . . .[19]

The *New York Post* referred to the incident as "barbaric indignities" in that "notorious local bastille known as the Women's House of Detention."[20] Always careful to avoid the lurid, the reportage of *The New York Times* also glossed over the details: "Commissioner of Correction Anna M.

Kross has ordered an investigation into charges by a Bennington College Freshman that she had been denied the right to contact her lawyer and had been humiliated by a doctor who examined her at the Women's House of Detention." The most that the *Times* would convey of the details was that "the internal examination was brutal."[21]

CONSCIOUSNESS RAISING: THE FOUNDATION OF ANTI-RAPE ACTIVISM

Dworkin's personal experiences and the stories she heard from other women in subsequent years became the basis for her anti-rape writing and activism in the 1970s. The same was true of countless other women. Learning from personal experience and listening to one another provided the knowledge and theory at the heart of the radical feminist movement. From the time the very first group met in Chicago, in 1967, women vowed that they would no longer take direction from men as to what was just or unjust, important or unimportant. Nor were they willing to engage in abstract analyses of the conditions of sexual oppression. Women learned to speak about rape in small groups and large. When they spoke they "went right to the sorest wounds," says Susan Griffin, author of one of the earliest feminist articles on rape.

> The stories we heard of women who, after being raped, were hounded by the police in a kind of inquisition as if the woman had provoked the rape, created a terrible pain in us. We moved to act there, to stop the bleeding there. After numerous speak-outs were held, in which women stood up and told of having been raped, and then abused by the police and the judicial system, after giving ourselves the so desperately needed time to speak about a long hidden injury, we worked to change these more outrageous injustices inflicted on us by the very system which claimed to protect us.[22]

A key moment was the Speak-Out on Rape, organized by the New York Radical Feminists in January 1971. According to Susan Brownmiller, this speak-out marked the beginning of rape as a feminist issue. In a 1972 interview with Martha Weinman Lear for *The New York Times Magazine,* she said:

> I must say, at first I didn't see it as an issue for us. . . . I thought prostitution was much stronger. But then one of our women was raped, hitch-hiking home from a college weekend. I was appalled at her getting herself into such a position. We had huge discussions on that, asking ourselves, how culpable was she? Then we organized a "Speak-Out on Rape," and different women stood up and told how they'd been raped. One woman described how a medical student took her "to see the residents' quarters," and raped her. Afterward, he said, "I'm sorry that happened. I suppose we should go out and eat." And what enraged her in retrospect, she said, was that *she went.* You see, what we all realized was that women accepted the fact that men are conditioned to be rapists, but they *don't* accept the fact that they are conditioned to be *victims.*[23]

Gail Sheehy attended the speak-out as a reporter for *New York Magazine.* Summarizing the gist of the thirty or forty "chilling accounts," Sheehy concluded that most women who are threatened with rape "usually succumb, seldom scream, rarely report it and almost never see their assailants convicted." Sheehy went to the speak-out thinking she was "rape-free" and came away flooded with memories of her own past. Several women talked about childhood experiences: sexual abuse by older boys, being fondled in a movie theater by an old man, being kissed by the orthodontist, being forced to "snuggle" with a father's drunk friend.

Listening to the stories, Sheehy realized how common sexual abuse was in the lives of little girls. The shame and guilt carried away from such incidents, she remarked, "makes the rapist's job much easier later on."[24] This was an astute observation for its time. Even today, very few people understand the helplessness many women feel when confronted with an abusive male. Little do they understand how the trauma a child victim feels can flood the psyche of the adult victim, rendering her inert once again. Going inert can also come from a lifetime of being taught to be deferential and polite.

Feminists were aware of the reality of acquaintance rape from the beginning. At the speak-out women described their rapists. They were men they knew—friends, schoolmates, a gynecologist, a psychiatrist, a therapist, husbands, and dates—as well as strangers and intruders. "The central revelation" of the follow-up conference held a few months later was that "the violent rapist and the boyfriend/husband are one. The friend and lover commits rape every bit as much as the 'fiend' prowling the street."[25]

Feminist understanding of rape was first articulated by Kate Millett in her book *Sexual Politics,* published in 1971. According to Millett, the sexual is first and foremost political. Her analysis of sexuality as portrayed in the work of Henry Miller, Norman Mailer, and Jean Genet shows with concrete detail the degree to which male-defined sex was obsessed with power. "Coitus can scarcely be said to take place in a vacuum," she says,

> . . . although of itself it appears a biological and physical activity,
> it is set so deeply within the larger context of human affairs that it
> serves as a charged microcosm of the variety of attitudes and values
> to which culture subscribes. Among other things, it may serve as a
> model of sexual politics on an individual or personal plane.[26]

Millett uses the term politics here to refer to "power-structured relation-ships, arrangements whereby one group of persons is controlled by an-other."[27] By stressing the political nature of sexual relations, Millett departed significantly from the evolutionary approach to human sexuality and offered women a way for thinking about human sexuality that stressed the strength of childhood training and cultural expectations. Following the work of Robert Stoller, Mary Jane Sherfey, and John Money, who in turn had been influenced by Margaret Mead and Ruth Benedict, she separates biological sex from social gender.[28] This division was compatible with the anthropological finding, first demonstrated by Mead, of the variation in the patterning of masculinity and femininity in tribal societies showing how lightly linked temperament was to biological sex.[29]

Millett argued that male domination works by denying women control over their bodies through making abortion illegal, through the threat of rape, and through wife-beating. Her analysis of the meaning of rape would become the intellectual impetus behind the anti-rape movement: "In rape, the emotions of aggression, hatred, contempt, and the desire to break or violate personality, take a form consummately appropriate to sexual politics."[30] Feelings of hostility toward women, she notes, are part of the social construction of gender. Thus, men learn to be sexually aggressive and women sexually passive. The job for feminists was to retrain themselves so that they could experience themselves as people, not as individuals trying to live up to an ideal female type.[31]

When Robin Morgan went on a promotion trip around the country following the 1970 publication of *Sisterhood Is Powerful,* she found women working on issues like rape, child care, abortion, and gynecological care. She set up The Sisterhood Is Powerful Fund, which dispensed the royalties from the book to women's projects. It was the first feminist grant-giving foundation. Money from the book helped fund the first rape-crisis center, the first battery shelter, the first incest abuse center, and some of the first feminist alternative newspapers and magazines. Such activities showed the degree to which grassroots activism had spread across the country.[32]

In April 1971, the New York Radical Feminists organized a conference on rape as a follow-up to the speak-out. The conference was attended by seven hundred women. The increase in rape was discussed as was the evidence that nationally, the conviction rate for rape was decreasing. At the final plenary session, women agreed on the following series of points, which would make rape a permanent concern of the feminist movement.[33]

1. All women are subject to rape wherever they go. Rape is an act of violence and contempt against women and not a sexual act. Women are most subject to rape by the average man, not by some strange sex fiend.

2. Girls are socialized to be passive and not to protest or tell about being raped. Female children are the great majority of the victims in incest and child molestation cases.

3. Women are made to feel guilty if they are raped. To exculpate themselves, men imply women really want to be raped.

4. The law reinforces secrecy and the sense of shame by requiring the testimony of another person in addition to the victim. This is because of the myth that women want to fantasize about being raped and also that men are entitled to obey their impulses because women have seduced them.

5. Women are seduced into sleeping with their male therapists, having been told this is part of the "cure."

The proposals suggested for dealing with the problem of rape included a rape hot line that women could call if attacked and which would offer psychological comfort as well as guidance as to hospital and courtroom procedures. This idea was an early model for rape crisis centers.[34] Another idea was the proposal to repeal all laws dealing with sex offenses, including prostitution and homosexuality. In addition it was suggested that rape laws be changed so as to include wives as possible victims under the definition of rape.

THE NECESSITY FOR LEGAL REFORM

The problems women faced in the courtroom were widely publicized as a result of early feminist activity. A case reported by *Time* in 1972 was typical. In this case, the alleged rapist had confessed to raping two college students. Yet he was acquitted because the confession was ruled inadmissible during the trial. The issue during the trial was whether the girls had resisted "sufficiently." After the verdict, one of the victims claimed that she, not the defendant, was the one tried in the courtroom. These kinds of problems led *Time* to conclude that "rape remains the least punished of all American crimes of violence."[35]

During the 1960s the legacy of Hale and Wigmore still dominated the courtroom. In a 1965 book entitled *Sexual Behavior and the Law,* Samuel G. Kling, a legal expert, sought to educate the general public about false accusations. There are many motives prompting women to make false charges of rape, he explained, rehearsing the familiar litany: "One of the strongest is that 'hell hath no fury like a woman scorned.' " Adopting Wigmore's authoritative style, this author noted that some women, like some men, "seem unable to accept rejection with anything remotely resembling equanimity." Rejection for these women is "always a personal affront to the ego, not to be tolerated." Women simply cannot understand that a "male may reach a point of satiety, saturation, or sheer boredom." They retaliate by charging rape.[36]

As late as 1970, the following comment appeared in a *University of Pennsylvania Law Review* article: "Women often falsely accuse men of sexual attacks to extort money, to force marriage, to satisfy a childish desire for notoriety, or to attain personal revenge. Their motives include hatred, a sense of shame after consenting to illicit intercourse . . . and delusion."[37]

In a 1975 New York case, a judge argued that the defendant's "predatory conquest" of the resisting female was seduction, not rape, on the grounds that since "the dawn of history, men with clubs have grabbed women, willing or unwilling, by the hair to have their way with them." The defendant was not convicted because his acts were "closer to a permissible seduction than a forceful rape, despite evidence that the defendant deceived the victim as to his real identity, lured her under false pretenses to an apartment he did not own, threatened that he would kill and rape her, lied to the police, and escaped from their custody."[38]

Judicial bias made it mandatory for a complainant to present corroborating evidence of her charges. In New York State, for example, Section 130 of the penal law stated that "A person shall not be convicted . . . solely on the uncorroborated testimony of the alleged victim."[39] New York's corroboration rule was the most stringent in the country in requiring that "every material element of a rape—penetration, force and the identity of the rapist—must be corroborated by evidence other than the victim's testimony." As Martha Weinman Lear pointed out in her *New York Times Magazine* article, if a woman was raped in New York and her TV was stolen, a man could easily go free on the rape charge and be convicted for stealing her TV.[40] One is not surprised to read that a typical year during the 1960s in New York yielded only twenty rape convictions in the entire state.[41]

Hale's cautions were still read to the juries in many states and his guidelines followed in assessing the complainant's credibility. In addition to the corroboration rule, a rape complainant had to demonstrate that she had resisted. Although the nineteenth-century requirement of "utmost resistance" had been relaxed in some courts, all still looked to the woman's resistance as a sign of nonconsent. Force was defined more often as that which "might reasonably be supposed sufficient to overcome resistance, taking into consideration the relative strength of the parties and other circumstances of the case." In New York, however, resistance still had to be "to the utmost." In most courts the defense was allowed to investigate the complainant's reputation as before. Finally, the promptness in reporting the charge continued to be used as evidence of the veracity of an allegation.[42]

The study of the American jury based on more than 3,000 fifties trials, published in the 1960s by Harry Kalven, Jr. and Hans Zeisel of the University of Chicago Law School, provided important evidence that the legal establishment was not unanimously anti-female. This study showed that judges were much more likely to convict in rape cases than jurors, whether the case was "aggravated" or "simple." Additionally, this study demonstrated the degree to which popular values rather than the law rules in rape cases involving acquaintances.[43]

The fate of Wigmore's 1940 advice regarding psychiatric examinations of complainants is summarized in the 1970 revision of his Law of Evidence. The judicial system was far from unanimous in its response to Wigmore's suggestions. In 1956, for example, one judge warned against needless embarking "on an amateur's voyage on the fog-enshrouded sea of psychiatry." This sort of pessimism about the role of psychiatry had resulted in widespread criticism and eventual repeal of the sexual psychopath laws in the 1960s.[44] A 1966 California decision stated that it would be inappropriate in "many instances" to require a psychiatric examination. One of the reasons given is that it would deter victims of sex crimes from reporting them. The general tendency followed in most courts was to leave the question of allowing psychiatric testimony regarding the credibility of a witness to the discretion of the trial judge.[45]

During the 1970s, law review writers increasingly questioned the focus of rape trials on the victim rather than the defendant. The author of one particularly interesting article reveals the extent of the bias by applying the questions routinely asked of rape victims to a fictive robbery victim.

Mr. Smith, you were held up at gun-point at the corner of First and Main?

Yes.

Did you struggle with the robber?

No.

Why not?

He was armed.

Then you made a conscious decision to comply with his demands
   rather than resist?

Yes.

Did you scream? Cry out?

No, I was afraid.

I see. Have you ever been held up before?

No.

Have you ever *given* money away?

Yes, of course.

And you did so willingly?

What are you getting at?

Well, let's put it like this, Mr. Smith. You've given money away in
   the past. In fact you've quite a reputation for philanthropy. How
   can we be sure that you weren't *contriving* to have your money
   taken from you by force?

After a few more questions to Mr. Smith about what he was wearing
and where he was walking, at what time, the final question asks: "In
other words, Mr. Smith, you were walking around the streets late at night
in a suit that practically advertised the fact that you might be a good
target for some easy money, isn't that so? I mean, if we didn't know
better, Mr. Smith, we might even think you were *asking* for this to
happen, mightn't we?"[46]

FEMINIST ACTIVISM FOR LEGAL REFORM

One of the first sustained political efforts of the feminist movement was
to change outmoded rape laws. This activity brought groups of radical
feminists together with members of NOW. In February 1973, the Sixth
Annual National Conference of NOW, meeting in Washington, D.C.,

voted by acclamation to establish the National Task Force on Rape—the only resolution passed by acclamation of the conference body. During the following two years, the number of chapters actively involved in the rape issue grew from fifteen to two hundred. This kind of organization provided the impetus for rape law reform in many states.[47] Feminists sought support from traditional political organizations such as the League of Women Voters and the American Civil Liberties Union. Had they not done so, the backlash against feminism might have blocked rape reform legislation in many states.[48]

Between 1974 and 1980 almost every state passed some form of rape reform legislation. The purpose of changing the law was to secure more convictions and protect the interests of the victims. The reform movement was controversial and did not sail easily through the mostly all-male state legislative bodies. In some states reform efforts were more successful than in others. Despite the variation, some common trends may be noted.[49]

In general, defense attorneys were no longer able to probe into a victim's sexual history at will. The prompt reporting and corroboration requirements were dropped by most states. In many states, rape was redefined in gender-neutral terms so that same-sex rape and female-to-male rape became part of the law. Rape was also defined in some states so as to include spousal rape, which meant that rape involving people who knew one another would be more seriously addressed. Often rape was defined in terms of objective circumstances "in order to move the focus of the trial away from the victim's behavior and character."[50]

To make it easier to obtain a conviction, many states defined offenses in terms of degree in order to establish "gradations of penalties," under the theory that juries were reluctant to convict when the penalty could be as severe as the penalty for murder. According to psychologists Julie A. Allison and Lawrence S. Wrightsman, in 1971 capital punishment was a potential punishment for a rape conviction in sixteen states and by the federal government. This number was reduced to three after the 1972

Supreme Court decision in the case of *Furman* v. *Georgia,* when the states were forced to review their capital punishment provisions. In 1977 the Supreme Court ruled in the case of *Coker* v. *Georgia* that capital punishment for raping an adult woman was "grossly disproportionate and excessive." Noting in its written decision that "in no time in the last 50 years has a majority of the states authorized death as punishment for rape," the Court concluded that the death penalty for rape went against public opinion. According to Allison and Wrightsman, due to juror reluctance, rape-reform advocates saw the abolishing of the death penalty for rape as positive.[51] In addition, reform advocates welcomed gradations of penalties because it allowed for the punishment of specific acts short of intercourse, such as sexual contact offenses.[52]

Although the efforts to abolish Hale's cautionary jury instructions were less successful at first, in time the majority of states eliminated them.[53] In 1975, for example, the Supreme Court of California unanimously deleted the "Lord Hale Instruction" requiring judges to tell juries that the uncorroborated testimony of an alleged victim must be taken with "caution" because her charge "is easily made and difficult to disprove." In the same year, a state law took effect barring inquiry into a woman's past sexual history unless it was pertinent to the immediate case. The California National Organization of Women was the prime mover behind these changes, supported by a fifty-year-old organization of women lawyers known as the "Queen's bench" and helped by feminist activists staging protests in the streets.[54]

In the case of New York, its strict corroboration rule first came under attack in 1972. By 1974 the rule was virtually eliminated, which meant that a complainant could testify without corroboration that the sex act had occurred, that it was without her consent, or that force was employed by the attacker. According to Linda Fairstein, head of the Manhattan Sex Crimes Prosecution Unit, the dropping of this rule gave the complainant "her day in court." The change meant that jurors were themselves charged with determining a complainant's credibility by listening to the testimony and observing her demeanor.[55] However, as we know from the outcome of the St. John's case, leaving to jurors the task of determining credibility based on their impressions of the complainant opens the door to popular stereotypes of how a complainant should act on the witness stand. New York retained only two situations in which corroboration was required: in cases where the victim was under seventeen or suffered from a mental defect or was incapacitated. The latter exception meant that corroboration was required in the St. John's case because of Angela's physical helplessness.

New York changed the rules on inquiring into a complainant's sexual history in 1975. The legislation drafted by Leslie Snyder and other lawyers declared that "evidence of a victim's sexual conduct shall *not* be admissible in a prosecution" for consummated or attempted sex offenses. Information about a complainant's past sexual activity was prohibited with the exception of five specified areas. According to Linda Fairstein, "this legislation was a tremendous effort to strike a fair balance between protecting the rights of victims and the rights of defendants in the rare circumstance when such evidence might indeed be relevant."[56]

The final change in the New York law took place in 1983 with the demise of the requirement that forcible compulsion be established by the complainant's "genuine" (not "feigned, or passive") resistance to "the utmost limit of her power." This requirement was first modified in 1977 by substituting the phrase "earnest resistance" in the place of "utmost resistance." In 1982 the requirement of earnest resistance was abandoned, which took the focus off the complainant's resistance. However, the new language still emphasized the importance of establishing "forcible compulsion" and the victim's fear of "immediate death or physical injury."[57]

It should be noted that none of the legal changes significantly altered the definition of rape. Nowhere was rape explicitly defined in terms of nonconsensual penetration alone. Force had to be present or evidence of a person's incapacity to consent due to physical helplessness, mental incapacity, or by reason of being mentally defective and thus, as stated in the

New York State law, "not able to make a rational, free-will determination to consent, or not able to communicate an unwillingness to consent, to sexual activity." Thus, the law is ambivalent about the importance of explicit consent, finding its absence definitive of rape only in cases of physical helplessness.

In the years after rape-law reform, there was no clear-cut evidence that it was having the impact feminists hoped for. In some states, the new legal procedures appeared to have increased the rate of reporting and the percentage of convictions. In Washington and Michigan, two states with comprehensive reforms, there was evidence of a significant increase in convictions as charged and a decrease in convictions for a lesser offense.[58] However, in other states no such gains could be noted. This was partly due to the fact that legal reform was uneven, affecting the courts in some states more than others. Even in the presence of significant legal reform, most researchers concluded that although legal reform might bring more cases to trial, the rate of conviction still depended largely on whether jurors were willing to view rape as a criminal rather than a moral issue. Because of juror prejudice, a study conducted in the early 1980s found, many prosecutors were unwilling to accept cases unless they conformed to the old pattern of forcible compulsion by a stranger and evidence of significant resistance by the victim.[59]

In the final analysis, equal justice in acquaintance rape will depend on refocusing the public's attention in general and that of jurors in particular from popular myths and the complainant's resistance to the defendant's behavior. The major questions should be "Did he obtain consent?" not "How much did she resist?" Getting jurors to take this point of view is nigh impossible given the prevailing stereotypes. As legal analyst Leigh Bienen observed in a 1980 article on rape reform legislation, the problems associated with the American attitude toward sexual consent "cannot be removed by statute when they are the result of deeply ingrained hostility toward women's sexuality, independence, and adulthood."[60] Bienen's conclusion is supported by the body of research initiated in the mid-seventies, which identified the scope of acquaintance rape, its causes, and most important, a deep ambivalence about the legitimacy of female sexual autonomy.

NINE

NAMING AND STUDYING ACQUAINTANCE RAPE

When it comes to my masculinity I get very defensive. Because I know that men are admired for having many partners, I set quotas—so many girls in one month. The joy of sex for me is the feeling of acceptance and approval which always goes with having sex with a new person.

—MALE COLLEGE STUDENT[1]

MARTHA McCLUSKEY WENT TO COLLEGE DURING A TIME WHEN FEMINIST activism for rape reform was well under way, however not yet widely publicized outside scholarly and legal circles. In 1977 she was sexually abused by a group of fraternity brothers while a student at Colby College. At the time, however, Martha thought that being assaulted by "normal white college men . . . was not significant" and she didn't understand it as "real violence." It wasn't until after graduating from Yale Law School that she wrote about the assault in an article in the *Maine Law Review* on "privileged violence in college fraternities."

It happened at the beginning of vacation, when her dorm was nearly empty. As she described it:

I am standing in the hallway looking out the window for my ride home. I turn around and my suitcase is gone; Joe and Bill from down the hall are laughing as they carry it away. I follow them. I hear a door lock behind me. They let go of my suitcase and grab me.

I am lying on the bare linoleum floor of Joe's bedroom. In the room are a group of Lambda Chi and KDR pledges who live on my hall; several of them are football players. Some are sitting on the bed, laughing. Two others are pinning my arms and my legs to the floor. Joe is touching me while the others cheer.

I am a friendly fellow-classmate as I reasonably explain that I'm in a rush to catch a ride, that I'm not in the mood to joke around; that I'd really like them to please cut it out. It takes a few long upside-down seconds before things look different. As I start to scream and fight I feel like I am shattering a world that will not get put back together. They let me go.

Later I don't talk about this, not even to myself. I sit near Joe and Bill in sociology and English classes. I don't talk in class.[2]

Starting in the 1970s, research on acquaintance rape conducted by psychologists, sociologists, and medical researchers began, and by the 1990s a significant body of knowledge on all aspects of sexual assault and abuse had been established. At first the research focused on the annual incidence and lifetime prevalence of acquaintance rape in order to establish the scope of the problem, but soon expanded to include causes, consequences, social and psychological costs, and prevention. The studies operated within the legal definition of rape as sexual intercourse, including oral or anal penetration, due to force, the threat of force, or by taking advantage of a person's incapacity to consent. Most studies focused on the heterosexual rape of females. However, in recent years attention has turned also to the heterosexual and same-sex rape of male victims. Least attention has been given to same-sex rape of women.[3]

THE EARLY STUDIES

Studies making a distinction between jump-from-the-bushes stranger
rape and rape involving people who know one another go back at least to
the 1950s. In 1952 the *Yale Law Journal* (discussed in Chapter 7) recognized that rape ranges from "brutal attacks familiar to tabloid readers to
half won arguments of couples in parked cars." Kalven and Zeisel's distinction between "aggravated" and "simple" rape in their national study
of fifties trials (see Chapter 8) was the first to demonstrate that a significant proportion (40 percent) of rape cases going to trial involved acquaintances. Both of these acknowledged that when the parties know one another a conviction is much more difficult. Kalven and Zeisel were able to
attribute the difficulty to juror prejudice by showing that judges were
much more likely than jurors to believe that the evidence warranted a
conviction in cases of simple rape.[4]

The most well-known of the early studies acknowledging the scope of
acquaintance rape was authored by sociologist Menachem Amir. Based on
an examination of police files of rapes occurring in 1958 and 1960, Amir
concluded that rapists are generally "normal" men. About half of all the
rapes were committed by men who knew their victims. Only 42 percent
of the rapists were complete strangers to their victims, and not all of the
victims resisted to the utmost.[5] More than half of the victims were sub-
missive during the rape; about one fifth of the victims put up a strong
physical fight; and another quarter actively resisted in some other way,
like screaming. Twenty percent of the victims were between the ages of
ten and fourteen, and 25 percent between fifteen and nineteen. The
younger the victim the less likely she was to resist.[6]

The first widely read feminist studies mentioning acquaintance or
date rape were authored by Susan Brownmiller and Diana Russell in the
mid-1970s. In her landmark study, *Against Our Will,* Brownmiller is the
first to use the term "date rape." The kind of interaction Brownmiller

labeled date rape was typical of men and women caught in the double bind of the sexual revolution. Men pressed their advantage thinking that all women now "wanted it," but nice girls hadn't yet learned to make a no stick. Brownmiller phrased the problem as follows:

> In a dating situation an aggressor may press his advantage to the point where pleasantness quickly turns to unpleasantness and more than the woman bargained for, yet social propriety and the strictures of conventional female behavior that dictate politeness and femininity demand that the female gracefully endure, or wriggle away if she can, but a direct confrontation falls outside of the behavioral norms. These are the cases about which the police are wont to say, "She changed her mind afterward," with no recognition that it was only afterward that she dared pull herself together and face up to the fact that she had truly been raped.[7]

Brownmiller's historic contribution to the anti-rape movement is in her valuable analysis of the cultural forces shaping female passivity when confronted with male sexual aggression and her conceptualization of rape as violence. Brownmiller urged a generation of young women to learn to say no and overcome their historical training to be nice. She recognized that date rapes hardly ever get to court and don't look good on paper because the "intangibles of victim behavior . . . present a poor case."[8] These are the kinds of cases that Kalven and Zeisel found usually ended in acquittals. Brownmiller admits that even with her feminist awareness she often feels like shouting, "Idiot, why didn't you see the warning signs earlier?" upon hearing such cases.

Before she began researching rape in the early 1970s, Diana Russell held the "crazed stranger" theory of rape, believing that rape was "an extremely sadistic and deviant act, which could be performed only by crazy or psychopathic people." The idea had never occurred to her that rape by a lover, friend, or colleague was possible. She learned differently in 1971 while she was attending the highly publicized rape trial of Jerry

Plotkin in San Francisco. Plotkin was a jeweler accused of abducting a young woman at gunpoint to his swank apartment, where he and three other men raped and forced her to commit various sexual acts.[9]

During the trial, which drew many feminist protestors, Russell began hearing stories from other women who had been raped but who had not reported the rape, fearing the treatment they would probably receive in the courtroom. The outcome of the Plotkin trial was a grim reminder of why so few were willing to report. The jury acquitted Plotkin because of the complainant's prior sex life, which was gone over in minute detail in the courtroom.[10] Convinced of the injustice of the verdict and aware of the need for further education, Russell embarked on a program of research that would produce two of the most important early studies of acquaintance rape.

Russell's first book, *The Politics of Rape,* was based on interviews with ninety women. In chapters titled "Lovers Rape, Too," "Some of Our Best Friends Are Rapists," and "Fathers, Husbands, and Other Rapists," to name just a few, Russell records women's experiences which demonstrate that rape is just as likely to occur between acquaintances as between strangers. The level of force employed during rape ranged from intimidation in some instances to extreme force in others. A typical case is reflected in one woman's statement that she put up as much struggle as she could, but he "used all of his strength, and he was very forceful and kept [her] down."[11] Another woman, who was raped by a fraternity brother, said she didn't scream because she was afraid he would call his frat brothers and "run a train" on her.[12]

The reasons these women gave for not reporting their experiences reflect the dominant belief that to do so would be embarrassing and useless. The first woman thought about going to the police but decided against it, believing that her accusation of rape would be impossible to prove. The woman who was raped by the frat brother told a close friend but remained silent otherwise, due to depression.[13] Another woman, who had been gang raped after getting into a car, told her brother, who called her a whore. When she told her husband many years later, he started punching her in the head. She never thought of going to the police, for fear of how her parents would react. One by one the women Russell interviewed gave similar reasons for not reporting.[14]

In 1978, Russell conducted a survey in San Francisco of 930 randomly selected women ranging in age from eighteen to eighty. Her results provided a statistical profile of acquaintance-versus-stranger rape in a diverse population of all social classes and racial/ethnic groups. The study followed the legal definition of rape in California and most other states at that time. Questions were asked about experiences of forced, nonconsensual intercourse as well as about experiences of "unwanted" sexual intercourse while asleep, unconscious, drugged, or otherwise helpless. The inclusion of the question about physical helplessness due to alcohol or drugs also was in keeping with the legal definition of rape in California. Russell was very careful to exclude from the rape category any experiences in which women reported *feeling* rather than *being* forced.[15]

Of the 930 women, 24 percent reported at least one completed rape, and 31 percent reported at least one attempted rape.[16] Russell used the term acquaintance rape as an umbrella term to distinguish rapes involving people who know one another from rapes involving strangers. Thirty-five percent of the women in her study experienced rape or attempted rape by an acquaintance (ranging in degrees of intimacy from casual acquaintances to lovers) as compared with 11 percent raped by strangers and 3 percent by relatives (other than husbands or ex-husbands.)[17] Only 8 percent of all incidents of rape and attempted rape were reported to the police.[18] These incidents were much more likely to involve strangers than men known to the victim.[19]

Another important early survey was conducted in 1978 by psychologist Mary Koss of nearly four thousand college students at Kent State University, where she taught. As a young psychology professor just starting out in the mid-seventies, Koss had read Susan Brownmiller's book on rape and felt that the next step should be a scientific study of the epidemiology of rape. When she first designed the Kent State study, Koss preferred the label "hidden rape" to "acquaintance rape" because of the growing recognition in law enforcement circles that rape was "the most underreported of major crimes." She chose to study "unacknowledged victims of rape," women who have experienced forced sexual intercourse but do not call it rape.

In criminology terms, the unacknowledged victim is the "safe victim." For law enforcement purposes it is always important to identify the kinds of people most likely to be safe victims in any class of crime so that they can be protected through educational programs informing them of their rights. At the time Koss embarked on the Kent State survey, government estimates suggested that "only 40–50 percent of the rapes that occur each year are reported to the police."[20]

Koss's goal was to determine the prevalence of hidden rape. For the survey, she identified four degrees of sexual aggression ranging from what she called "low sexual victimization" to "high sexual victimization" in order to separate gradations of sexual abuse.[21] The category labeled "high sexual victimization" was the category that Koss defined as rape. It included women who said they had experienced unwanted intercourse or penetration of the mouth or anus from a man or men who used or threatened to use physical force. Koss separated this category of rape victims into two types: women who acknowledged they had been raped and those who did not name what happened to them as rape. Koss found that 13 percent of the women interviewed answered yes to at least one of three questions asking them whether they had experienced forced penetration at any time since the age of fourteen. Only 6 percent of the women interviewed, however, answered yes to the question "Have you ever been raped?"[22]

Less than 5 percent of the men in the study admitted to using force. Those who admitted to using force were remarkably similar to the sexually aggressive men described in Kirkendall's 1961 study of college men. For example, like their 1950s counterparts, the Kent State males expressed attitudes illustrative of the double standard. They were more approving of sexual relationships with prostitutes and more disapproving of sexual freedom for women than the less aggressive men in the study.

They preferred traditional women, who were dependent, attention-seeking, and suggestible. Their first experiences with sexual intercourse tended to be unsatisfactory, but they expressed more pride in these experiences than the less aggressive men. When asked if they had sex the first time because it was socially expected, nearly half of the men in the sexually aggressive groups answered yes, as compared with only a quarter of the nonsexually aggressive men.

There were other differences between the types of men in Koss's study reminiscent of Kirkendall's findings. The highly sexually aggressive men were more likely to identify with a male peer culture. More were likely to be in fraternities than those reporting no or low sexual aggression. They were more insensitive to the woman's resistance and more likely to think that sexual aggression was normal sexual behavior, part of the game that had to be played with women. They believed that a woman would be only moderately offended if a man forced his way into her house after a date or forced his attentions in other ways.[23]

RECENT STUDIES

To see whether she could replicate her Kent State findings in a nationwide sample, Koss joined with *Ms.* magazine in a 1985 survey of 6,159 students on thirty-two college campuses. The results of this survey would play a significant role in stepping up anti-rape activism on college campuses, and in inspiring the campus section of the Violence Against Women Act, which would be introduced into Congress five years later.

The survey questions were similar to those Koss used in the Kent State study. This time, however, she included a question about unwanted sexual intercourse that occurred because of the effects of alcohol or drugs. The results showed the extent to which sexual behavior in a college population had changed since Kinsey's male and female studies in the 1940s and 1950s. For example, the percentages of college-age males who were having sexual intercourse rose from 44 percent, reported by Kinsey, to 75 percent, reported by Koss in the 1980s. For college-age females, the percentages changed from 20 percent, reported by Kinsey, to 69 percent, reported by Koss.[24] Morton Hunt, who conducted a survey of the sexual behavior of two thousand individuals in twenty-four cities in 1972, found a similar increase for college men, but a less marked increase for college women.[25]

The results of Koss's national study were widely disseminated and quoted after publication in the *Journal of Consulting and Clinical Psychology* in 1987.[26] Robin Warshaw's *I Never Called It Rape*, the first major book on acquaintance rape, was based on Koss's study. Warshaw reported that one in four women surveyed were victims of rape or attempted rape, 84 percent of those raped knew their attacker, and that 57 percent of the rapes happened on dates.[27] The women thought that most of their offenders (73 percent) were drinking or using drugs at the time of the assault, and 55 percent admitted to using intoxicants themselves. Most of the women thought that they had made their nonconsent "quite" clear and that the offender used "quite a bit" of force. They resisted by using reasoning (84 percent) and physical struggle (70 percent).[28] Only one quarter (27 percent) of the rape victims acknowledged themselves as such. Five percent reported their rapes to the police. Although many women did not call it rape, Koss reported that "the great majority of rape victims conceptualized their experience in highly negative terms and felt victimized whether or not they realized that legal standards for rape had been met."[29]

The results for the men were similar to what Koss had found at Kent State. One quarter of the men reported involvement in some form of sexual aggression, ranging from unwanted touching to rape. Three percent admitted to attempted rape and 4.4 percent to rape.[30] A high percentage of the males did not name their use of force as rape. Eighty-eight percent said it was definitely *not* rape. Forty-seven percent said they would do the same thing again.[31]

Koss's findings that men viewed the use of force as normal were corroborated by other surveys conducted on college campuses. For example, one study cited by Russell found that 35 percent of the males questioned about the likelihood that they would rape said they might if they could get away with it. When asked whether they would force a female to do something sexual she really did not want to do, 60 percent of the males indicated in a third college study that they might, "given the right circumstances."[32]

Convicted rapists hold similar beliefs. In a study of 114 rapists, Diana Scully found that many either denied that the sexual activity for which they were convicted was rape, or they claimed it hadn't happened. One told her the sexual activity for which he was convicted was "just fucking." Other rapists told her that men rape because they have learned that in America they can get away with it because victims don't report. Almost none of the convicts she interviewed thought they would go to prison. Most of them perceived rape as a rewarding, low-risk act.[33]

Since the early studies conducted by Koss and Russell, a number of additional scientifically designed research studies conducted on campuses in various states and in various communities reveal that an average of between 13 percent and 25 percent of the participating females respond affirmatively to questions asking if they had ever been penetrated against their consent by a male who used force, threatened to use force, or took advantage of them when they were incapacitated with alcohol or other drugs.[34] A more recent national study, published in 1992 by the National Victim Center, defined rape more narrowly by leaving alcohol and drugs out of the picture. Thirteen percent of this national sample of a cross-section of women reported having been victims of at least one completed rape in their lifetimes. Most of these women had been raped by someone they knew.[35]

ACQUAINTANCE GANG RAPE

In the 1980s quite a few cases of acquaintance gang rape were reported around the country. In the *Ms.* article announcing the results of Koss's

Kent State study, Karen Barrett describes an incident that took place at Duke University in the Beta Phi Zeta fraternity. A woman had gotten very drunk and passed out. Men lined up outside the door yelling, "Train!" Although the woman did not press charges, saying that she had been a willing participant, Duke moved against the fraternity after it was discovered that senior members had assigned a pledge the task of "finding a drunk woman for a gang bang."[36]

In Koss's national study she found that 16 percent of the male students who admitted rape, and 10 percent of those who admitted attempting a rape, took part in episodes involving more than one attacker.[37] In 1985 Julie Ehrhart and Bernice Sandler wrote a report for the Association of American Colleges describing such incidents. They found a common pattern. When a vulnerable young woman is high on drugs, drunk, or too weak to protest, she becomes a target for a train. In some cases her drinks might have been spiked with alcohol without her knowledge. When she is approached by several men in a locked room, she reacts with confusion and panic. As many as two to eleven or more men might have sex with her.[38]

In a survey of twenty-four documented cases of alleged college gang rape reported during the 1980s, psychologist Chris O'Sullivan found that thirteen were perpetrated by fraternity men, nine by groups of athletes, and two by men unaffiliated with any group. Nineteen of the cases were reported to the police. In eleven cases, the men pleaded guilty to lesser charges. In five of the six cases that went to trial, all of the men were acquitted. The only finding of "guilty" in the twenty-four cases she studied involved black defendants on football scholarships.[39]

In 1983, I began hearing stories describing gang rape on college campuses in several parts of the country. One such incident became the focus of my book *Fraternity Gang Rape*. The incident was brought to my attention by a student, whom I called Laurel in the book. Laurel alleged that she was raped at a fraternity party when she was drunk and too high on LSD to know what was happening. The local district attorney for sex crimes, William Heinman, concluded that a gang rape had occurred because from his investigation of Laurel's state during the party, "there was no evidence that she was lucid" and able to give consent. When her behavior was described to Judge Lois Forer, she also concluded that Laurel was "incapable of giving consent."[40]

The brothers claimed that Laurel had lured them into what they called an "express." Reporting the party activities that night, they posted the following statement on their bulletin board a few days later:

> Things are looking up for the [name of fraternity] sisters program. A prospective leader for the group spent some time interviewing several [brothers] this past Thursday and Friday. Possible names for the little sisters include [the] "little wenches" and "the [name of fraternity] express."[41]

One of the boys involved in the act, who lost his virginity that night, said that he thought what happened was normal sexual behavior, even though the trauma experienced by Laurel sent her to a hospital for a long period of recovery and kept her out of school for two years. He explained his behavior by referring to the pornography he and his brothers watched together at the house. "Pulling train," as they called it, didn't seem odd to him because "it's something that you see and hear about all the time."[42]

Another brother talked at length with me about what he thought happened. Tom [pseudonym] was adamant that it was not rape because Laurel did not name it rape at first. It was only later that she called it rape after talking to campus feminists, he said. He suggested that the real problem was "her sexual identity confusion" and that both men and women who are sexually confused indulge in casual sex. According to Tom, a lot of guys "engage in promiscuous sex to establish their sexuality," because male sexual identity is based on sexual performance. The male ego is built on sexual conquests as a way of gaining respect from other men. For men, he said, there was lots of peer pressure to be sexually successful.[43]

When I asked Tom about Laurel's bruises, he admitted that she had been bruised that night because she had taken acid and was dancing wildly. He added that sex always involves some degree of force, which also explained the bruises. He went on to say that "subconsciously women are mad that they are subordinate in sex and are the objects of force."[44]

WHAT WE KNOW ABOUT SEXUALLY AGGRESSIVE MEN

Sexually aggressive men, whether they be convicted rapists, men who admit that they would probably rape given the right circumstances, or men who admit that they have forced women into sexual intercourse, share a remarkably similar set of attitudes. Reviewing many studies, Mary Koss and Kenneth Leonard find that such men believe that sexual aggression is normal, that relationships involve game playing, that men should dominate women, that women are responsible for rape, and that relations between the sexes are adversarial and manipulative on both sides.[45]

In her survey of 6,159 students on thirty-two campuses, Koss asked questions that allow us to assess the kinds of attitudes held by sexually aggressive men in the 1980s. For example, the idea that no means yes is more likely to be believed by the males in Koss's sample who admitted to forcing a woman. Twenty-one percent of the males reporting *no* incidents of forced intercourse in Koss's national sample agreed with the statement that "many times a woman says no to intercourse because she doesn't want to seem loose, but she's really hoping the man will force her." This percentage increased to 52 percent among those males who admitted to forcing women into sexual intercourse. One quarter of the self-admitted rapists, as opposed to 11 percent of the nonaggressive men, agreed with a view similar to that articulated by Havelock Ellis that "being roughed up is sexually stimulating to many women." Finally, whereas 22 percent of the self-admitted rapists expressed agreement with the statement that "women have an unconscious wish to be raped," only 8 percent of the nonaggressive men agreed with this statement.[46]

The females surveyed in Koss's study were much less likely to hold these ideas whether or not they reported rape experiences. For example, of those who admitted to having experiences meeting the legal definition of forcible rape, only 20 percent expressed agreement with the statement that a woman says no "because she doesn't want to seem loose," but is "really hoping the man will force her," as compared with 17 percent of women who had not been raped. On the other questions about women liking to be forced, the female subjects also tended to respond in the same proportions as the nonaggressive men.[47]

My analysis of some of the other attitudes reported by Koss reveals some interesting findings that help to assess the degree to which the beliefs discussed in previous chapters have changed.[48] It appears that the majority of the members of Generation X hold egalitarian sexual beliefs. For example, a minority of males (18 percent) and an even smaller number of females (3 percent) agree with the traditional belief that a woman should be dominated by a man as expressed in the aphorism "a man's got to show the woman who's boss." Much more common is the lingering relevance of the nineteenth-century emphasis on female passionlessness. A high percentage of males (45 percent) and females (52 percent) agree with the statement that "a woman shouldn't give in sexually to a man too easily or he'll think she's loose." The concept of the "good girl" still exists in the percentages of males (30 percent) and females (21 percent) who agree that "a nice woman will be offended or embarrassed by dirty jokes." And yet, only a minority of males (23 percent) and females (12 percent) believe that a woman who takes the initiative in sex is a "slut."

The ideas of Freud and Ellis are evident in the popular idea held by 37 percent of the male and 31 percent of the female Generation Xers that men "have a biologically stronger sex drive," suggesting that men will be the aggressors in sexual relationships. Ellis's idea that women "love pain" is not so popular. Only 12 percent of the males and 11 percent of the females agree that "being roughed up is sexually stimulating to women." Only 9 percent of the males and 6 percent of the females agree that women unconsciously wish to be raped.

Anti-female attitudes, from Hale's to Hefner's, are also in the minority, yet prevalent enough to cause concern. Twenty-four percent of the men rate women as manipulative, "sweet and nice to a man until she has him," while 13 percent of the women agree with this statement. In addition, many men (29 percent) and women (24 percent) agree with the idea that women falsely accuse men of rape to get attention.

Most students of acquaintance rape agree that sociocultural factors and family background, as opposed to psychopathology or biological predisposition, explain the high incidence of rape.[49] To explain why some men adopt rape behavior and others don't, Koss and her colleague Thomas Dinero distinguish between "preconditions" and "releasers" of sexual violence. They found that childhood sexual abuse and preadolescent sexual activity were more likely to characterize the early life experience of the more aggressive men. The releasers they identified were frequent use of alcohol and pornography. Many more of the aggressive men admitted to drinking frequently, using drugs, and reading pornographic magazines than the nonaggressive men. Another important releaser was involvement in all-male peer groups with highly sexualized views of women.[50]

Using the same data, Koss, psychologist Neil Malamuth, and other colleagues attempted an even more complex analysis of developmental patterns that might explain the self-reported sexual coercion in Koss's sample. They suggest that the tendency toward coerciveness is due to early childhood experiences such as violence between parents and child physical and sexual abuse, which inspire feelings of shame and inadequacy regarding intimate relationships with the opposite sex. A hostile home environment affects sexual aggression through two paths. The first is through the adoption of a macho, hostile attitude toward women, which emphasizes "power, toughness, dominance, aggressiveness, and competitiveness as 'masculine.' " Such males are likely to be more controlling and aggressive toward women, and sex becomes one of the arenas where dominance and control are acted out. The second path leads to sexual aggression through the path of sexual promiscuity. Some men from hostile home backgrounds turn early to sexual promiscuity in order to gain peer acceptance and foster self-esteem. Males who look to sexual conquest for self-esteem are more likely to force girls into sexual acts.[51]

The relevance of sociocultural factors becomes apparent when one looks at the variation in the incidence of rape cross-culturally and within the United States. In a 1981 study of ninety-five band and tribal societies, I found that 47 percent were rape free and 18 percent were rape prone. I concluded that rape is part of a cultural configuration that includes interpersonal violence, male dominance, and sexual separation. In other words, rape is an expression of a social ideology of male dominance. Judging from rape statistics reported by Mary Koss and others, America is such a culture. In rape-prone societies, women have little power and do not participate in public decision-making. I show also that male sexuality tends to be aggressive when boys are taught to be tough and interpersonal violence is common.[52]

The sociocultural model is supported by evidence of variation in rape prevalence rates within the U.S. among ethnic groups and from one part of the country to another. For example, Koss reports a number of demographic and institutional factors related to prevalence rates. The number of women reporting sexual victimization was higher in the Great Lakes and Plains states and at private colleges and major universities. Rates also varied by ethnicity, with the highest reported by white women and the lowest by Asian women.[53]

Sociocultural factors exert a powerful influence in shaping notions of masculinity for some males. Insecure young men forced to display their masculinity for other males are more likely to buy into the popular social message that sexual performance defines masculinity. Robin Warshaw quotes at length from a Haverford College senior thesis written by Erik Johnke explaining how it is possible for men to have sex with a woman who is resisting vocally and physically and believe that it is not rape. Johnke describes sexual interaction on a typical date as primarily adversarial, like a football game in which the object is to gain the most territory toward the goal of sexual intercourse. Every time the man's date "submits to his will," he believes he has "advanced," and every time she does not he feels that he has "suffered a retreat." Echoing the old ideal of passionlessness, Johnke writes that because the man knows that good girls don't, ". . . he attempts to pressure her into saying 'yes.' . . . When she finally says, 'no,' he simply may not listen, or he may convince himself that she is just 'playing hard to get' and that she really means 'yes.' "54

Power, masculinity, and sexual performance provide the building blocks of the masculine persona in the dating game Johnke describes. The game confuses sexual megalomania with manhood. In the 1980s a young man told me that he couldn't commit to a woman because he needed sexual conquests to confirm his masculinity. In college he adopted the practice of setting quotas for himself. He had to find a certain number of new girls to have sex with in a specified time period. For him the joy of sex did not come from the sex act itself, but from the feeling of acceptance and approval that comes with a new conquest.

Whatever personal problems caused this young man to think of masculinity in this way, the atmosphere of his fraternity encouraged his beliefs. He lived in a house that kept a symbolic penis, in the shape of an orange cone-shaped object, in the room where the brothers held their meetings. The symbolic phallus in such settings draws males together. Songs, stories, and rituals celebrating sexual violence also join isolated, insecure males in the bonds of brotherhood. Friendship and gamesmanship are facilitated by singing songs with lyrics like "She died from sucking a Phi Psi cock, Shove it in and shove it out, Quit fucking about." When feminists on campus object, they are dismissed as humorless.55

The phallus as organizing symbol is seen in the following comments made to me by a fraternity pledge who admitted that he joined the fraternity primarily to find comradeship and a sense of belonging to compensate for his sense of isolation:

We . . . liked to share ridiculously exaggerated sexual boasting, such as our mythical "Sixteen Kilometer Flesh-Weapon," and double-entendre plays on sexual performance. Example: "How was the exam this morning? *Much too long!* Yeah, that's what *she* said!" Even when this got embarrassingly out of hand (such as when we sent party invitations to alumni, promising to supply imported women "with big breasts and small brains"), it was always fun to laugh over this stuff together. By including me in this perpetual, hysterical banter and sharing laughter with me, they showed their affection for me. I felt happy, confident, and loved. This really helped my feelings of loneliness and my fear of being sexually unappealing. . . . We acted out all of the sexual tensions between us as brothers on a verbal level. *Women, women* everywhere, feminists, homosexuality, etc., all provided the material for the jokes.[56]

It is important to emphasize that being a member of a fraternity per se is not related to sexual assault. In a study of college alcohol use, fraternity affiliation, and athletic participation, Koss and John Gaines found that regular use of alcohol and nicotine were the most important predictors of sexual aggression. This study also confirmed the evidence of prior research that suggested the importance of participation in organized athletics in the lives of sexually aggressive men. Taken together these three factors were more important than fraternity affiliation.[57]

Fraternity communities can promote or discourage rape-supportive attitudes. Rites such as those described above, as well as abusive initiation rituals in which pledges learn that their manhood depends on toughness, aggressiveness, and "cleansing" the feminine from their bodies, encourage misogyny. For example, a ritual was described to me in which the pledges were put through mind-altering exercises designed to "cleanse" the "fag," the "nerd," and the "pussy" from their bodies. The humiliating physical acts of this ritual can be likened to induction into a religious cult in which homophobia and misogyny supply the most important conditions for membership.[58] The effect of such rituals can be devastating to a male's sense of respect for women.

As destructive as fraternities can be, however, they can also be constructive agents for change. Despite the abuses, the institution provides one of the few surviving examples of a small, face-to-face community where young males can learn responsible sexual behavior. However, there is little incentive for fraternities to play this role as long as social life is structured on the promiscuous paradigm of the sporting-male culture of the nineteenth century, where shared sensual pleasure is a mask for male bonding.

THE PORNOGRAPHY CONNECTION

Pornography is as important now for facilitating male bonding as it was in the eighteenth and nineteenth centuries. In my research on gang rape in college fraternities, the pornography connection was very clear. For example, one of the brothers involved in the alleged gang rape discussed in *Fraternity Gang Rape* explained the sexual behavior that took place with the following comment:

> We have this Select TV in the house, and there's soft porn on every midnight. All the guys watch it and talk about it and stuff, and [gang banging] didn't seem that odd because it's something that you see and hear about all the time. I've heard stories from other fraternities about group sex and trains and stuff like that. It was just like, you know, so this is what I've heard about, this is what it's like, what I've heard about.[59]

The connection between pornography and rape was part of feminist analysis and discussion as early as 1970, if not before. Kate Millett characterizes pornography as antisocial, antisexual, and antifemale. She describes the "virility cult of Nazi male culture" in terms that are reminiscent of the American sporting-male culture and sadistic fraternity initiation rituals such as I encountered in my study of gang rape.[60]

In 1974 Robin Morgan wrote about pornography as the theory of male sexual sadism, and rape as the practice.[61] That same year Andrea Dworkin published *Woman Hating,* in which she argues that pornography is not pro-sex, but rather represents a view of womanhood: "of what a woman is, what she needs, her processes of thinking and feeling, her proper place." That place is sacred submission to the male, joy in pure suffering, and in giving the body in service "to be ravaged, exploited, and totally possessed." According to Dworkin, books like the *Story of O* are "of astounding political significance," emblematic of the "Judeo-Christian values of service and self-sacrifice and universal notions of womanhood."[62]

In her 1981 book, *Pornography,* Dworkin continues her critique of pornography through analyses of the work of the Marquis de Sade and Alfred Kinsey, among others. In this work she critiques pornography as the "mass-marketing of woman as whore," as "hole" and "object." For Dworkin, the putative freedom pornography promises to women "is in being massively consumed, denied an individual nature, denied any sexual sensibility other than that which serves the male."[63]

Those who reject Dworkin's ideas because of the intense media backlash against her would do well to take a look at the culture of pornography up close. I had this opportunity in the early 1980s when a University of Pennsylvania student organization brought pornographic movies to campus twice a year as a money-making enterprise. In 1984, for example, the year that the pornography industry grossed $7 billion, the student organization grossed $3,000, more than it made from any other business venture. Sitting in the audience during one of these films and listening to the male reaction, it is hard not to agree with the feminist analysis of pornography as encouraging male violence against women. What transpired that night was not about sex, it was about a masculine ethos—a celebration of male sexual power—in a coeducational setting.

Before the showing of *Deep Throat,* Linda Lovelace, its star, was brought by Penn's Women's Center to speak. Nearly two thousand people attended her talk. She spoke about her imprisonment during the making of the film, the beatings she suffered, and pointed out that the film shows the bruises on her body.

Two days later protestors, mostly female, and moviegoers, mostly male, showed up to see the film. The atmosphere was rowdy, and although it was against university rules, many males came carrying beer cans. Throughout the screening the voices of the film were drowned out by the constant din created by males chanting, "Bruises, bruises."

While waiting for the film to start, mindful of the protestors outside, men in the audience yelled, "We can have our fun," and "Hey, we're here to see Linda. We're gonna love her bruises." A chant went up, *"Deep Throat, Deep Throat,* let's go, Quakers, let's go." Men excitedly pointed to one another in the audience, yelling names and strutting around. "Hey, Smith, hey, Jones, what are you doing here?" "Psi Omega's here!!"

One man stood up and shouted, "Hey, you girls out there," referring to the protestors, "watch out for the popcorn trick," referring to a movie in which a man sticks his erect penis in a popcorn box and offers popcorn to the woman next to him.

Once the movie started, the audience cheered and shouted, "Bruises, bruises" as Linda appeared on the screen in a short dress. Deep husky voices shouted, "Blow job, blow job," "Black leather," "Jerk off, jerk off!!" The "bruises" refrain was especially deafening in those scenes where they were clearly visible. At one point, a man shouted, "Ugly bitch," and another added, "She's really ugly all over, including her bruises."

The audience cheered whenever Linda did a "deep throat" blow job. One man yelled, "Why can't my girlfriend do that?" During another blow job, a man screamed, "I'm *horny!!"* "Fuck her," another voice chimed in.

Almost all of the women present as spectators left the theater before the end of the film. The scene played out their worst fears of what getting caught in a locker room after a particularly nasty game and becoming the object of male wrath might be like.

After it was over, some of the protestors interviewed males as they left. The reaction they encountered was mixed. Some expressed little enthusiasm for the movie and admitted they wouldn't go to another porn film. One was disgusted by the whole scene, yet he felt that it should be shown on campus. Another was bored, saying, "It makes sex very mechanical." Another male, a freshman, came up to the protestors and said in a coaxing tone, "Come on, she must have enjoyed some of that," referring to Linda Lovelace. "Look at her facial expressions. She never looked like she was upset. She had only one bruise on her thigh." He concluded, "I'd go to another porn film. It really looked like she was getting into it."

The difference between reactions expressed during the screening with those expressed afterward illustrates very different attitudes toward sex. The bored and disgusted reactions demonstrated a disassociation from the mechanical, emotionless nature of the acts displayed. The verbal sexual aggression demonstrated a way of thinking, knowing, and perhaps experiencing sex that conforms closely with feminist analysis of pornography. Desire is projected onto women along with a host of attitudes that support rape behavior: no means yes, women secretly desire to be forced, a woman always wants it, and women have an unconscious desire to be raped. These are the same attitudes that Mary Koss found to be related to self-admission of rape behavior. In another study, Martha Burt describes these attitudes and summarizes the research demonstrating that they are related to juror insensitivity to rape victims.[64]

This research and my own study of gang rape suggests that pornography must be understood as producing a way of thinking about sex, not just a way of being sexually. Thus, when we ask about the impact of pornography, we must ask about its effect not only on sexual aggression, but on sexual epistemologies as well, a point which I take to be the central contribution of Andrea Dworkin's and Kate Millett's analyses of pornography.

In a 1993 article, Neil Malamuth of the University of California in Los Angeles, who himself has conducted some of the major research on the effects of pornography, summarized the findings of more than a decade of research on the relationship between the use of pornography and the practice of sexual aggression. Based on these findings, Malamuth concluded that "[t]here seems to be scientific support for the hypothesis of harmful effects on some men of certain types of pornographic stimuli." According to Malamuth, the research results suggest that the impact is greatest when the portrayals include violent and degrading material. The impact of exposure to pornography is also more evident with subjects, who for reasons of early family background and childhood experiences of abuse or delinquency, "already have some risk of being attracted to sexual aggression or similar behavior."[65]

By 1990, when Angela was invited up to Michael's room, knowledge of acquaintance rape was well established on most college campuses, but not well known to the public at large. Public intrigue with the subject was sparked by Patricia Bowman's allegations in the spring of 1991 that she was raped by William Kennedy Smith at the Kennedy compound in West Palm Beach. Between the time of her allegations in March 1991 and the trial that December, more than one thousand articles on date and ac- quaintance rape appeared in the popular press. In comparison with the three articles published ten years earlier, this number is astounding.[66]

The interest generated by Anita Hill's appearance in the fall of 1991 before the Senate Judiciary Committee was another indication that Amer- ican society was ready to consider the "woman problem." Occurring a few months apart, the first St. John's trial, Anita Hill's appearance, and the trial of William Kennedy Smith were benchmarks of a new era in the long struggle for women's rights. These events, along with the Violence Against Women Act, which was formally introduced in Congress earlier in the year, educated the public and helped lift the stigma of being a victim of acquaintance rape and sexual harassment even as they demon- strated how deeply the stigma still reached.

Although Patricia Bowman's courtroom experience was hardly en- couraging for other women considering bringing charges, the public dis- cussion she initiated led to a reconsideration of the boundaries of accept- able male sexual behavior. The public soul searching had an undeniable influence on the outcome of the second St. John's trial, which took place in February 1992. In all likelihood, the outcome of the Mike Tyson trial, which ran concurrently with the second St. John's trial, was similarly affected by the new public concern. This conclusion, however, is only partially hopeful because the old stereotypes were as evident in the trial of Mike Tyson as they were in that of Smith. Even as women started to make public that it was no longer to be a no-means-yes sexual culture, the continuing power of stereotypes indicated how far America still had to go.

TEN

THE
CONTINUING POWER
OF STEREOTYPES

A MONTH BEFORE THE TELEVISED PROCEEDINGS OF THE WILLIAM KENNEDY Smith trial, Anita Hill appeared before the Senate Judiciary Committee hearings on the nomination of Clarence Thomas. The attention showered on Anita Hill was even more unprecedented than that paid to Patricia Bowman. On the lowest rung of America's sexual-status hierarchy, here was an African-American woman claiming that America's newest candidate for knighthood, an African-American male nominated for a seat on the highest court in the land, harassed her sexually. In keeping with the American tradition of silencing women who bring charges against an American hero, the members of the Judiciary Committee tried to keep her allegations of sexual harassment hidden from the most public forum of the televised hearings.

The questioning of Hill ran through a litany of nineteenth-century stereotypes. Senator Howell Heflin asked her character witnesses whether she brought charges because she was vindictive, had a "martyr-type complex," wanted to be a "hero," was a "spurned or scorned woman," or was "out of touch with reality." Senator Biden clarified Hefflin's meaning by asking directly whether it was possible that Professor Hill felt a romantic interest in Clarence Thomas. Perhaps her charges could be understood in terms of Shakespeare's phrase, "Hell hath no fury like a woman scorned," Biden suggested. Anxious to set the record straight on such matters, the senator from Wyoming pointed out that William Congreve was the author of the famous quotation.

Clarence Thomas's wife, Virginia, also labeled Hill a "scorned woman." "In my heart, I always believed she was probably someone in love with my husband and never got what she wanted," she told *People* magazine after it was all over. Along the same lines, but reverting to stereotypes of the 1930s, Senator Orrin Hatch of Utah suggested that only "a psychopathic sex fiend or a pervert" would do what Anita Hill charged. White House aides sought to discredit Hill's story further by suggesting that she was lying, fantasizing, or a disappointed careerist. More than one source suggested that she was mentally unstable. Senator Specter announced, for example, that he had an affidavit from a man alleging that Anita Hill was unstable because she had a problem with being rejected by men she was attracted to.

In the early 1990s these two women, Patricia Bowman and Anita Hill, reluctant witnesses though they were, illuminated the dark side of American sexual relations and facilitated a nationwide discussion on the subordination of women to male-defined sexual norms. Although neither won their cases, the two women and their supporters demonstrated that women were ready to contest the norms that rendered them helpless not only in sexual situations in the office but in the aftermath of nonconsensual sex.

The willingness of Patricia Bowman and, later, of Desiree Washington to come forward with their stories and the relative ease with which Smith and Tyson were indicted showed that women and law enforcement officials were ready to name forced, nonconsensual sexual intercourse rape irrespective of the relationship between complainant and defendant. Law professor Susan Estrich's influential book, *Real Rape,* published in 1987, argued strongly that the distinction between "simple" and "aggravated" rape cases was spurious, "that a 'simple' rape *is* a real rape," and that the law needed to give equal attention to both.[1] Feminist activism in rape crisis centers, which taught more and more women their legal rights, together with acquaintance rape prevention efforts and reform legislation conspired to place sexual aggression on the national agenda for discussion and action.

THE TRIAL OF WILLIAM KENNEDY SMITH

The discrepancy between the reform law and feminist activism for female sexual autonomy on the one hand, and juror attitudes and public opinion on the other became patently obvious during the widely reported proceedings of the trial of William Kennedy Smith in the fall of 1991. The case was intriguing because it showed both the stability of old ideas and the changes introduced by the new.

The story Patricia Bowman told the Palm Beach police was a typical example of acquaintance rape as defined by feminists and by the rape reform laws in most states, including Florida. She described force and lack of consent. She told Detective Christine Rigolo that she met William Smith at Au Bar, they danced, and she gave him a ride home to the Kennedy estate. He invited her in and the two walked down to the beach. As she stood on the moonlit beach looking at the stars with Smith, Patricia Bowman remembered feeling shy. It was a beautiful, crisp spring night, early in the morning after Good Friday. They kissed but she didn't think that the kisses were an invitation to anything. Then Smith said he wanted to go for a swim and asked her to join him. She thought this was odd because it was so cold. Besides, she couldn't swim. She said no and turned her back as he was taking off his clothes. When he moved toward the water, she started walking toward the steps to leave. She didn't realize that Smith was behind her until he tackled her.

She told Rigolo, "And I went up the stairs and . . . it was like a little hallway going up and I was starting to come out. I got pulled down and he grabbed my . . . my ankle. . . ."

She thought she hurt her rib when she fell on the top of the stairs. She remembered thinking, "This guy plays a little bit too rough." She got up and started to run toward the house. She didn't know where she was. Bowman said that as she ran "he caught me again and tackled me and I fell to the ground out by the pool, which is on the south side of the house.

"He tackled me and then he had my dress up and his hands in my pants and . . . he raped me," she said. When he tackled her she was on her back facing him. He pressed his shoulder against her chest so that she couldn't move.

"And I was yelling no and to stop and he wouldn't and I . . . he might have been yelling at me something but I don't know what it was . . . all I know is I was just screaming no and to stop and . . . and I couldn't figure out why he wasn't stopping and why nobody was helping me," she said.

Five-foot-six, weighing 130 pounds, Patricia Bowman was unable to move him. She didn't know whether he ejaculated, but she felt him inside of her. He was partially erect and she felt his hands trying to get her hands away from him or maybe he was trying to guide his penis, she didn't know.

In addition to describing the act in the taped statements, Patricia Bowman provided a written description:

He had me on the ground. He was on top of me—he was very heavy. My chest hurt. He had pushed my dress up, had his arms over my shoulders. I was screaming no, trying to get out from beneath him. When I couldn't do that I used my hand to try and keep him from entering me. He was not fully erect. He entered me, but not fully, and I felt him ejaculate (I think). I felt something wet near my legs. I think he rolled off of me. I ran into the house through the living room door to the kitchen and hid next to the water cooler. There was a phone there. I called Anne to get me out of there. I heard him yelling for me.[2]

"Anne" was Anne Mercer, who had accompanied Patricia Bowman to Au Bar earlier in the evening. Later, she described to Detective Rigolo Bowman's condition when she arrived at the estate. "She was roughed up and hysterical and I think [her] dress was torn on the bottom and she was just hysterical." She added that Bowman was "shaking and crying."

Detective Hohnholz of the Palm Beach sheriff's office, who was the first law enforcement official to observe Patricia Bowman's condition, corroborated this description. According to him, Bowman "was extremely upset . . . very emotional . . . crying a lot . . . scared . . . she was emotional to the point that she couldn't even hold a cup of water with one hand without spilling it . . . she had to use two hands."[3]

Bowman went to the sheriff's office at the suggestion of rape crisis counselor Denny Abbott, whom she had called as soon as she got home, hoping to get help to calm down enough to pick up her child, who was spending the night with Bowman's mother. This is a crucial point in the story because it shows the role of the rape crisis counselor in encouraging the victim to report. Abbott advised Bowman to make a police report so that she could get a medical exam. Remembering that Smith had told her that no one would believe her, Bowman balked at the idea of going to the police. She felt she couldn't face going through what they put rape victims through. Abbott convinced her that it was not right to be raped, and she agreed to meet him at the Palm Beach County sheriff's office that morning.[4]

Detective Rigolo also described Bowman's state when she met her. As she wrote in the incident report, "the victim appeared extremely distraught, nervous and upset. She also exhibited pain." Her hands, legs, and feet were visibly shaking. To Rigolo it seemed that the victim was in a state of shock, appearing to be on "the verge of hysteria at times and at other times in her own world."[5]

Rigolo's first step was to take Patricia Bowman to Humana Hospital for a rape kit examination, which consisted of an oral swab, fingernail scrapings, drawing blood, taking hair samples, and combing the pubic area for the suspect's hair. A vaginal exam was conducted, and an X ray of Bowman's chest was taken because she was complaining of discomfort in that region. Detective Rigolo was advised that a nonmotile spermatozoa was observed and that there was a possible fracture of the victim's seventh rib. The victim also had an obvious bruise on her right leg, where she said that the suspect had grabbed her as she was walking up the stairs from the beach. Later, additional bruises were observed around the site of the first bruise on the right leg. Bruises were photographed on the victim's arms and back. According to Rigolo's report, "one set of bruises appeared to be like that of five fingerprints."[6]

Bowman expressed an interest in pressing charges during the second interview with Rigolo. "I did not want to be raped," she said. "I want that man to not rape again and I told him no. I told him to stop. I tried to push him off of me and out of me and he wouldn't stop. And I don't care if he thinks nobody's gonna believe me. He raped me, he did." She added, "I'm ninety eight and one-half percent sure that I want to prosecute."[7]

The investigation took five and a half weeks. William Kennedy Smith, Ted Kennedy, and Patrick Kennedy had all left Palm Beach before they could be interviewed. Blood and semen samples had to be collected from William Smith. There was some confusion over the fact that among the items taken from the estate to prove that Patricia Bowman had been there and wasn't fantasizing the whole thing was an expensive vase, which at first authorities thought might have been stolen. Later, it was returned. In addition, there were many discrepancies to be checked out. The timing of the event according to Patricia Bowman did not correspond with Smith's or Patrick Kennedy's account. Patrick Kennedy claimed to have been in bed and not to have seen Patricia Bowman when she came to the estate, yet she saw him twice. Michelle Cassone, who accompanied Patrick Kennedy to the Kennedy estate that night from Au Bar, said that she saw a nude woman on the beach early in the morning. It would be some time before it was determined that this woman was not Patricia Bowman.

Finally, on May 8, 1991, Detective Rigolo presented a probable cause statement to State Attorney David Bludworth and Assistant State Attorney Moira Lasch. The probable cause was accepted by Bludworth the next day and a warrant was issued for the arrest of William Kennedy Smith for one felony count of sexual battery and one misdemeanor count of battery. In the news conference announcing these charges, Bludworth explained that sexual battery, Florida's legal term for rape, is "our most unreported crime." Bludworth summarized the highlights of the case, mentioning that "the woman passed two polygraph tests on her statements to police." He also stated that a medical examination "documented bruises on her legs, shoulders and arms."[8]

William Smith's response was to deny that any offense had been committed. In Washington, D.C., where he was working as an intern at Georgetown University Medical Center, he issued a statement saying, "I'm very tired because I've been in the hospital all night taking care of people who have real problems. So I've got some perspective, but obviously I'm very sad about the events today. And I'm worried about my family and obviously my future and my friends."[9]

NAMING THE VICTIM

During the weeks of the investigation the media frenzy replayed every woman's nightmare of what might happen if she charged a well-connected man with rape. Patricia Bowman's character was trashed and her name revealed on *NBC Nightly News* and by *The New York Times*. At first the *Times* and other news organizations had kept to their usual policy of not naming the complainant in rape cases. Then, when a London tabloid published Patricia Bowman's name and photograph, the American supermarket tabloid *The Globe* jumped on board and did the same. NBC News felt called upon to follow *The Globe*'s example by featuring all the information reported by *The Globe,* including Bowman's picture, in its nightly newscast of April 16. Michael G. Gartner, president of NBC News, explained that the action was taken to better inform the public. "We do not mean to be judgmental or take sides," he said in a prepared statement, "we are merely reporting what we have learned."[10]

NBC's decision persuaded the *Times* to abandon its usual policy, and the next day it published Bowman's name in a lengthy profile. The article was a late-twentieth-century version of what can happen when an allegedly working-class girl charges a man like William Kennedy Smith with rape. In some respects it was a twentieth-century repeat of Lanah Sawyer's fate in the eighteenth century. Sending the subliminal message that a working-class girl will do anything to bag or milk a rich man, the article opened with the observation that Smith's accuser, although "born into a modest working-class family," had "moved sharply up the economic scale 10 years ago after her divorced mother remarried a wealthy industrialist." Having noted that she had come into wealth through her mother's marriage, the article continued with other implicitly unsavory aspects of Bowman's life: she moved "from Ohio to Florida, where she held jobs sporadically, took college classes occasionally, had a child and moved into a house near Palm Beach that was bought for her by her stepfather."[11]

The *Times* ended up with considerable egg on its face because of this article. In her column for the *Times,* Anna Quindlen pointed out that the profile on Bowman was not only "not informative but punitive." "If we had any doubt about whether there is still a stigma attached to rape, it is gone for good," she wrote. "Any woman reading the *Times* profile now knows that to accuse a well-connected man of rape will invite a thorough reading not only of her own past but of her mother's, and that she had better be ready to see not only her name but her drinking habits in print," she concluded.[12]

In an op-ed piece in *The New York Times* Susan Estrich pointed out that publishing the woman's name and the stories about her made it all too clear that acquaintance rape was not yet considered "real rape." It was still the victim who came under attack, not the defendant. "The right question in rape cases," she wrote, "is not what she did wrong, but what he did; not what she's done in the past, or with whom, but what happened that night; not what she thought, but what he did." The questions that had to be asked were simple, she said. Was there force? Was their sexual intercourse? Did he know or not care that she was not consenting? If the answer to these questions is yes, she said, the police should charge rape. Nothing else, certainly not the victim's taste for "café society," mattered, she concluded.[13]

The *Times* responded to its critics by issuing an apology—of sorts. Max Frankel, the executive editor, expressed regret. "We did not sufficiently guard against the imputation that we were saying 'She deserved it.'" An "Editor's Note" was published saying that the article had not explicitly asserted that the woman's background should not be taken as evidence of the veracity of her charges.[14]

Once Smith was charged, Patricia Bowman reacted strongly against the fact that her name had been revealed. Had she known this would happen, she said in an interview, she might not have reported the incident.[15] "When you're a rape victim, you have to go through a process of recovery, and that process just completely stopped when I saw my name," she said.[16] State Attorney Bludworth, citing "the chilling effect of printing, publishing or broadcasting the victim's name" because it encourages victims not to report, charged *The Globe* with violating Florida law by publishing Bowman's name the same day charges were brought against William Kennedy Smith.[17]

After Smith was charged, *The New York Times* published a glowing piece on his background, describing him as a fine young man from a distinguished family, a devoted, hardworking medical student. Interviews with friends established that he was "a good reliable guy," "a thoughtful conversationalist," a "calm and easygoing young man" who "wouldn't hurt somebody." Of the five women interviewed for the article who had dated Smith, three asserted "vehemently that the William Smith they know could not have tackled, pinned and raped the woman, in what she described . . . as a ferocious attack that left her bruised and aching."

We are not told, however, what the two other women had to say because they refused to comment, fearing the effect it might have on their careers and their families.[18]

The Washington Post was a little more forthright in its profile of Smith published the same day. It was widely known that William Smith did not have such an unblemished record. There were anonymous tips that he had assaulted other women. The *Post* did some digging and found that when Smith drank heavily his personality changed "from quiet and thoughtful to aggressive and difficult." A former girlfriend revealed that she broke up with Smith because of his behavior when drunk. In interviews with several male and female friends, Smith's personality was described as "charming," "sweet," and "unassuming" when he was sober but was known to "change dramatically when he drank." None of these individuals would permit their names to be published. The remainder of the lengthy article described Smith's intelligence, compassion, hard work, and dedication to poor patients.[19]

THE TRIAL

The trial was an example of how a woman's reputation can be dragged through the mud even in the face of the legal reform that explicitly forbids such information into court. Smith's defense team proved masterful at inserting subliminal messages suggesting that Bowman was a sexually experienced false accuser who, if she didn't ask for it, at least deserved it. All of this despite Florida's rape reform law and a judge who seemed very much in charge of the courtroom proceedings.

Florida was at the forefront of rape reform legislation when it passed a new law in 1974. Prior to 1974, Patricia Bowman's case would probably not have been accepted for prosecution. Under the old law, rape was defined as having "carnal knowledge" of a person "by force and against his or her will." The 1974 law abolished the offense of rape and replaced it with the crime of sexual battery, defined as "oral, anal, or vaginal penetration by, or union with, the sexual organ of another or the anal or vaginal penetration of another by any other object." Force was divided into degrees that defined both the crime and the severity of the sentence. The statute no longer spoke of the crime as being "against the will" of the victim, but instead focused on consent. Consent was defined as "intelligent, knowing, and voluntary consent," not to include "coerced submission." The law recognized that "a victim might be physically unable to communicate unwillingness to participate in an act."[20]

Under the new law, William Kennedy Smith was charged with one count of second-degree sexual battery. Second degree referred to a lesser use of force, which was not likely to cause "serious personal injury." Because he had no prior criminal record, had he been found guilty Smith would have faced a prison term of no more than four and a half years.

One of the most important provisions of the new law was called the "rape victim shield." This provision stated that the victim's testimony need not be corroborated and that evidence of prior sexual conduct was not admissible, except under certain circumstances. The circumstances had to establish "a pattern of conduct or behavior on the part of the victim which is so similar to the conduct or behavior in the case that it is relevant to the issue of consent."[21]

The Smith defense team argued that aspects of Patricia Bowman's past showed a similar pattern to her conduct with respect to William Kennedy Smith. Roy Black, the head of the defense team, argued that Bowman suffered from a sexually related "psychological disorder" that led her to make false charges against Smith. He asked Judge Mary E. Lupo for permission to examine "all relevant records of psychological or psychiatric treatment" that she might have received. He told news reporters that he had uncovered "strong and compelling evidence" that she was "mentally or emotionally unstable" and that this psychological condition cast doubt on the believability of her allegations. He claimed that she suffered from a "severe emotional disorder" and "a deep resentment of men" resulting from a variety of traumas that included alleged abortions and her having been sexually abused as a child.[22]

Under the new rape law, Lupo prohibited the defense attorneys from posing any questions about Patricia Bowman's past consensual relationships. But the judge did agree to consider a request permitting Smith's lawyers to explore Patricia Bowman's statement to the police that her natural father physically and emotionally abused her and that a caretaker sexually molested her at the age of eight. This ruling established an image of Bowman as a mentally unstable false accuser, which continued to haunt her in the press. According to the judge's ruling, the defense would have to show to what extent the childhood abuse explained her emotional or physical condition immediately following the reported March 30 rape.[23]

Despite Judge Lupo's ruling against admitting Bowman's past sexual history, Roy Black was able to introduce this evidence through the back door. Questions about her bar-going habits painted a certain picture, as did her underwear, which Black asked the jurors to examine for tears to show that Smith had not forced her. As the black Victoria's Secret panties and sheer black bra with blue satin trim were passed from hand to hand to be checked for tears or stains, along with the newly bought Anne Taylor dress, it was obvious that another, more important message was attached to the show. Over the objection of the prosecution, the jurors also saw the T-shirt Anne Mercer gave Bowman to wear home after she changed her clothes at her house that morning, which bore the words: MADONNA—BLONDE AMBITION, and I THINK I AM A SEXUAL THREAT.[24]

Through these clothes and his cross-examination of Anne Mercer, Roy Black left the indelible impression that this unattached young woman, who had left her illegitimate child at her mother's for the night, was out for a night on a town famous for its bars frequented by rich men and fortune-seeking women. All of this without ever explicitly getting into Bowman's past sexual history.

Moira Lasch, on the other hand, was never able to get one iota of William Smith's past sexual patterns into the courtroom even though three women had come forward to say that between 1983 and 1988 he had allegedly raped one and assaulted the other two. The Florida law includes a provision called the "Williams rule," which allows prosecutors to offer evidence of the defendant's prior acts similar to those alleged in the pending case if they show a striking and detailed similarity to the offense charged. However, if the judge finds that this evidence is relevant solely to prove bad character or propensity, it cannot be entered into testimony. Lasch argued that the encounters described by the three women in sworn depositions were very similar to the allegations brought by Patricia Bowman.

Arguing before Judge Lupo, Lasch pointed out that in all four cases Smith charmed the women, "fostered trust in them" by showing interest in their personal lives. It was only when they were alone that he assaulted them, insisting later that he had done nothing wrong. "He followed a plan, a scheme in attacking these victims," Lasch said. To bolster her argument Lasch presented charts comparing the details of the four stories.[25] Judge Lupo, however, was not swayed by the similarities and ruled that they did not constitute a pattern within the meaning of the law, and this evidence was not allowed at the trial.

Many legal experts felt that by itself this ruling won the case for the defense. Without the evidence supplied by the other women, most commentators and criminal lawyers predicted an easy win for the defense— the word of a seemingly nice young doctor against that of a woman he picked up at a bar. But they agreed that if jurors heard about the three previous alleged crimes, the image of the nice boy would evaporate. Anna Quindlen of *The New York Times* remarked that taken together the statements of the three women "present a portrait of a man whose idea of foreplay is force."[26]

Alan Dershowitz put it in stronger terms.

If jurors in the Smith case learn of the three previous alleged crimes, they will no longer think he is a nice boy. They will think that maybe one woman or even two could be overreacting, mistaken or on a vendetta. But all four? No way. This guy is a rapist, the jurors will think, even if the evidence is less than entirely convincing.

They will see the Florida woman as someone who finally had the courage to blow the whistle on Mr. Smith."[27]

Interviews with jurors after the acquittal showed that while Patricia Bowman's past history probably made a difference, nothing that might have been brought out about William Kennedy Smith would have changed the strong sympathy the jurors felt for him and his family. All of them had been in Smith's camp from the very beginning. Four of them wept after the announcement of the verdict. Foreman Thomas J. Stearns, Jr., a former army paratrooper who had earned seven Purple Hearts in Vietnam and who cited war heroes as his idols, burst into tears the moment the verdict was announced. For Samuel Celaya, one of the alternate jurors, the high point of the trial was Ted Kennedy's testimony. Demonstrating how much sympathy can play a role, he expressed how deeply moved he was by Kennedy's testimony and by being so close to him physically.

Lea Haller, an attractive woman of thirty-seven, always impeccably dressed, sporting brightly polished nails, also cried. She owned a wholesale cosmetics company and gave facials during the trial when the jury was sequestered. According to her, the evidence just wasn't there. The testimony of the three other women had no bearing on this case, she said. Patricia Bowman either lied, was influenced by the wrong people, or had difficulty with reality. William Kennedy Smith was too charming and too good-looking to have to resort to violence for a night out, she said. She and Roy Black were seen together at one of the Palm Beach nightspots after the verdict. Later they appeared together on *Donahue*. Much later, according to Black, a year after the trial, they started dating. Both denied having any romantic interest in each other during the trial. Eventually, they married.

REACTION TO THE VERDICT

The public verdict among many in the media was that the evidence was not there to convict. Amy Pagnozzi of the *New York Post* said on Ted Koppel's *Nightline,* "If I was a juror, I would have definitely voted not to convict him and I would have returned the vote probably very rapidly as well." However, Pagnozzi added that she felt Smith was guilty due to the information from other women who alleged to have been assaulted by Smith. By the end of the trial several more women had come forth.[28] One of these women, Nancy Narleski, appeared on *The Jane Wallace Show* in Philadelphia the day the jury reached its verdict. On the basis of such information, Pagnozzi felt that Smith was guilty.

Susan Estrich also felt that there was not enough evidence to convict. She said that Smith was "a particularly credible witness" and the judge's decision to exclude evidence about the other women "was a damaging blow to the prosecution's case." Estrich pointed out that the verdict did not mean the jury thought "she had lied, it concluded that the prosecution had not made out its case against him."[29]

Given the testimony, Susan Brownmiller concluded that "there was reasonable doubt." She never saw this as a date-rape case but as a "celebrity rape case." She said she was impressed with Bowman's testimony, but found his "plausible." "My conclusion," she said, "just sitting there watching CNN, was this was a case of bad exploitative sex, but that's different from rape."[30]

Barbara Egenhauser, an assistant district attorney in Westchester County, New York, who specializes in prosecuting sex crimes, thought Moria Lasch could have done better. She felt it was "a winnable case if it had been presented in a certain manner." She feared that the verdict would have a "chilling effect" on other victims coming forward.

Rape crisis specialists also called the verdict "chilling." Many reported getting calls from rape victims saying that after watching the trial they decided not to divulge their names in rape prosecution. Others said that they would not go to the police because of what happened to Patricia Bowman.

In the fall of 1992 Patricia Bowman appeared on *Larry King Live* and said that she had no regrets, she would do it over again. Calling William Kennedy Smith her accuser as well as her offender, she said she would report the same crime and go down the same road because of her firm belief that if a woman is raped she has to seek justice.

"Despite all that happened?" Larry King asked.

"Despite all that happened, I would still do it again. And I still advocate any victim going forward, reporting the crime, and prosecuting."[31]

"THE TWO MIKES"

The second St. John's trial opened with jury selection on January 27, 1992, the same day that jury selection in the Mike Tyson case began in Indianapolis. J. Gregory Garrison, the lead prosecutor in Tyson's case, was fond of saying that Tyson picked the wrong city to rape in. In Indiana rape is rape whether strangers or acquaintances are involved and no matter who the man is. Sentencing for rape is stiff irrespective of the amount of force: where no weapon is used and the victim has no serious injuries, ten years is common.[32]

In New York comparisons between the two cases were inevitable, with some reporters referring to "the two Mikes." Indeed, the trials were similar in a number of significant ways. Desiree Washington and Angela shared the same starry-eyed innocence, gullibility, and trust. Both had led sheltered, religious lives and both believed that the American dream would work for them. Just as striking was the similarity between Judge Patricia Gifford in Indianapolis and Judge Kenneth Browne in Queens. Both judges created an atmosphere in the courtroom that could be called pro-justice, strikingly different from the pro-defense atmosphere of Palm

Beach and Long Island City. In their conduct and demeanor on the bench these judges demonstrated that acquaintance rape was not a legal joke. Watching them in action, one felt confident that both sides would get a fair hearing. They were both modern-day examples of the dedication shown by the Earl of Bridgewater more than three centuries before.

Several weeks before jury selection in the second St. John's trial, Adam G. pleaded guilty to sexual abuse in the second degree in return for a sentence of three years probation and community service. When he went before Judge Browne on January 7, with his lawyer, Peter Bongiorno, he admitted to touching Angela's breast "without her consent" at a time when "she appeared intoxicated." He testified that when this happened Andrew D., Walter G., Matthew G., and Thomas D. (Tommy) were in the room.

Judge Browne put the question of consent and physical helplessness very specifically.

"She was in no condition, as far as her sobriety was concerned, to give her consent or permission about anything, was she?"

Adam answered, "That is correct."

The prosecution was glad to have Adam G. behind them, and to deal exclusively with Michael, whom they believed set the whole thing up. They knew their case was not strong against Michael, especially on the charges of sodomy and sexual abuse. But they felt they had a good case for the charge of "unlawful imprisonment by acting in concert" with Walter and Andrew to restrain Angela.

The testimony presented at the trial spoke to the issue of consent and physical helplessness. The public finally heard that Michael had told Dean Jose Rodriguez of St. John's that Angela was "drunk" and Detective Vito Navarra that Angela was "like a rag doll" when he left the house. Tommy testified that he was on the landing standing behind Walter, Andrew, and Matthew watching Michael during the alleged sodomy act. However, he testified that he was able to see what actually transpired in the room only one third of the time. He said that he saw Angela's head moving from side to side when Michael's penis was in her mouth, which could be interpreted as consensual oral sex. However, just before he testified to seeing Angela's head moving from side to side he described her arms as "just to her side," which could be interpreted to mean that she had already been rendered physically helpless before her head started to move and it was Michael's pelvic motion that caused the movement.

Tommy's testimony also included important details with respect to the charge of "acting in concert." When Michael left the room, Andrew and Walter talked "close" together in a "low tone of voice" on the top step leading to the room. Then, when Michael returned he conversed with Andrew and Walter at the entrance to the room. Tommy remembered that Michael and Walter talked in "a low tone of voice" for fifteen to twenty seconds. Tommy said that after Michael talked softly with Walter and Andrew, he heard Walter say "he was going over to the girl." Michael then left, saying in a loud voice, "I have to leave." Tommy testified that Walter and Andrew "went into the room and Walter put the girl into a sitting position."

At this point trial testimony ground to a halt because Judge Browne would not allow Tommy to testify to the acts that took place after Michael left. They had all they needed for the charge of acting in concert, the judge said, pointing out that Tommy had testified that Michael brought the girl to the house, talked with Walter and Andrew in "sotto voice," and then loudly proclaimed he was leaving. Beyond this evidence of Michael's acting in concert, Judge Browne wouldn't budge, despite Reese's argument that he needed the sex acts of the co-defendants to show that because of her condition discernible during these acts, "she couldn't possibly have consented [to Michael]." The judge's decision meant that Tommy could not go on to describe the subsequent acts nor could the other eyewitnesses be called.

With the mainstay of their case gone, Reese and Gentile felt they had no choice but to negotiate a plea, which Barry Levin, the defense attorney, had been holding out as a carrot since jury selection. Both Levin and Michael were very worried about Judge Browne, fearing that if Michael was convicted on anything the judge would send him away for the max.

In a long and painful talk with Angela, the prosecutors explained that the plea would be consistent with her story and their theory of the case. It would distinguish Michael from the others who had pleaded guilty, because Michael would plea to sexual misconduct, the misdemeanor version of sodomy. This meant that Michael would admit to being guilty of an act of sodomy, not sexual abuse by means of touching, as Joe and Adam had done. The negotiated plea with Michael would also include an admission of guilty to unlawful imprisonment. This meant that Michael's case would be distinguished also by conviction on two misdemeanors. In exchange, Michael would receive probation not to exceed three years, and five hundred hours of community service with counseling. There would be no jail time, however, which the DA had wanted but Levin refused.

The next day, February 11, Reese informed the judge that Angela had decided to accept a plea from Michael. Judge Browne was willing to listen, but wasn't about to approve anything unless Angela agreed to it.

When Angela came into Judge Browne's chambers he stood up, his six feet dwarfing her tiny frame, and addressed her formally.

"I understand, young lady, you have a feeling this should go a certain way."

In Angela's eyes, Judge Browne not only stood at the peak of the pyramid of judicial power, he also embodied the epitome of moral authority. She spoke reverently to him, as she might to an archbishop presiding over a High Mass.

"If I can't tell the whole story of what happened, Your Worship, to me the plea is okay," she said, speaking in a tiny voice.

"You understand the rule of law sometimes prevents us from doing what we'd like to do," Judge Browne explained more gently.

"I understand, Your Worship," Angela replied.

The judge asked her to step outside for a moment while he conferred with his law secretary. When they came back, Judge Browne agreed with the plea. "I'll approve the plea," he said. "Set it up, gentlemen. I'm doing this on the complainant's wish."

It was about 11:30 A.M. The plea negotiation had been going on all morning and everyone but the jury knew it was in the works. Once the courtroom was prepared, the spectators and the jurors seated, the door opened and Angela came in and sat on the opposite side of the aisle from Michael's parents, one row back. As the proceedings started, she leaned over and placed her head down on the back of the bench in front of her as if it were a pew in a church and she was at morning Mass. Occasionally, she turned her head in the direction of Michael's mother. The two had never met, but Angela had often thought of calling her to express sympathy for what she was going through. As much as she felt compassion for Michael's mother, Angela was glad that today some sort of justice would be meted out in the courtroom. She hoped that Michael would tell the whole story and that she would be vindicated.

Michael's mother was not feeling at all compassionate toward Angela. She was furious. The family believed Michael was being railroaded and the trial was motivated by politics and reverse racism.

As Michael stood before Judge Browne reciting the details of his plea, it was obvious that his mother was deeply agitated. As he spoke, admitting to all the acts Angela had alleged, she looked angrily over at Angela's bowed head and said with pure hatred in her voice, "Look up, Angela, you won."

In answer to questions posed by Judge Browne, Michael said that he gave Angela three drinks and when she said she didn't feel well he massaged her shoulders and her head to make her feel better. He said that he started kissing her neck.

"And then what did you do?" the judge asked.

"And after we were kissing I stood up and I put my penis in her mouth," Michael answered. "We engaged in oral—I engaged in oral sex," he said, correcting himself.

"Now, at a time when she was just about drunk; is that right?" Judge Browne asked.

"Right," Michael answered.

"And you placed what where?" the judge asked.

"I put my penis in her mouth," Michael answered.

After the judge's questioning, Reese asked Michael to describe Angela's condition when he placed his penis in her mouth.

"She appeared drunk," Michael answered.

Referring to the sex act, Reese asked, "Did she give you any permission or authority to do that?"

Michael answered, "No."

Judge Browne also went over the charge of unlawful imprisonment, asking Michael if he "acted in concert with certain other persons."

"Yes," Michael testified. "I got her drunk with the intent to relax her —restrain her."

"You did what?" Judge Browne asked.

"I gave her drinks to get her drunk to relax her," Michael answered.

"She couldn't get up and go anywhere, could she?" Judge Browne asked.

"No."

"And, as a matter of fact, just about that time here comes three or four of your buddies beeping up the staircase; is that right?" Judge Browne continued.

"Correct," Michael answered.

"And at the time that you left, you left her in a condition whereby she could not remove herself from that predicament? Isn't that so?"

"Yes," Michael said.

In further questions from Reese, Michael admitted that he "left her on the couch," and that "her top was up," exposing the upper portion of her body.

"You intended to get her drunk?" Reese asked.

"Correct," Michael answered.

At the end of Michael's plea, Reese felt it was important to explain why Angela had agreed to accept the plea. Addressing the court in a speech meant for the spectators, he explained that Angela had asked to be present in the courtroom "to listen to these admissions from this defendant that she's been waiting such a long time, twenty-three months, to hear.

"We are accepting this plea primarily because of Your Honor's evidentiary rulings, which I know you made in accordance with the law," Reese said.

Reese ended by noting that Michael's admission of guilt represented "the fourth person to come forward and agree with the complainant that the sexual contact and conduct engaged in that night was indeed without [her] consent."

When it was over, Angela was ushered out of the courtroom while the rest remained seated and Michael sat in the defendant's seat. Michael tried to follow, hoping to speak to her. Later, he sought Reese out and asked to meet with Angela, who was in Reese's office. "I just want to talk to her," he said. "I want to tell her that everything is okay in my heart and I hope everything is okay in hers."

As Michael left the courtroom, one of the women in the back sitting with the anti-rape activists yelled, "Rapist!" A huge scuffle resulted. Michael's father leapt out of his seat and yelled to court officers, "What about them! Douche bags! I'm a fine, upstanding citizen. What about them?" he repeated, pointing to two feminists sitting with a group of protestors at the back of the courtroom.

Michael's mother was beside herself when she heard the word "rapist." She flew at the women, ready to fight any and all of them. "He's pleading to things he didn't do," she yelled, sobbing. "Black bitch. I don't want my son to be called a rapist. Dyke! No one calls my son a rapist."

On Valentine's Day, three days later, Peter Reese received a simple pink and red Valentine card with a little handwritten note from Angela thanking him.[33]

THE OTHER MIKE

Jeffrey Modisett, the first Democrat to hold the office of Marion County prosecutor in twelve years, made two key decisions in the Mike Tyson case. He picked Judge Patricia Gifford to be presiding judge and J. Gregory Garrison as the special prosecutor to try the case. Judge Gifford knew the law inside out, having helped draft the Indiana rape reform law. She was the first woman in Indiana to prosecute sex crimes as part of a separate sex-crimes division, which she initiated in the seventies. In one of the few remarks quoted in the press, she said, "The law in Indiana is pretty clear, and it never mentions whether a defendant or a victim are acquainted."[34]

Prosecutors respected and trusted Judge Gifford. They knew if they lost in her court it was because the evidence wasn't there or the jury was asleep. Garrison was comfortable trying Mike Tyson before her because she would make it a level playing field. "Nobody, but nobody pushes her around in the courtroom," he said. "She'd have stuck me in the lock-up as fast as she'd have stuck Vince Fuller." In her courtroom both sides could count on a fair trial. Later, when Alan Dershowitz tried to appeal Tyson's conviction, he got nowhere with his argument about Judge Gifford's conduct of the trial.[35]

Jeffrey Modisett hired Garrison on as lead prosecutor at $20,000, which worked out to about $70 an hour as compared with the $500 an hour Vincent Fuller, Tyson's prominent D.C. lawyer, was reputedly paid. Garrison was ideal for the job. He hadn't lost a jury case in two decades and he wasn't one to let some high-price Eastern lawyers come in to "kick a little Indiana backwoods ass," as a prosecutor who watched the trial said. He was a red-headed, "fire-in-the-belly" homeboy who knew how to speak to an Indiana jury. He pranced around in the courtroom, got angry, and spoke from the heart always without notes. Next to him, Vince Fuller, best known for having defended John Hinckley, who tried to assassinate President Ronald Reagan, looked like a snitty Eastern intellectual.[36]

It was clear from Garrison's remarks that you didn't have to be a feminist to send a man to jail for acquaintance rape. For him no always means no and his head wasn't filled with ideas that saw a yes lurking behind every no. He told the jury that going up to a guy's room at two in the morning wasn't any different from getting a flat tire in the wrong neighborhood and having your head bashed in by a robber. Is that your fault? he asked each perspective juror.[37] For Garrison the case was about justice, the law, and protecting the budding flowering of true womanhood he saw in Desiree Washington.

Garrison reminded me of the fire-and-brimstone preachers of the old moral reform societies. "Society has fallen apart and people don't respect women anymore," he said. Sounding like a man straight out of the cult of true womanhood, he said women were responsible for civilization and for keeping men from acting like a bunch of beasts, for jerking them around until they started behaving themselves. The Old West was a jungle until women brought education, the church, culture, and smarts, he said. The sexual revolution had only betrayed women by turning them into sex objects. Feminism was all right with Garrison so long as it stopped at the vote and equal pay for equal work. He showed more respect for Judge Gifford than most men show for their female superiors, yet he also called her "the Ice Queen," as if you couldn't be a real woman on a judge's bench. It's when girls want to fight, be paratroopers, carry M-16s, and give up their identity as women that Garrison started getting apoplectic about feminism.

Desiree Washington fit easily into Garrison's category of the true woman. For him she was a "beautiful child with nothing to hide—one hundred and six pounds, five feet five inches tall—just a little twig, little tiny voice, sweet beautiful eyes." Mike Tyson was the epitome of the animal with his wild, salacious advances to every and all women he set eyes on. Tyson's defense played up this image of Tyson. The defense strategy promoted just about every stereotype in the book of the oversexed black male, figuring that the jury would blame the complainant for being so dumb as to set foot in Tyson's limo.

The case was pretty much open and shut as far as Garrison was concerned. The details just didn't fit with someone who went out knowing or even suspecting that she would end up in Tyson's bed. If anything, she might have thought she would be the one to tame the wild beast in Tyson. When Desiree met Tyson, he was wearing an orange button saying TOGETHER IN CHRIST on his shirt. When he first asked her to go out he offered to take one of her roommates from the Miss Black America pageant along too. Her understanding of Tyson's intentions was further bolstered by seeing him praying with the Reverend Jesse Jackson.

When Tyson called her at 1:30 A.M. and invited her out, she was in bed and didn't want to go. She invited him up to her room, but one of her roommates nixed that idea. She agreed to go out with Tyson only after he told her he was leaving the next day. Thinking they would go to the parties celebrating the opening of Black Expo, an annual weeklong celebration of black culture, she hurriedly put on some clothes over her pajama undies and took her camera along to take pictures.

After she got into the limo, Tyson took her straight to his hotel. They went up to his room because he said he had to get something. In the room, he asked about her background, her family, and her feelings for him. She began to feel very uneasy when he told her that she really turned him on. On the witness stand she testified that she told him she was "not like the girls he must be used to hanging out with." She asked to use the bathroom and when she came out he was on the bed in his underpants.[38]

He said, "Come here," she testified. "And he grabbed my arm; and he was like, 'Don't fight me. Come here.' And then he stuck his tongue in my mouth." "He was disgusting," she said.[39]

Garrison led her through the rape itself. She had to tell all of the gory details. Not a sound in the courtroom. The testimony was riveting, painful to hear. She fought back tears, and didn't break down once. She was "almost too perfect," one journalist reported, "a little prissy." She testified that in the months after, she was plagued with nightmares. Garrison asked her how long she had had that problem. "I still do, sometimes," she answered. For Garrison this part of her testimony was "the most powerful moment" in direct examination he had ever experienced as a lawyer."[40]

Minutes after the end of the rape, she was seen by a bellboy coming out of Tyson's room, who testified that she looked "confused, scared, [carrying] her shoes in her hands." "She was looking around like she was lost," he testified. The woman limousine driver waiting for them downstairs also happened to be professionally trained to counsel rape victims. She testified that she knew something was wrong with Desiree when she came back to the car. She "came out in a hurry," she testified. Her hair was messed up. "She looked like she was disoriented. She looked all frantic . . . like she might have been in a state of shock. . . . She seemed scared." She kept repeating, "I don't believe him. I don't believe him. Who does he think he is?"[41]

Desiree's testimony was the heart of the State's case. She looked beautiful on the witness stand. She was wearing a conservative gray silk suit. Her hair was all fixed up. Before her testimony, she prayed with her family and with Garrison, just as Angela had prayed with Reese and Reverend Herbert Daughtry, who attended the St. John's trials with members of the black community. Garrison could hear a loud gasp in the courtroom when she walked through the doorway. She was little, only a few pounds over one hundred. Next to Tyson's 260-pound hulk she "looked more like a girl than a grown woman." Garrison was sure that anyone with half a brain was thinking, "What are we talking about? Sex? Wait a minute."[42]

The physical evidence was damning. As Garrison and co-author Randy Roberts reported, "[i]n rape cases 10 to 20 percent of victims suffer some kind of vaginal injury." This was true in the case of Desiree Washington. The physicians who testified for the prosecution explained that the internal injuries she suffered almost never happen during consensual sex. One of them said that in the two thousand to three thousand pelvic examinations he had carried out he had seen the kind of vaginal abrasions she had sustained only twice in women saying they occurred during consensual sex. The second physician testified that he had completed more than twenty thousand pelvic examinations and had never seen such abrasions as a result of consensual sex.[43]

The defense case robbed Tyson of all individuality and civility and turned him into the common stereotype of the sex-crazed black man. Numerous witnesses attested to Tyson's lecherous attitude toward women, and how he touched, manhandled, or propositioned every woman he met at the Black Expo. The implication was that Desiree was an intelligent woman and should have known that Tyson was after only one thing.

Tyson testified that he made his intentions clear to her from the moment they met. Contradicting her story, he testified that when she agreed to go out with him, she said, "We can go to a movie or dinner or something." In response, he testified that he told her: "I want to fuck you." And she answered, "Sure, give me a call." Tyson testified that this was his way with women. "I just want to know what I'm getting before I get into it," he said.

In cross-examination, Garrison brought out that this story was inconsistent with the one Tyson had told the grand jury. In his grand jury testimony, Tyson stated that when he made the date with Desiree he had said only, "I want to be alone with you. I want you." Tyson told the grand jury that he didn't like to be so blunt as to come straight out and say, "Want to screw?"

There were other important discrepancies between Tyson's two sworn testimonies. He told the grand jury that his bodyguard, Dale Edwards, had been in the parlor of his suite during the entire time he was in the bedroom with Desiree. But witnesses had testified that Edwards was not in Tyson's room at all. In his trial testimony, Tyson changed his story and said that he didn't really know, but thought that Edwards was in the room. At which point Garrison shot back, "Kind of like supposing that somebody wants to have sex with you but you don't really know, isn't it?"

Trying to get Tyson angry so that the jury could see how he would react, Garrison came very close to him at one point during the cross-examination. When he saw Tyson getting angry he walked back to the prosecution table, leaving behind a piece of Desiree's clothing near him. As he was returning to his seat, Tyson flicked the clothing away with rage. As Garrison records, this motion with its momentary hint of violence was not lost on the jury.[44]

The defense argument was that Desiree Washington cried rape when she realized that it was "no more than a one-night stand."[45] In his direct testimony, Tyson testified that he asked Desiree to stay the night. According to Tyson, when she chose to go back to her room he didn't walk her to the limousine because he was too tired. She became "irritated" when he remained in bed. "I told her that was the way it was," Tyson testified. "If you don't want to use the limousine, you can walk."[46]

In his closing argument Garrison poked holes in this theory by pointing out that if Desiree wanted Tyson so badly, she would have accepted his invitation to spend the night.

In addition to employing "the scorned woman" theme, the defense claimed that Desiree Washington was a "gold digger." They called witnesses who testified that Desiree had talked about Tyson's money, and that although he was dumb and ignorant he was rich.[47] In his opening, Fuller had said that she had hired a civil lawyer to pursue a civil case against Tyson and pointed out that if Tyson was convicted, a civil lawsuit could make Desiree Washington a very wealthy woman.[48]

Dershowitz also went after the gold-digger theme in his appeal on behalf of Tyson. However, as Garrison pointed out in his book on the case, it would be foolish to file criminal charges if one's goal was a civil case. The burden of proof is less in a civil case, and the chances of winning an acquaintance rape case in criminal court were less than fifty-fifty. Besides, if Desiree Washington wanted Tyson's money, she would have accepted the million-dollar offer she got to drop the charges.[49]

The jury's decision to convict Tyson was reached in ten hours. They concluded that "clearly consent had not been given." They believed her story about going to parties. They wondered why Tyson's bodyguard, who was reportedly outside the bedroom that night, had not been called as a witness to corroborate his story.[50] The jurors also said that they were convinced of Tyson's guilt after hearing him testify. Gary Thomas, a thirty-year-old insurance salesman quoted by *The New York Times,* said, "His own testimony convicted him. Up until then I thought that the girl put herself in a vulnerable position. I thought that she didn't have a case, but when Mike Tyson took the stand, he convicted himself."[51]

The defense strategy of painting Tyson as a lout with women clearly backfired. But one wonders whether the same jury would have convicted Tyson had he been white and a little less forthcoming about his boorishness with women. Did racial stereotypes or the evidence convict Tyson? Given the emotion expressed by the Smith jury and their comments that his prior acts would have made no difference to their decision, it is doubtful whether William Kennedy Smith would have been convicted on the evidence against Tyson.

On the other hand, if the Tyson verdict was based on the evidence rather than on racism, it is clear that the defendant's prior sexual behavior can make a difference in acquaintance rape trials. However, this was precisely the area most rigidly excluded in the William Kennedy Smith and the St. John's trials. In both cases, the complainant's worthiness upstaged careful consideration of evidence of guilt. In the Smith case, for example, the issue of force and consent was lost in the fog of Roy Black's trial presentation of Patricia Bowman's reputation and his ability to cloud important issues such as the medical testimony about her bruises. Other issues were also muddied or forgotten altogether. For example, Smith testified that Patricia Bowman wore no panties, yet she testified that he pushed her panties aside, entered her, and then withdrew. The forensic evidence corroborated her story more closely than Smith's. Tests showed that her panties were saturated with semen and that there was semen on the back lining of her dress, which was consistent with her statement to the police that she felt "something wet" between her legs. If the focus had been more solidly on the physical evidence, perhaps the public and the jury would have understood why there was semen on panties that William Kennedy Smith testified had been removed prior to any sex acts.

• • •

The high-profile cases of the early 1990s demonstrated that despite rape law reform, justice continued to allude rape complainants. Although false reports of rape were estimated to be the same as for other major crimes, the complainant was placed on trial in the modern courtroom as she was a hundred years ago.[52] Justice will be served only when the scrutiny shifts from the complainant—her reputation, her alleged sexiness, abortions, childhood sexual abuse, or what she might have said hours earlier, etc.— to the defendant's behavior. Did the defendant obtain consent? Did the defendant go ahead despite an expressed no? Did the defendant know whether the complainant consented? These are the questions to be answered in determining whether a crime was committed.

In most states it would be necessary to ask in addition, Was force used? However, there is a growing trend to interpret or rewrite rape statutes so that a woman's no is sufficient to establish nonconsent. A controversial state supreme court decision in Pennsylvania, for example, caused lawmakers to change the state's rape statute to criminalize nonconsensual sex in the absence of force. In the case in question, Robert A. Berkowitz, a student at East Stroudsburg University, was accused of raping a fellow student who testified that she did not physically resist or scream, but repeatedly said no. Berkowitz was found guilty of rape and indecent assault and sentenced to prison for one to four years for rape. On appeal, the Superior Court of Pennsylvania overturned the rape conviction on the grounds that the evidence was "insufficient to convict appellant of rape" because force had not been established. The Pennsylvania Supreme Court upheld the lower court's opinion and argued that the Pennsylvania rape statute requires the elements of actual or threatened "forcible compulsion." Saying no was not "relevant to the issue of force," the court concluded. According to the court, "Where there is a lack of consent, but no showing of either physical force, a threat of physical force, or psychological coercion, the 'forcible compulsion' requirement" under the Pennsylvania rape statute "is not met."[53]

Demonstrating that rape reform activism was still very much alive, ten months after this decision was handed down in May 1994, Pennsylvania's House of Representatives gave final legislative approval in March 1995 to a bill popularly labeled the "no-means-no legislation." Although the bill kept forcible compulsion as an element in the definition of rape, which was defined as a first-degree felony, the no-means-no provision created the new offense of "sexual assault." Sexual assault was defined as a "felony of the second degree" and applied to persons who engage "in sexual intercourse or deviate sexual intercourse with a complainant without the complainant's consent."[54] Under this legislation Berkowitz could have been convicted of a crime punishable by a prison term of up to ten years and a fine not exceeding $25,000.

Negative reaction to the passage of this legislation from *Philadelphia Inquirer* reporters Tanya Barrientos and Lini S. Kadaba reflected another trend of the 1990s.[55] As Anita Hill and Patricia Bowman increased public consciousness of sexual harassment and date rape, a backlash against anti-rape activism became more evident. Displaying typical backlash rhetoric, the *Inquirer* reporters referred to the "shark infested waters of modern dating." Interviewing students in the Philadelphia area, they described supporters of the bill as coming "from elite and staunchly politically correct campuses." "Women *do lie,*" the article announced in its opening sentence, quoting from an interview with one of the students who was against the bill. "In the real world of dating," the reporters concluded, "sometimes *no* really means *yes.*" Similar ideas are being widely expressed in the 1990s crusade against anti-rape activism. Part of the conservative trend of the Reagan-Bush era, the crusade seeks to resurrect the old sexual stereotypes as eternal verities, illustrating that the reaction summarized by Susan Faludi in her book *Backlash* applies as much to women's progress toward equality in the sexual arena as it does in other areas.

ELEVEN

THE CRUSADE AGAINST ANTI-RAPE ACTIVISM

THE MEDIA CRUSADE AGAINST THE ANTI-RAPE MOVEMENT THAT BEGAN IN 1990, and shows no sign of letting up any time soon, levels the charge of "politically correct sex" at sexual offense policies on college campuses and the idea that no means no. The crusade refashions the thought of Havelock Ellis and Freud, with some new ideas thrown in for a modern audience. As part of the resurgence of nineteenth-century social Darwinism during the Reagan-Bush era, the critics argued that male sexual aggression is "natural" and that feminists turn women into victims with their claims of "male oppression." This was a little like Newt Gingrich's charge that the Democratic Party tended "to identify victims and purport to relieve their victimhood" in the 1995 political debates over social welfare and affirmative action.[1] In the sexual arena, one could also see the conservative goal of scaling down restrictions imposed by "big government" in the critique of campus sexual offense policies on the grounds that individuals should devise their own rules and women could manage on their own.

The conservative critique ballooned in 1991 in response to stepped-up efforts to get a Violence Against Women Act passed in the Senate and House. Camille Paglia and Katie Roiphe, most noted for their attacks on the alleged "date-rape hysteria," rose to media stardom on the wave of the backlash. Arguments over the incidence and prevalence of date rape and an attack on "gender feminism" became an important part of the critique, bringing in Berkeley professor Neil Gilbert and Clark University professor Christina Hoff Sommers. Although all of the individuals involved in the backlash made it a point to say they abhor rape, all of them showed more concern with condemning feminists than with finding solutions.

Just below the rhetorical surface one detects an unmistakable nostalgia for the old hunt-pursuit-capture model of male sexuality—a desire to reinstate sexual difference by resurrecting belief in the manly seducer and his counterpart, the compliant, sensuous woman. The rhetoric condemns anti-rape activists as neo-Puritans, prudes, or dykes. College students attending Take Back the Night marches or participating in peer education programs on campuses are called "victims" of feminist propaganda. Like the labels "wimp" or "poor worm" applied to effeminate or sensitive men in earlier decades, these labels diminish females who take an active interest in their sexual autonomy. Like the Salem witches, modern women seeking greater sexual self-determination are prime targets for attack—especially from other women. As Jon Wiener, who summarized the date-rape backlash for *The Nation* in 1992, noted: "Women journalists can go far if they attack feminism."[2]

THE CRUSADE BEGINS

It wasn't until after the Violence Against Women Act first underwent hearings in the Senate Judiciary Committee in June 1990 that the fervor against anti-rape activism took hold. Feminists played an important role in drafting and lobbying for this act. Its passage on September 13, 1994, can be counted among the most significant victories achieved by modern feminism.[3] Senator Joseph Biden's impassioned speech when he introduced the act in 1990 showed that it was not meant as a token gesture. "Violent crime against women happens every day in the country," he said.

"Over the past ten years the rape rate has risen four times faster than the national crime rate," he noted. Calling violence against women an "epidemic" that had to be stopped, Biden said that women are "losing a fundamental human right—the right to be free from fear." Biden claimed that the legislation he was introducing would attack "the problem in all forms—from rape cases to domestic violence, from everyday assaults to murder" and at all levels of society: "from the home to the streets, from the criminal justice system to the prison system."[4]

The act included three major titles: safe streets for women, safe homes for women, and civil rights for women. Two additional titles—safe campuses for women and equal justice for women in the courts—were added later. Biden considered the most important provision to be the one addressing women's civil rights. Pointing out that "97 percent of all sex assaults in this country are against women," he said the bill would "fill a gap in our civil rights laws by defining gender-motivated crimes as bias or hate crimes and amending Federal civil rights laws to say that such attacks violate a woman's civil rights."[5] "Making a certain action a civil rights violation means our society believes that action is morally obscene, that we have made a value judgment against it and will not tolerate it anymore," Senator Biden told *McCall's* magazine. According to Biden, if women have to change their lives to accommodate the fear of rape while men don't, "that's not equality."[6]

The civil rights provision of the act was widely hailed by feminists as a major step forward for women. Using Patricia Bowman's allegations against William Kennedy Smith as an example, feminist legal scholar and activist Catharine MacKinnon painted a vivid picture of the potential consequences of giving women a civil rights remedy. Had Patricia Bowman had this provision at her disposal, her case would have been entirely different. As is true in all civil cases, she would not have had to prove her charges "beyond a reasonable doubt" but only by "a preponderance of the evidence." But most important, the testimony of the other women barred from testifying against Smith would have become part of the evidence used to prove Smith's gender bias. Patricia Bowman's statement that she went through with the case to prevent Smith from "doing it to someone else" would not have been treated as vindictive but rather as the very point of bringing a civil rights case. Roy Black's attempts to discredit Patricia Bowman's character would have been "exposed as gender bias." Recognizing rape as a systematic act of sex bias is a powerful tool for ending violence against women, which could be likened to recognizing lynching as an act of "racial bigotry," MacKinnon concluded.[7]

After Biden introduced the Violence Against Women Act in June 1990, three hearings were conducted by the Senate Judiciary Committee during the summer and fall. The first focused on gender issues in rape cases; the second examined the issue of acquaintance rape on college campuses; and the third concentrated on crimes of domestic violence. Mary Koss testified about the results of her national survey during the second hearing at the end of August. She also explained why government statistics on rape were unrealistically low. This was important for those whose knowledge of rape in America was based on these statistics alone. She pointed out that inadequate collection procedures resulted in "a false picture of rape as an infrequent crime and, as a result, blunts societal concern about the extent to which American women are victimized."[8]

The first missive of the date-rape backlash began with an article by journalist Stephanie Gutmann in the July 1990 issue of *Reason,* a magazine of Libertarian thought published by the Reason Foundation in Los Angeles, California. It is impossible to tell whether this article was a coincidence or a direct response to the news that the Violence Against Women Act was being drafted. It is telling that the article was quickly reprinted in the October issue of *Playboy,* suggesting that the laissez-faire philosophy of the Libertarians had a ready ally in *Playboy*'s philosophy of sexual freedom.

Three years before Katie Roiphe published *The Morning After,* Stephanie Gutmann expressed concern that women might start blaming men for a night of bad sex instead of examining their own ambivalent feelings. Describing two hypothetical incidents—one of forcible sex, the other of sex without consent—Gutmann distinguishes between "rape and seduc-

tion, between sex offense and offensive sex." Referring to the FBI definition of rape as "carnal knowledge of a female forcibly and against her
consent," Gutmann is concerned that feminists are broadening the definition of rape to include no means no when the issue is not so clear-cut and
no might mean yes. She fears that broadening the definition of rape is
unfair to men and unhelpful to young women, who might be too quick to
turn ambivalent feelings about sex into a charge of rape.

Like Roiphe, Gutmann argues that the evolving definition of rape
emphasizing no means no only reinforces female passivity and the notion
that females are victims. Expanding on what she calls the "redefinition of
rape," Gutmann suggests that there is a tendency to broaden the definition of rape to extremes. As an example of the trend, she refers to a
statement that appeared in a 1985 training guide for a student-produced
video made at Swarthmore College to teach students about acquaintance
rape. The video was shown to incoming freshmen in acquaintance rape
workshops teaching sexual communication. Women students were encouraged to say no clearly and male students to make their intentions
clear. For discussion purposes the student author of the manual included
the following statement, which Gutmann quotes as follows: "Acquaintance rape . . . spans a spectrum of incidents and behaviors, ranging
from crimes legally defined as rape to verbal harassment and inappropriate innuendo."[9] Gutmann implies that this is Swarthmore's definition of
rape.

After Gutmann's article was published, *Reason* printed a response
from two Swarthmore students stating that Gutmann's article "drastically
misrepresents the ideology, purpose, and methods" of the Swarthmore
workshops. Nevertheless, the phrase "inappropriate innuendo" stuck as
the feminist definition of date rape, appearing in numerous articles for
several years thereafter as an example of fuzzy-minded, victim-obsessed
feminism. Swarthmore College repeatedly tried to set the record straight
in letters to editors and interviews, pointing out that the statement did
not appear in the video itself, was never part of Swarthmore's sexual
offense policy, and was never given to students as a definition of rape.[10]

THE RISE OF CAMILLE PAGLIA

After the summer and fall hearings on the Violence Against Women Act, a substitute bill was prepared that was voted on favorably by the Judiciary Committee and formally introduced on the floor on January 14, 1991, by Chairman Biden and twenty-five senators. Two weeks later two major articles appeared two days apart. The first article, written by Camille Paglia for *Newsday,* initiated a media assault on "date rape hysteria." The second article, by Eric Felten of *The Washington Times,* sparked a numbers war over the prevalence of date rape, which had already been started by *Playboy* and would be taken up by Neil Gilbert and repeated by Katie Roiphe and Christina Hoff Sommers in their books.[11]

Camille Paglia's rise to media stardom after the publication of her op-ed piece in *Newsday* is a case study in the backlash phenomenon. Overnight, she was thrust into the limelight as an expert on date rape. Calling herself an "antifeminist feminist," Paglia was a logical spokesperson for a counter-offensive against date-rape activism. She proved to be an excellent player in the ongoing game, which began during the Reagan-Bush era, of highlighting divisions among feminists in order to suggest that feminism was no longer a potent force for change. Paglia's appeal was in her ability to bring arguments about human nature back to the simplicity of social Darwinism and its suggestion that life is a struggle between the weak and the strong.

Central to her argument, and expressed in a whirlwind of media interviews and op-ed pieces during 1991, is the "naturalness" of male sexual aggression. Reminiscent of Havelock Ellis, she boldly claims that "hunt, pursuit, and capture are biologically programmed into male sexuality." She describes male sexuality as a "powerful, uncontrollable force," which "cannot be regulated"—all hormones and aggression, "the most creative cultural force in history." Walking into a fraternity party is to walk into "Testosterone Flats, full of prickly cacti and blazing guns," she says. In addition to the testosterone, young women have to reckon with the fact that fraternity brothers might be motivated by the "fun element" of rape, "especially the wild, infectious delirium of gang rape."[12]

In the opening pages of her 1990 book, *Sexual Personae,* Paglia expresses a vision of the sex instinct more outdated than either Freud's or Ellis's by giving eroticism an independent existence, calling it a "realm stalked by ghosts," a force that subjects males and females alike to its elemental, dark power.[13] "In the beginning was nature," she proclaims. Paglia's reading of nature as violence, lust, and hierarchy, and a place where "brute force is the law, a survival of the fittest," hearkens back to Hobbes's *Leviathan,* published in 1651. She concludes that although society is constructed to guard mankind from these elemental powers, it can erect only a weak edifice against the sex and violence that is natural in man.[14]

The rapist, then, is the man who has been reduced to a state of nature. Take away the trappings of social conditioning and all men will rape, Paglia suggests, reflecting a simplistic universalism. "Rape is the sexual expression of the will-to-power, which nature plants in all of us and which civilization rose to contain." Paglia seems ambivalent about whether rape is a good or bad thing. On the one hand, she says rape is male nature responding to the lure of female sexuality, which she calls "nature's red flame." On the other, she says, "the rapist is a man with too little socialization rather than too much." She comes down enthusiastically on the side of nature when she lectures feminists working for equal rights that there can be no such thing as sexual liberation or sexual equality because by nature "we are hierarchical animals." "Sweep one hierarchy away, and another will take its place." If we try to institute sexual freedom, she suggests, we will end up with sadomasochism. No matter what we do to fight the dark hierarchical forces of eroticism, nature will rule in the end.[15]

Paglia counsels young women to either go with the flow or get out of the way of "aggressive, unstable, combustible" masculinity. She advises that the best protection for women is to understand the laws of nature:

"It is woman's personal responsibility to be aware of the dangers of the world." Male sex is one of those dangers. "Wake up to reality," she tells women, sounding like a modern-day Krafft-Ebing: "Male sex is hot." Her advice to women who can't deal with male sex and who expect protection from the law is simple: "Stay home and do your nails."[16]

If a girl wants to have fun, she should accept the inevitable, take the risk. Getting raped is no worse than getting beat up in a dark alley. Rape should be treated as an assault. Women who go crying to their mothers or to a rape counselor are immature. Like the early sex researchers in the Ellis tradition who claimed that women who are psychologically devastated by rape didn't have the proper attitude toward sex, Paglia claims it should not be the rapist who is blamed for a woman's rape trauma, but feminists trying to sell the idea that sex can be benevolent, a wonderful thing between two equals. "The only solution to date rape," she advises, is "female self-awareness and self-control."[17]

If a woman takes the risk and gets raped by an acquaintance, it is her fault, not the fault of the man who assaults her. "The girl in the Kennedy rape case," as she refers to Patricia Bowman, was "an idiot" for going to the Kennedy compound late at night. She, not Smith, should have been charged—for ignorance. "Because everyone knows that Kennedy is spelled S-E-X." She dismisses Patricia Bowman as just another one of those "overprivileged people" who wanted the world "to be a bowl of cherries." Survival in the exhilarating domain of male power means putting up with the likes of William Kennedy Smith.[18] Paglia was not any kinder toward Anita Hill. She dismisses her as "a delicate flower," whose charges against Clarence Thomas showed that America was "still burdened by its Puritan past."[19]

The phallicism and violence of Paglia's romanticization of male sexual aggression are a reminder of the mythology of violence that inform our history and that became, as Richard Slotkin writes, "the structuring metaphor of the American experience." More than metaphor, Slotkin notes that violence was the means men relied on to regenerate their fortunes and their spirits in the New World.[20] As Paglia spoke about the natural-

ness of male aggression, testimony was presented concurrently in the
Senate Judiciary Committee hearings about an epidemic of violence
against women. According to Biden, the evidence was overwhelming:

> One out of every five American women will be raped during their
> lives. More women will be beaten by their husbands this year than
> will get married; flight from domestic violence is the number one
> reason why women are homeless. Assaults against young women
> have risen 48 percent in the past 15 years, while assaults against
> young men have actually fallen by 12 percent.[21]

Paglia's ideas provided academic fodder for the paramilitary culture of
post-Vietnam America and its anti-feminism, a mannish woman jousting
with nasty feminist warriors. She was the female Ollie North of the right,
larger than life like Howard Stern, the designated hitter to clear the field
of foggy-minded feminism. She was as necessary as Clarence Thomas to
give the appearance of change in the white male club of the right.

John Leo, conservative columnist for *U.S. News & World Report,* who
was fond of attacking "femino-puritanism" and the new campus rules,
expressed his awe of Paglia, calling her "quite brilliant," and her book
"stunning and eccentric." He embraced her notion of the biological basis
of the hunt-pursuit-capture nature of male sexuality because it helped
him explain all the flack he was getting for his "male chauvinism." According to Leo, there were two colliding views of rape: "the traditional or
biologically-based model," which he espoused, and "the feminist male-
oppression model" asserted by his detractors. Leo also leaned on Stephanie
Gutmann for corroboration of his view that "feminist academics" produce
"deeply flawed studies with ludicrously broad definitions of date rape that
force the numbers to rise." Although Leo knew from a call to Swarthmore
that the "inappropriate innuendo" definition of date rape alleged by Gutmann was a misrepresentation, he still quoted Gutmann to make his
point: "The real story about campus date rape is not that there's been any
increase of rape on college campuses, at least of the acquaintance type, but

that the word 'rape' is being stretched to encompass any type of sexual interaction."[22]

Leo's trivialization of date rape and his glorification of Paglia's biological essentialism are puzzling given his characterization, some six months later, of the St. John's verdict as a "total miscarriage of justice" (see Chapter 1). There is an important lesson contained in this contradiction. It appears that Leo responds philosophically to the rhetoric of date rape and with compassion and a sense of justice when confronted with the reality of specific cases. Yet one could argue that his reduction of male sexual behavior to biology and hormones encourages the sexual behavior he decries in the St. John's case, which places young males in a sexual double bind. Believing in the necessity of venting sexual energy due to a presumed biological imperative, males find themselves in a courtroom when that necessity leads them to transgress the line of consent.

THE NUMBERS GAME

One week after Paglia's first attack on date-rape feminism appeared in *Newsday,* Eric Felten wrote a long article in *The Washington Times* that was an attack both on the Violence Against Women Act and Mary Koss's research. The attack against Koss had actually started in *Playboy* the previous October and November after she testified before the Senate Judiciary Committee.

Koss's finding that one in four women indicated that they had experienced rape or attempted rape since the age of fourteen was the focus of much of the backlash in the numbers arena. The one-in-four statistic was based on the finding that 16 percent of the women students interviewed in her national sample claimed they had experienced unwanted sexual intercourse due to force, threat, or the use of drugs or alcohol. An additional 12 percent had experienced attempted unwanted sexual intercourse due to force, threat of force, or alcohol. Hence, her often quoted result of one in four.[23]

In the same October issue in which Gutmann's article is reprinted, *Playboy* describes these results and objects to the fact that "43 percent of the women classified as rape victims by Koss's students had not realized they'd been raped." An article in the following issue repeats Koss's statistics and raises a second criticism, namely that Koss used "an overly broad definition of rape," a comment that confused Stephanie Gutmann's critique of the feminist "redefinition of rape" with the narrow legal definition of rape Koss actually used.[24]

In his article for *The Washington Times,* Felten repeats these objections and adds that Koss's figures are much higher than those collected by the Bureau of Justice Statistics, notorious among rape researchers for its methodology, a notoriety specifically discussed by Koss in her testimony before the Judiciary Committee and included in her later response to Neil Gilbert. Felten begins his article by dredging up the old fear of the false accuser, citing a case at George Washington University of a student who falsely reported that a woman she knew had been raped at knifepoint on campus by two young black men. He goes on to confuse the findings of two surveys conducted by Koss, suggesting that she cites the numbers incorrectly, when in fact it is he who misrepresents Koss's findings from these two surveys.[25]

Ostensible academic support for the attack on Mary Koss was provided by Berkeley professor Neil Gilbert in articles published in *The Wall Street Journal* and *Public Interest* later the same year. Without specifically referring to them as sources, Gilbert repeats the criticisms of *Playboy* and *The Washington Times.* He also dwells on the lower figures reported by the Bureau of Justice and the FBI, which Koss had addressed in her Senate testimony. He objects to Koss's inclusion of a question on alcohol. He is particularly concerned, like the other commentators, with the fact that so many "whom the researcher defined as having been raped did not perceive of themselves as victims." He adds that nearly half of these women "had sex again with the men who had supposedly raped them." Furthermore, more than three quarters of the men identified as having committed rape "disagreed with the researcher's interpretation of the incidents."[26]

In his *Wall Street Journal* article, Gilbert's goal is mainly political when he warns the public against "radical feminists" who want to convince us that "a silent epidemic of sexual assault has infected college campuses throughout the country." He is concerned that this hysteria has contaminated the Violence Against Women Act, which he says offers "more than a symbolic gesture of concern for this problem" by appropriating $80 million over the next four years "to make campuses safer for women." Gilbert fuels the reader's opposition to the act by suggesting that date rape activists on college campuses condone false accusations of rape.[27]

Gilbert cites the well-known fact that few women report rapes to the campus police. However, it is also well known that while few rapes are reported to the campus police, a great many are reported to campus women's centers, where women go for counseling. For example, Angela's first thought was not to go to the campus police but to a trusted nun. Experience on many campuses teaches students who seek vindication by going to the police or to campus administrators that they are in for one long headache. Administrators may drag their feet, the alleged assailant may not cooperate, the student judicial system may not be equipped to deal with rape; meanwhile, the complainant is often pressured or intimidated into dropping charges by the alleged assailants or their friends. Angela had to drop out of school because she was constantly running into members of the lacrosse team, who would follow her to class and around campus telling her "nothing happened."

Gilbert's attack on Koss demonstrates his awareness of the political stakes in rape-crisis feminism. "The rape crisis movement's agenda is to change social perceptions of what constitutes acceptable intimate relations between men and women," he states. Yet, according to Gilbert, the feminist goal is to turn "the slightest pressure" into an "inappropriate use of force," to define "sweet talk and efforts at verbal persuasion" as "coercive," and to define the "faintest demurral" as a no. Gilbert follows Gutmann in characterizing the feminist idea that no means no as "an effort to reduce the awesome complexity of intimate discourse between the sexes to the banality of 'no means no.' " Before appropriating "millions to support the crisis centers that form the backbone of this movement," Gilbert warns, Congress should "study the data more carefully."[28]

KOSS'S RESPONSE TO GILBERT

In several articles, Koss takes up Gilbert's points one by one. She discusses the major problems with the two federal sources of rape-incidence data (meaning the number of cases that appear in one year), which Gilbert cites to argue that rape is not the problem feminists make it out to be. First there is the data presented in the FBI Uniform Crime Reports. These data only cover *reported* rapes. Even the compilers of the Uniform Crime Reports caution that their statistics underestimate the incidence of rape. According to them," [e]ven with the advent of rape crisis centers and an improved awareness by police in dealing with rape victims, forcible rape is still recognized as one of the most underreported of all index crimes."[29]

The second source is the Bureau of Justice Statistics National Crime Victimization Survey (NCVS). This survey is a nationwide, household-based crime-victimization survey designed to determine the true amount of crime, including both reported and unreported cases. The estimate of rape-victimization rates for the year 1989 based on this survey was 1.2 per 1,000 women and girls. This is extremely low compared with the figures Koss found for her college sample. In a twelve-month period she estimated an incidence rate of 50 per 1,000 college women of one or more attempted or completed rapes.[30]

Koss gives several reasons why the NCVS undermines full disclosure of rape by survey participants. First, the compilers of the NCVS themselves recognize that violence or attempted violence involving family members is underreported because of the presence of family members during the interview. Second, interviewers used for NCVS data collection are not trained to handle sensitive issues and are not consistently matched in ethnicity or gender with respondents, which undermines rapport and trust. Third, the NCVS is presented as a survey of "crimes." The compilers of NCVS acknowledge that violence involving family members or close friends may not be considered a crime. Finally, no specific questions about rape are actually asked. For example, after being asked whether they were physically assaulted or attacked with a weapon, respondents are asked, "Did anyone *try* to attack you in some other way?" This is the closest the survey gets to asking about rape. Just recently, a new question was added that mentions a "sexual attack." Since this question appears in a context of attacks involving guns, knives, baseball bats, and other physical objects, Koss objects to it on the grounds that it fuels the stereotype of stranger rape and is unlikely to obtain information on acquaintance rape.[31] Finally, according to Koss, "The compilers of the NCVS themselves now agree that their methodology undermines self-disclosure of sexual assault and results in underdetection of rape."[32]

In August of 1995, the Bureau of Justice Statistics issued new estimates of the rates of violence against women based on a new survey designed "to produce more accurate reporting of incidents of rape and sexual assault and of any kind of crimes committed by intimates and family members." The revised survey yielded two very different findings compared with previous reports. First, the number of rapes and attempted rapes reported for the year 1992–93 doubled. Secondly, contrary to previous findings that more than half of rapists were strangers, the new survey found that nearly 80 percent of rapes were committed by someone known to the victim, the same percentage of nonstranger rapes reported by Koss and by numerous other researchers.

These changes demonstrate the degree to which information on the incidence of acquaintance rape is dependent on the types of questions asked. The number of rapes reported by the new survey, however, was still far lower than figures reported in other studies. While the redesigned survey is an improvement, researchers maintain that it still underreports rape. For example, Lynn Hecht Schafran, director of the National Judicial

Education Program, commented in a *New York Times* op-ed piece dated August 26, 1995, "Although the redesigned Justice Department survey is a vast improvement, its methodology is not as sophisticated as that used in the 'Rape in America' study." (See Chapter Nine.)

Mary Koss responded to Gilbert's criticism about including a question on the use of alcohol in her survey by eliminating the question. The results showed that rape prevalence (meaning the percentage of women who said they had experienced rape in their lifetime versus the number of rapes reported in one year, such as calculated by the NCVS), was reduced from 12 percent to 8 percent for attempted rape, and from 16 percent to 11 percent for completed rape.[33] Thus, without the question of alcohol, one-in-five in Koss's survey reported that they had experienced force in attempted or actual acts of sexual penetration since the age of fourteen.

Koss dismisses Gilbert's argument that individuals who did not think of themselves as rape victims should not be included in the rape estimate. She argues that "failure to embrace the correct legal term for a victimization certainly does not mean that the incident itself never happened." She notes that victimization surveys carried out by criminal justice researchers find that it is quite common for the general public to be unaware of "correct definitions of legal terms such as *rape, larceny, burglary,* and *robbery.*" According to Koss, although women who have "endured sex against their will may fail to realize that legal standards for rape have been met," this does not therefore mean that they do not feel victimized. Of the rape victims identified by Koss, very few (only 10 percent) "contended that they did not feel victimized by the experience."[34]

With respect to the discovery that many victims have sex again with the man who raped them, Koss reports that "87 percent of the victims eventually ended their relationships with the men who raped them." Since she didn't ask questions about the nature of the relationships with the males who perpetrated the assault, she was unable to pursue this topic more specifically. One study she cites, however, suggests that a woman is more likely to continue a relationship after an assault with a man whom she has known for some time as opposed to a casual date.[35]

In support of Koss it is important to note that many studies confirm her findings. Studying populations in communities across the nation, researchers have found rape prevalence figures of 24 percent in Minnesota; 24 percent in San Francisco; 28 percent among college-educated women ages eighteen to thirty-nine in Los Angeles; 25 percent for African-American and 20 percent for white women in Los Angeles County; 23 percent in Charleston, South Carolina; and 14 percent in a national sample.[36] The repetition of similar results in many samples speaks to the issue of validity. In survey research, "validity" refers to conformity of the survey questions with the event being measured. Usually, this is tested by comparing the replies from independent samples. Based on this criterion, Koss's data are valid when compared with data collected in similar studies.[37]

Koss notes that despite the wealth of data confirming her national survey, Gilbert concludes that her data "have provoked a 'phantom epidemic.' " "To reach this conclusion," she says, "Gilbert has to ignore not only the literature reviewed above, but also the entire body of research by Kanin and colleagues that documents a 20 percent–25 percent prevalence rate for sexual assault among college students going back over a twenty year period."[38]

Koss's results are supported by another recent national study of sex in America, conducted in 1992 and published in 1994. The authors of this study criticize the National Crime Survey's methodology for the same reasons outlined by Koss. The study was conducted by three social scientists, professors Robert T. Michael, John H. Gagnon, and Edward O. Laumann. With a staff of 220 interviewers, a random national sample of 3,432 individuals was interviewed over a period of seven months. The authors purposely did not use the term "rape" but chose instead to ask about "forced sex." They found that "large numbers of women say they have been forced by men to do something sexually that they did not want to do."[39] The numbers they cite fall within the range of many other studies: "22 percent of women were forced to do something sexually at some time," while "just 2 percent of men were forced."[40]

The authors caution that due to the broad scope of the question they asked, "the reported experience involving force may not constitute rape in the legal sense or in the minds of the female respondents." "Whatever the relation to rape," they suggest that "it is of considerable interest to find that as many as one in five women do consider themselves to have been forced against their will to do something sexually."[41]

The authors believe that this finding is relevant to the debate over whether date-rape statistics are inflated. "Is there a forced-sex crisis or is it a nonissue, whose perceived incidence is inflated beyond all bounds?" they ask. Referring to the Antioch Sexual Offense Policy, much discussed in the media during 1993 for its requirement of getting affirmative consent (see next chapter), they conclude as follows:

> Our data reveal that the Antioch rules, much as they were ridiculed by pundits and comics, may have arisen from a valid problem. Although, clearly sexual interactions between men and women are fraught with ambiguity and potential conflicts, there is something more going on than a few misunderstandings.[42]

VOICES OF THE NEW GENERATION: KATIE ROIPHE

In November 1991, Katie Roiphe joined Gilbert and Paglia in the barrage against feminism, adding Princeton to the list of institutions whose date-rape activism is misrepresented. Like so many of the rape-crisis detractors, Roiphe also raises the specter of false accusations in her book *The Morning After,* citing the same story told by Felten and adding another from Princeton. For those familiar with Princeton's history regarding the issues Roiphe raises, her account is remarkably one-sided and ahistorical.

From the time that Princeton went coed in 1969, it was widely recognized that its strong male tradition competed with issues of gender equality. In 1979, Sally Frank brought a lawsuit against Princeton and three of its thirteen eating clubs on the grounds that they discriminated against her on the basis of her gender. When she tried to join the clubs she was verbally and physically harassed. Eventually one of the clubs was dismissed from the case when it agreed to admit women members, and Frank won a key victory against the other two in June 1986, when a judge found they discriminated against women.

Sexual harassment was an ongoing problem for women at Princeton. In a 1981 interview with *The New York Times,* Claudia Burke, a student activist, described what she said was a "typical and average incident of sexual harassment" at Princeton. A male student living in her dormitory "rushed naked into her room and grabbed her sleeping roommate." Although there was a sexual harassment policy, Burke felt it was "just a token gesture" and complained of the secrecy surrounding the outcome of complaints regarding specific incidents.[43]

In April 1987, discontent with Princeton's sexual offense policy boiled over in reaction to an incident that occurred during the annual Take Back the Night march. The march moved through the campus to nine sites where acts of sexual violence were said to have occurred. As marchers walked past the eating clubs, a number of male undergraduates began harassing them. One student dropped his pants, others threw beer at the marchers and screamed, "We can rape whomever we want." The incident sharpened debate over the extent to which physical and verbal abuse of women existed on the Princeton campus and whether the university was taking appropriate steps. A few days later, about six hundred people gathered to demand immediate action by the university, including hiring a trained rape crisis counselor to oversee the university's sexual harassment policy and direct sexual assault victims to appropriate counseling services.[44]

The protest resulted in the creation of an office for sexual harassment and assault counseling. When she took the job as director, Myra Hindus had no idea of the extent of the problems she would be faced with. From the first day she arrived, students came in for counseling and to air other personal problems. The cases ranged from sexual harassment between peers to faculty-student harassment to acquaintance rape. Students also sought counseling for previous abusive sexual experiences. Incest, for example, is an issue many college counselors are confronted with. By the time Hindus left, in 1990, just before Roiphe arrived, the office staffed by her and a part-time assistant was handling more than two hundred of these kinds of cases a year.

To respond to the demand for more education, Hindus put together a peer education program of twenty-five to thirty students, one third of whom were males, and renamed the office the Sexual Harassment/Assault Advising Resources and Education office (SHARE). Each year there was a Take Back the Night march attended by eight hundred to one thousand people, a sizable number given a total student population of six thousand. During these marches Hindus heard dozens of heartbreaking stories. Contrary to Roiphe's experience in her first march at Princeton, in 1991, not one of these stories was ever recanted while Hindus was at Princeton. Rather than acknowledging the powerful stories of so many, Roiphe devoted considerable attention to one isolated incident, in which a student did recant her story, to argue that "students are willing to lie" to be part of the emotion of the moment.[45]

In the spring of 1990, overwhelmed by the demands for SHARE's services, Hindus asked for her part-time assistant to be changed to full-time. When the university refused, citing lack of funds, student supporters of SHARE volunteered to fund-raise to pay for the position. Again, the university refused. Student insistence on the expansion of the SHARE staff escalated, with students circulating petitions and holding large rallies for weeks. The protest culminated when twenty-nine students, mostly rape survivors, staged a sit-in in the president's office. Still, the university would not waiver and Hindus left. Without strong leadership, the SHARE program was vulnerable. Roiphe arrived that fall as a new graduate student and sided with the university's efforts to downplay the need for SHARE. In *The Morning After,* Roiphe says that the "idea of a rape epidemic" has gone beyond polemics and has started to affect "real students and real financial decisions on college campuses." Hindus, however, was talking about a staff of two individuals for a campus of six thousand students.[46]

In a 1991 op-ed piece for *The New York Times* titled "Date Rape Hysteria," Roiphe claims that talk about rape was "a fashionable leftist mask" and a "neo-puritan preoccupation." Roiphe suggests that, like their grandmothers, anti-rape activists assume that "men want sex, women don't."[47] It's hard to tell what she means by this statement, since the whole point of date-rape activism is to give women sexual self-determination and confidence. While still director of SHARE, for example, Hindus says she promoted "a positive sense of sexuality" and differentiated between consensual and nonconsensual sex. According to her, one of the things that made the SHARE program so successful was that "we encouraged people to explore their desire, become more comfortable with their bodies, and tap into their sense of themselves as strong and powerful." Similar pro-sex attitudes are commonly found in the campus anti-rape movement all over the country.

Although Roiphe doesn't reach as far back in time as Camille Paglia to make her arguments, some of her views echo the 1920s masculinization of sexual culture. For example, she objects to the American College Health Association's advice to women to communicate their limits, on the grounds that it reiterates Victorian prudery.[48] In the 1920s this was a common charge used by men to convince women to join the movement for sexual freedom. Women who didn't respond readily to sexual advances were called prudes then, also.

Is Roiphe suggesting that women don't need to communicate their limits because they are always ready or eager for sex? If this is so, then they would also have no need to be clear when a man is offensive, another piece of advice she finds objectionable. Are women never to resist, to say what they want, and make clear what they find offensive? Being ready for sex at all times hardly adds up to female sexual agency. How can a woman be the strong, sensual, autonomous, pleasure-seeking woman Roiphe describes if she is not allowed to communicate her likes and dislikes?

Roiphe's logic places women in an impossible double bind—damned by her as prudish for verbalizing limits and damned by others as "wanting it" for remaining silent. As we have seen, no matter whether they speak or remain silent, women lose in the courtroom. The woman who communicates her likes and dislikes verbally is easily identified as the loose Messalina; the silent woman is the one who invited the attack.

In *The Morning After* Roiphe lodges two major complaints against "rape-crisis feminists." First, she claims that the concept of taking back the night, where survivors tell stories of abuse, perpetuates the myth of female innocence and rape as "a fall from childhood grace."[49] This charge is hard to comprehend in light of the fact that rape is often a tragedy of youth, the existential crisis that robs girls and young women of their innocence long before they may be ready. Koss's finding of one-in-five refers to women's experiences since the age of fourteen. Many of the studies cited in previous chapters of this book indicate the degree to which young girls have been the targets of incest or rape. The survey conducted by the National Victim Center found that 29 percent of all forcible rapes "occurred when the victim was less than 11 years old, while another 32 percent occurred between the ages of 11 and 17."[50]

These statistics are troubling. The childlike (not childish) traits that accompany innocence and vulnerability are vanishing human qualities. Angela's night at the Trump was, among other things, a tragedy of the abuse of innocence. What kind of people might we be, what kind of society might we become if violence against women were reduced to a minimum and women found their own way into adulthood? Might not women be more confident, more self-assured, less frightened and lost; men more sensitive and compassionate? Roiphe claims that date-rape feminists victimize and infantilize women, yet one can suggest that her masculinized view of sex robs us all, male and female alike, of empathy for human vulnerability.

We also must ask about the effect of the "Beavis and Butthead" sexual mentality on the sexual development of impressionable young males. The St. John's case provides a potent reminder that if the American sexual culture can be a sexual mine-field for young women, it is also a trap for their male peers. Sexual freedom without responsibility and empathy for one's partner has created too many sexual nightmares from which males as well as females may never fully recover.

Roiphe's second major complaint is that anti-rape feminists induce "passivity and victimhood" in their conception of the feminine.[51] This is pure fantasy. What could be more liberating for women then to give them the sense that their consent or lack thereof is honored by males and backed by the law? In her book *Real Rape,* Susan Estrich argues that consent should be redefined as no means no so that women can be exempt from the necessity of physical resistance in order to indicate nonconsent. According to Estrich, the emphasis on resistance as in the no-means-yes conception of consent only enforces "traditional views of male aggressiveness and female passivity."[52] A law recognizing that no means no would cut out the game of his scoring and her struggling, and make sexual interaction more mutual.

I have the sense that Roiphe is not only angry at date-rape activists, but more broadly at the constraints the world of today imposes on searching, exploring, youthful females. Her experiences at Harvard and Princeton provide a vivid account of the heavy burden of risk imposed on young women who seek sexual freedom in the 1990s, not just because of the warnings delivered by date-rape activists, but because of the ever-present reality of sexually transmitted diseases, including HIV. The irony in Roiphe's attack is that by silencing women who want to discuss the implications of a sexual encounter, she may also be cutting off discussions of safe sex.

Anti-rape activism on college campuses manages to combine sexual liberation with sexual responsibility. What Roiphe calls the "programmed message of the anti-rape movement" actually helps young women feel more comfortable and sure about asking a partner to use a condom, and young men to be more thoughtful about unprotected and undiscussed sex. I welcome any message that helps young women and men feel confident enough in their sexuality to make their options con-sensual safe sex or no sex.

It is shameful that efforts on campuses such as Princeton and Swarthmore and the many others maligned by the anti-feminist crusaders are misrepresented rather than praised. Roiphe and Paglia manage only to trap women ever more tightly in the old sexual double binds. Once damned as prostitutes if they tried to negotiate sex on their own terms, women are now called femino-puritans if they claim sex rights, while those who play by the old rules are still damned as loose or sluts if they appear too willing. If they seek greater communication with casual part-ners, they are accused of making sex a contract and violating the natural law of spontaneous sexual expression. Yet if they seek an abortion to end the unwanted pregnancy that might result from lack of communication, they are then condemned by anti-abortion advocates as violators of bibli-cal injunctions.

As mentioned above, men are also in a double bind. The unthinking sexual aggression encouraged by Paglia and celebrated in pornography can easily turn men into rapists in the eyes of their partners and the law. The messages males learn from pornography about when women "want it" do not necessarily apply to real women. If he goes ahead on the basis of what he has learned from watching porno videos with his buddies, a man may find himself in the courtroom. If we add HIV and STD's and the unwanted child that might result from wordless sex, the feminist stress on communication is a small price for men to pay.

After Roiphe's book was published, another diatribe against anti-rape activism appeared, in Christina Hoff Sommers's book *Who Stole Feminism.* In her chapter "Rape Research," Sommers summarizes many of the points made by Gilbert and makes a distinction between violent rape (which she regards as "real" rape) and date rape (the kind "gender feminists" write about). Sommers distinguishes between sex offenses and offensive sex in her distinction between penetration by a baseball bat as opposed to pene-tration by a finger. According to Sommers, the first is rape and the second can happen in a "heavy petting situation." The boy may have behaved badly, but "Is he a rapist?" she asks.[53] According to many state laws, such as the New Jersey law reviewed in the next chapter, the answer is yes. Any unwanted penetration is rape.

Sommers is critical of an illness she calls "gender feminism," which she compares with "gender equity." She defines gender feminism as the " 'Second Wave' doctrine," which she claims is held by most current feminists, "that women, even modern American women, are in thrall to 'a system of male dominance.' " More palatable to Sommers is the gender equity that she says characterized the feminism of the nineteenth-century Seneca Falls women, whose concern was "the attainment of full legal equality." The difference between the two is mainly in the understanding of the source of female subordination. Sommers claims that gender feminists attribute the problem to universal male oppression, while gender equity feminists "focused on specific injustices of the kind that social policy could repair by making the laws equitable."[54]

Contrary to Sommer's claims, academic feminism is by no means unanimous on the subject of universal male oppression. The debate in anthropology on this subject reveals another approach, followed in this book, which Sommers does not mention.[55] Applied to the study of female subordination and violence against women, this approach is more concerned with the analysis of social supports for egalitarian and nonegalitarian relationships than with positing male oppression. Because it is based on the assumption of social variability, by its very nature this approach falls outside of the gender feminism Sommers decries.

Sommers is committed to ending male violence, but she is against change in the gender-based rights and common attitudes that I argue perpetuate violence against women. Fearing divisiveness, Sommers is reluctant to challenge male-defined privileges and norms for sexual behavior. Thus, she faults the Violence Against Women Act because of its sensitivity to gender issues, which she believes does social harm "by accepting a divisive, gender-specific approach to a problem." This leads her to divert attention from male violence against women to other issues such as same-sex violence. Violence against women "is not caused by gender bias, misogyny, or 'patriarchy,' " she states. She fears that saying so "can obscure real and urgent problems such as lesbian battering or male-on-male sexual violence."[56] Are we to assume by this statement that same-sex violence is more a problem than heterosexual violence? Clearly, the numbers indicate otherwise. Not that same-sex violence is a problem that can be ignored, but it is disingenuous to use it to divert attention from heterosexual violence.

Social change for sexual equity cannot be achieved without changing gender-based prejudices and privileges. Beginning with Matthew Hale, I have shown in this book that American norms for sexual behavior and the response to rape have been determined by socially entrenched gender stereotypes. We can recall, for example, that men have never been referred to as Messalinas, scorned, vindictive, blackmailers, passionless, hysterics, pathological liars, or hypersexual in or out of the courtroom. To ignore the degree to which these and other stereotypes have shaped the American response to rape only perpetuates the very problem Sommers claims she is devoted to solving.

Sommers, however, does not see it this way. The true nature of rape, she suggests, is that it is "perpetrated by criminals, which is to say, it is perpetrated by people who are wont to gratify themselves in criminal ways and who care very little about the suffering they inflict on others." "The real challenge we face in our society," she adds, "is how to reverse the tide of violence."[57] I agree, but I am absolutely stumped after reading Sommers's book as to how she plans to go about doing so. Since she says the problem is not related to gender issues, we are thus prohibited from questioning the assembly-line approach to more and better sexual outlets and the gender stereotypes communicated in pornography and sexology. We are also not allowed to question the cult of masculinity, the bias against women in the courtroom, or civil rights violations on the basis of sex. All of these are gender-related issues, part of the very gender feminism she abhors. Beyond the criticism she levels against feminism, Sommers offers no solutions. One comes away from her book aware of the issues dividing modern feminism, but in the dark as to how to solve continuing inequalities.

Despite the backlash, the anti-rape movement continues to grow. Some call it the new sexual revolution. On campuses and in secondary schools the focus is on peer counseling and education. Unlike the feminism of the sixties, both sexes are involved. In the new movement, women learn to respect their sexuality so that they feel safe in saying yes and confident in making a no stick. Men teach each other to respect a woman's no. For the first time, same-sex acquaintance rape is also becoming part of the common discourse around sexuality.

This movement promises to change American sexuality because many of the participants and leaders are individuals just beginning their sexual life cycles. The give-and-take of sexual communication being taught by peer educators and the open recognition of issues of sexual orientation on hundreds of college campuses promise to make sexual parity part of the American sexual mainstream. If the movement succeeds, we will see another corner rounded in the history of American sexuality, one which makes it possible for men and women to exercise sexual choice with a greater understanding of their sexual orientation and interests as opposed to acting in response to peer pressure or popular sexual myths. How close we are to rounding that corner can be assessed by examining some of the more innovative campus, legislative, and legal developments at the dawn of the twenty-first century.

TWELVE

AFFIRMATIVE CONSENT

We conclude, therefore, that any act of sexual penetration engaged in by the defendant without the affirmative and freely-given permission of the victim to the specific act of penetration constitutes the offense of sexual assault.

—SUPREME COURT OF NEW JERSEY, 1992

For the purpose of the policy, "consent" shall be defined as follows: the act of willingly and verbally agreeing to engage in specific sexual contact or conduct.

—ANTIOCH COLLEGE SEXUAL OFFENSE POLICY, 1993

"AFFIRMATIVE VERBAL CONSENT," "FREELY GIVEN AGREEMENT," AND "sexual communication" are the operative words of an emerging sexual paradigm that promises to close the door on two hundred years of stereotyping female sexuality. Under the affirmative consent standard, women would not have to resist, and their alleged sexiness, desire, or silence could not be translated as a yes. The new standard is based on the assumption of an equal rather than an asymmetric sexual partnership. Women will no longer need to prove to anyone that they are not sluts. They can be just as aggressive as men in pursuing sexual relationships and they too will be held up to the affirmative consent standard. The same holds true in same-sex and group sexual behavior.

Today, the desirability of affirmative consent is widely taught in peer-education workshops on college campuses and in secondary schools. Its necessity is at the basis of the well-known and highly controversial sexual offense policy at Antioch College. Its legal implications are increasingly discussed in law review articles. In a few states affirmative consent has been incorporated into addenda in the rape laws. The philosophy behind affirmative consent and its implications for women's sexual autonomy is extensively argued in a precedent-setting 1992 New Jersey Supreme Court decision. The principles enunciated in this decision and increasingly reflected in campus debates and secondary-school sex education are as important for releasing women from male sexual dominance in the late twentieth century as the call for "free love" once was for releasing women from Victorian sexual restraint.

PEER EDUCATION: THE NEW ACTIVISM

Peer education is the new form of student activism. Increasingly, on campuses all over the country, fraternity brothers, athletes, and sorority sisters work side by side with males and females from the general student population conducting rape awareness workshops on the importance and meaning of sexual consent. Many of these programs owe their existence to sixties-style protests, sit-ins, speak-outs, or more guerrilla–like tactics such as spraying messages signed by the "Woman's Army" on campus walls.

Brown University drew national attention in the fall of 1990 when "rape lists" started to appear on its bathroom walls. Scrawled graffiti style, these lists named up to thirty males who had allegedly assaulted campus women. Brown's president, Vartan Gregorian, responded by issuing a statement declaring that "the route of graffiti and anonymity, whether against men or women, is not an acceptable substitute for either due process or justice." To encourage students to come forward, Gregorian promised that the university would provide assistance to those who wanted to institute judicial proceedings. He also recommended that the Code of Student Conduct be amended to classify sexual assault as a "major offense."[1]

At the same time, a peer education program was initiated as a preventative measure to combat the problem of sexual assault. Organized by Toby Simon, associate dean for student life, the program attracted one hundred student volunteers the first year and in time became so successful that its workshops, "Sex Without Consent," were in demand in secondary schools throughout New England.[2]

In the fall of 1994 Toby Simon presented a demonstration workshop at a plenary session of the Fourth International Conference on Sexual Assault and Harassment on Campus, held in the New Jersey suburbs outside Philadelphia. Sponsored by the Safe Schools Coalition, Inc., this conference and the annual student-run Campus Sexual Violence conference, also in its fourth year, are part of the growing anti-rape movement in the nation's educational establishment. The audience gathered for Simon's plenary session represented a broad cross-section of professionals and students working in the movement—counselors, health workers, campus security, sorority and fraternity leaders, school administrators, rape crisis staff and volunteers, as well as activists and peer educators from many campuses.[3]

Simon chose a workshop structured around an interactive drama performed by members of Brown's Cast of Color, created to attract students of color into the peer-education program so that the workshops would not be strictly composed of white and middle-class students. The skit presented a typical date-rape scenario with all the ambiguity and uncertainty about whether the act displayed is rape, sex without consent, or bad sex. Four African-American students performed the roles of two male and two female characters: Malik and Calvin; Denise and Ceecee.

The skit starts out with Denise scheming with Ceecee to meet Malik, a good-looking guy in her bio lab. They decide to have a small party. The plan is for Ceecee to invite her boyfriend, Calvin, and ask him to bring his friend, Malik. Denise tells Ceecee to be discreet. She doesn't want Calvin or Malik to get the wrong idea.

Things go wrong from the start. Calvin is suspicious when Ceecee asks him to invite Malik. "Why?" he asks. "To make it even," Ceecee responds. Denise gets on the phone and explains to Calvin that she just wants to get to know Malik, nothing else. "Don't tell Malik I want him or anything like that, because that's not what it's about," she tells Calvin. "Gotcha," Calvin says.

Calvin calls Malik to invite him to the party. To entice him, he says, "She's on you, man, *on you.*" Very interested, Malik responds, "I'll be ready, man."

The next scene is the party. Denise and Ceecee have drunk most of the beer and alcohol provided by Calvin and Malik. Denise is feeling very dizzy. She and Ceecee go into the kitchen to fix some food. While they are out of the room, Malik thanks Calvin for the invitation.

"I'm really glad I came," he says. "Denise is sweet and beautiful. Hey, man, she really seems to like me."

Calvin reassures him. "Man, she's really on you."

Malik asks Calvin to leave them alone so that he and Denise can get to know each other. Calvin agrees and asks him if he has protection. He and Ceecee then retire to the bedroom.

Left alone with Malik, Denise is feeling real dizzy. Malik asks her if she wants to lie down. She answers that she would like to sit down. He massages her back and they kiss.

As Malik starts groping her, Denise breaks away. "Malik, wait a minute, just take it a little slow, eh," she says.

"I'm taking it slow," Malik responds. "Feeling good?"

"I'm fine," Denise says in a suggestive tone.

But as Malik continues groping her body and feeling her breasts, she says in a raising voice, "Malik, Malik, Malik, take it slow."

"I'm taking it slow," Malik answers somewhat annoyed. "You know what Ceecee and Calvin are doing right now?"

"I don't care what they are doing," Denise answers.

"I have protection," Malik says.

"Wait a minute, wait a minute, that's not what it's about," Denise says with a good deal of certainty in her voice. "It's about . . . we can have a good time, but that's not what it's about."

"But it's okay," Malik says as he continues. "Just relax."

"I'm relaxed," Denise says more annoyed. "Malik, *please.*"

Malik's voice raises. "We're here alone. Take it easy. Just relax. Everything is going to be okay."

As Malik continues, Ceecee cries out Malik's name three times. The third time her voice is loud and anguished as he penetrates her. Then there is a long silence.

The scene shifts first to Denise and then to Malik ruminating on what happened. Denise's voice is sad and hurt as she says that before she knew it Malik was having sex with her. It took only a few seconds and it really hurt. When it was over, she says that she didn't look at him and started crying. When he asked her what was up, she told him to leave.

Malik's version is quite different. One thing led to another, and before he knew it they were having sex. It wasn't great, but it was okay. At first he felt that she was a little slow to get with it, but after a while she seemed like she was enjoying herself. It didn't last that long. Afterward she was kind of silent and he figured she wasn't in the mood to talk. Since he had something else to do, he got up to leave and said that he would call her the next day.

In the next part of the skit, members of the audience ask a series of questions. The moderator, in this case Toby Simon, reads a relevant statistic to provide further information regarding particular questions. The first questioner asks Denise to explain what she thought Malik understood when she said "slow down." Rather than answering this question, Denise explains what she meant. According to Denise, "slow down" meant no.

Asked the same question, Malik responds that when Denise said "slow down" he complied, but then things got heated back up.

The next questioner asks Malik to explain what he understood when Denise said, "It's not about that," regarding the condom. Malik answers that he thought she meant she was on the Pill. He admits that he also thought that maybe she didn't want to have sex, but then they started kissing again and it became very clear to him that she wanted sex.

In response to Malik's answer that he "thought" she was on the Pill, Toby Simon reads a fact. "Three out of one thousand college students are HIV positive and one million teens become pregnant each year."

Denise is asked how she was feeling while it was going on and why she didn't make a big protest.

She answers, "I like Malik. The kissing was fine. But I pushed him away. I didn't feel like I had to give in but I froze."

Malik is asked how he would have reacted differently had he known that Denise would be so upset. "I'd feel bad," he answers. "That's not the kind of guy I am. I was concerned about her silence afterwards. I wouldn't have done it if I knew."

"Why didn't you ask her what she meant by 'slow down'?" someone asks.

"This isn't a debate—we were in the mood, there was music, we were dancing. If she had said stop, I would have stopped," Malik answers.

Someone asks Denise whether in hindsight she would have done something different.

A little annoyed Denise responds, "I don't understand why I did something wrong. I asked someone to come over. We had a good time. I don't see what's wrong with kissing someone. But I didn't ask for sex."

The key phrase is "I didn't ask for sex." The point of the skit and the discussion with the audience is to take an ambiguous situation and use it to teach sexual communication. The emphasis is not just on teaching women to say no but on teaching men to be sensitive to the signals that mean no and to wait for the verbally expressed yes.

Stepping out of character, the skit members explain that they know

Malik's act doesn't meet the legal definition of rape. But their program is not about the law or how to win a conviction, they say. "It's about teaching men respect, safety, opening up dialogue, and above all, it's about how men make themselves vulnerable if they rely on implied consent," Jeremi Duru, who played Malik, explains.

After the question-answer period I talk with Jeremi and ask how male students usually respond to the scenario. Do they think Malik did something wrong? Was it rape? Was it assault? Jeremi answers that most believe it was rape because it was clear that she was not interested in having sex. "True, she didn't say 'no' and she didn't say 'stop,' but she didn't say 'yes,' and she said 'slow down' and she pushed me," he points out. "As Malik and as myself," he continues, "I feel it was rape."

I ask Alysia Turner, who played Ceecee, whether she feels the workshop format is changing the way students think about sex at Brown and at the secondary schools they visit. She is very firm when she answers, "Yes, I do, I definitely do." The skit and the discussion help people to "examine their sexual behavior, especially the way they interact with people of the opposite sex," she says. They learn to be "more aware of what's going on." "Communication is the key," she says. "Especially listening for the yes."

Jacques Louis, who played Calvin, explains to me the sexual mentality that they are trying to represent in the skit. He calls what Malik was doing to Denise "hitting." "If you're hitting this and hitting that—if you're kissing and fondling a little bit here and a little bit there, why not? That's the game. You want it and she wants it, then why not?"

I ask why they use the word "hitting." "Because it's nothing more than a physical act," he responds. "It's a game where the goal is to score with as many women as possible. Women are just dolls in this game, they have no kind of brain, no kind of decision, and we have all the power. We're up at bat and we're scoring. Women are like the playing field and men are the players."

Jacques volunteered as a peer educator at Brown because he would like to see these attitudes change. He believes that the lack of respect black males show to women is an extension of the lack of respect they have for themselves. "If you can't respect yourself," he says, "how can you respect a woman or someone else? . . . What use is self-worth, anyway," he asks, "if you know you'll probably be dead by age twenty-five?" Jacques sees as his job to try and open new ways of thinking, to turn guys on to education, to try to unshackle them from the chains of the "17-dude" mentality, where a guy's got to have seventeen girls to feel any self-worth.

For himself, Jacques says that verbal communication is vital, "a real turn on." In the workshops, he tells guys how it makes him feel. "It's the biggest boost you will get, to hear a girl say yes. When you hear a yes, your thing goes so much up, especially when she says, 'yes, yes, yes,' or when she says, 'I want this.' "

Alysia, who is listening, smiles and shakes her head. Her eyes light up. "It's really sexy to say yes," she says. "We've got to get away from this image in our culture of the man who just knows what to do with nary a word. A guy who thinks he can read a girl's mind or that he knows what she means and goes ahead is probably assaulting her," she concludes.

THE ANTIOCH SEXUAL OFFENSE POLICY

In the fall of 1990 "womyn" students at Antioch College initiated an action that resulted in its famous sexual policy emphasizing affirmative consent. Always at the cutting edge of social issues, Antioch students of the 1990s are passionate about sexual freedom. The major goal of the women who initiated the discussion leading to the policy was to make the Antioch campus safe for women. Their concern arose from the school's response to a date rape in which the offender was allowed to remain on campus and received no punishment other than a request that he seek counseling.

Eventually, as the policy was hammered out in meetings involving administrators, faculty, and students, other issues were added: choice, freedom, rights, and sexual communication. According to anthropologist Melinda Kanner, who teaches a human sexuality course at Antioch, students don't talk about sexual freedom per se, they talk about "their own choice," and the exercise of rights. Students want rules so that they can enjoy freedom, Kanner notes. The sexual offense policy, she says, "was designed not to restrict freedom, but to make some kind of accord so that freedom could be enjoyed and rights exercised."[4]

Contrary to popular assumption, the Antioch community is neither prudish nor puritanical. As anyone who visits Antioch soon finds out, the atmosphere is one of sexual openness. The sexual culture at Antioch is one of the reasons the student leaders I interviewed give for the necessity of a sexual offense policy. The policy stresses verbal consent and the necessity for obtaining it every step of the way and for every act. The language is nongender specific and is written to apply to same-sex partners, group sexual activity, and the abuse of men by women.

According to Alan E. Guskin, Antioch's president at the time the policy was drafted, the sexual offense policy defines sexual freedom for the 1990s. "Dealing with sexual matters in an open and direct manner is a defining issue for students of the nineteen-nineties," he says. As he understands the policy, which he worked on with students, sexual freedom for students in the 1990s is not about gratification independent of one's partner. In an article defending the policy, Guskin quotes an Antioch male student who upon hearing about the policy said, "This policy means I can't get what I want when I want it." In response Guskin writes: "He is right! But, is this freedom or license?"[5]

Karen Hall, director of the Sexual Offense Prevention and Survivors' Advocacy Program at Antioch, is the main administrator in charge of providing services to "victims/survivors" of sexual violence and their significant others. She also plans a variety of educational programs on sexual violence and personal safety. In the two years that the policy has been in place, she says there have been dozens of incidents, most of which were handled through informal discussions, counseling, or mediation. The purpose of her office is to help facilitate sexual communication and prevent sexual violence. Students are encouraged to come forth with problems they may be having with certain individuals, but who may not wish to make charges under the policy. The discussions with students are part of the educational process of helping students to relate to their sexual partner as a human being rather than as an orifice. Most of the complaints are by women against men, but some complaints are brought by men. Most commonly, complaints by men involve alcohol. They pass out drunk and a woman starts trying to have sex with them. Sometimes men come forward because they have been abusive or know that they might be and want help. The fewest number of cases are those involving same-sex relationships.[6]

Joan Chappelle, head of the counseling center, confirms the figures cited by Karen Hall. In a population of a little more than six hundred students, there were as many as fifteen sexual offenses in the 1993–94 academic year, of which only one or two might actually be reported through the policy. Students are either protective of one another or they would rather discuss the issues face-to-face in mediation sessions or receive counseling. Thus, the policy serves as an educational tool and helps to open dialogue between sexual partners. Chappelle believes that student awareness of policies like Antioch's helps prevent rape on college campuses.[7]

Students express a range of opinions about the policy. The majority support affirmative verbal consent. A few were adamantly opposed on the grounds that it is "demeaning toward women." "It implies that women can't handle themselves when it comes to sexual encounters," Erica Stautiniger says. Erica agrees with the idea that "if someone says no and the other person doesn't stop, that's rape," but she feels that you don't have "to get a verbal yes, certainly not every step of the way, because there are other forms of consent."

Andy Abrams, who graduated in 1993, supports the policy fully. During the year that news of the policy hit the media, Andy was a community manager, an elected leadership position, which put him in touch with student opinion. Andy believes in the importance of trust in sexual relationships. According to him, trust grows out of verbal communication and is the essence of pleasure. He likes the fact that the language of the policy is gender neutral and recognizes same-sex as well as female-to-male sexual assault. Requiring mutual verbal consent makes him feel that he doesn't have to perform just because a woman comes on to him. He feels that sex is much better when people talk about it. "If you're not talking openly with your partner," he says, "you don't know what's comfortable and what's not. You don't know what's enjoyable and pleasurable." Andy believes that nonverbal magic just doesn't work in sex despite all the hype about it. Not talking about your sexuality "leaves a lot of room for discomfort," he points out. "Sex requires talking and communication, especially when your goal is safe sex and protecting yourself from diseases."[8]

Sierra Levy, who graduated in 1994, was a peer advocate at Antioch for two years, a job that involves supporting students who bring charges under the policy. Sierra served as peer advocate in the first case brought under the policy that went as far as the Hearing Board solution, rather than ending with the more usual mediation process. She is a strong supporter of the policy because she believes it creates "subject-to-subject relationships, rather than subject-to-object relationships." In her opinion wordless sex plays into the pornographic ideology, in which men think they know what a woman wants because of what they've heard from other men or gotten from pornography. "Verbal communication makes women sexual subjects," she says. "It helps people vocalize their internal dialogue," so that they become knowledgeable agents in the sexual exchange.[9]

Kristine Hermann, another student leader, is also a strong supporter. "Antioch is trying to dispel the myth that sex has to be mysterious, romantic, all animal instinct. . . . How can you communicate that you're HIV positive if you don't talk about sex?" she asks. "We want to make sex as safe as possible, that's our goal."[10]

Tex Clark, outspoken on all issues that matter to her, is also a strong believer in the policy. She says that people who don't use the policy by obtaining affirmative consent risk being reported by their partners. Proud to be an out lesbian, Tex has been going out with the same woman for nine months. Tex always asks for consent "at each increasing level of physical intimacy as the policy says." "I think it's smart and it's right," she says. "It's a cool way to be and I have a better time when I know I'm doing OK." For Tex, following the policy is not a matter of being careful but of "respect and communication."[11]

Another student, also an out lesbian, described an incident of sexual assault, which she chose not to report. When she first came to Antioch, she was very naive about sex, she told me. This is an important point, because as anthropologist Melinda Kanner notes also, students are often very naive sexually when they enter Antioch. According to this student, who chose to remain anonymous, the policy helped in the education process. It is not just about reporting, but a tool for learning to express one's self sexually, to be able to say, "This doesn't feel OK," or "We need to talk about this." Although she was raped by her partner, for a number of reasons she chose not to report the incident. It happened after they had broken up and she visited her one last time before moving to another state. Her former lover put a lot of emotional pressure on her to have sex, and despite her verbal resistance and physical struggle went ahead anyway. Although she was angry, hurt, and traumatized by what happened, she chose to talk it out with her former lover, to make it clear that what happened was wrong. Afterward, they managed to remain friends.[12]

I also talked with a male student who was brought up on charges of sexual imposition (defined as sexual contact) under the policy. Surprisingly, perhaps, this student expressed full support of the policy. He recognized that he was at fault immediately. He said, "I was angry at myself for violating [her]; I was angry at myself for violating the standards of the community." Before the incident he had always followed the policy; indeed, it had been his "personal policy" even before there was a campus policy.

Explaining his version of what happened, he made an interesting slip.

"It all happened really quick. I kissed her and placed my tongue in my [sic] mouth and she immediately pulled away. And I let go—and felt terrible."

Although innocuous, this slip suggests that the source of sexual assault may lie in the unconscious blurring of boundaries between self and partner, so that the partner becomes indistinguishable from the self.

Continuing his explanation of what happened, this student added, "In one minute I got turned on. . . . I couldn't believe that I had crossed a boundary with a friend."

Interestingly, he ascribed that one-minute slip as not being under his conscious control but due to "the release of a chemical in the brain called dopamine." Thus, although he supported the policy and did not contest the charges against him, he rationalized his actions with a biological explanation rather than searching for the psychological reasons that may have led him to cross the boundary and act toward his partner as if she were but a part of the self.

LEGAL DEVELOPMENTS

The fine points of consent reflected in the attitudes voiced at Brown and Antioch demonstrate a significant change in the traditional response to acquaintance rape. For the first time the American debate about sex is focusing on *language* rather than on animal instinct or nonverbal cues, such as how she looked, what she wanted but never actually verbalized, or how she acted. The debate transforms sex from a purely physical activity —"hitting," as Jacques Louis, the Brown student, called it—to one fraught with human meaning. It's a human issue, students point out, involving a host of considerations—trust, health, the possibility of pregnancy, personal emotions, responsibility, personal autonomy, peer pressure, ignorance, and vulnerability. Sex takes place in a context larger than the act itself, with potential consequences beyond immediate pleasure.

Even the pleasure itself is questioned as students realize that the way sex, especially wordless, casual sex, is represented in the American sexual culture may be more hype than real.

Clearly America has come a long way on the rape issue. This is true not only on college campuses but in the legal community as well. The saga of the changing definition of rape is nowhere better reflected than in a 1992 New Jersey Supreme Court decision that chronicles change in that state's definition of rape from the eighteenth century, when its first rape law was devised, to the present. The fact that this unanimous decision raises many of the issues discussed by students suggests to me that the American sexual culture is at the threshold of a new era in the long and painful evolution of women's sexual autonomy.

The case involved a juvenile who was found delinquent for committing sexual assault in 1990 and then appealed. The superior court, appellate division, reversed the conviction in 1991. The State then appealed to the Supreme Court of New Jersey, which reinstated the original conviction for delinquency in 1992. The case involved a fifteen-year-old girl, C. G., and a seventeen-year-old boy, M.T.S., who were temporarily residing in the same house. At approximately 11:30 P.M., C. G. went to her room on the second floor to sleep. According to her testimony she went to sleep and woke up to find M.T.S. on top of her, her underpants and shorts removed. She said "his penis was into [her] vagina." She said that she immediately slapped him and "told him to get off [her] and get out." She did not scream or cry out. She testified that he complied in less than one minute after being struck. After he left, she said she "fell asleep crying" because she "couldn't believe that he did what he did." She didn't tell anyone until the next morning, at 7:00 A.M., because she was "scared and in shock." As soon as her mother heard the story, M.T.S. was told to leave the house.[13]

According to M.T.S., C. G. had encouraged him repeatedly to "make a surprise visit up in her room." He did so and they started "kissing and all." They undressed each other and continued kissing and touching for about five minutes. M.T.S. said that he was on top of C. G. and "stuck it in" and "did it [thrust] three times, and then the fourth time [he] stuck it in, that's when [she] pulled [him] off of her." M.T.S. said that when she said, "stop, get off," he "hopped off right away." When he asked C. G. what was wrong, M.T.S. said that she slapped him. M.T.S. testified that she said, " 'How can you take advantage of me' or something like that." When he told her to calm down, he said that she told him to get away from her and began to cry.[14]

The New Jersey law defines "sexual assault" as the commission of "an act of sexual penetration with another person" accomplished by any one of a number of circumstances, among which is the use of "physical force or coercion." At the original trial, the court interpreted "physical force" as meaning "sexual penetration of the victim without her consent." The appellate division's decision, however, stated that the statute "requires some amount of force more than that necessary to accomplish the penetration" to establish sexual assault.[15]

The original trial court concluded that C. G. was not sleeping, but had consented to the kissing and heavy petting but not to the actual sex act. The Supreme Court agreed that the trial court had proven second-degree sexual assault "beyond a reasonable doubt." It disagreed, however, with the appellate division's finding that "non-consensual penetration does not constitute sexual assault unless it is accompanied by some level of force more than that necessary to accomplish the penetration."[16] According to the Supreme Court's decision "physical force in excess of that inherent in the act of sexual penetration is not required for such penetration to be unlawful."[17]

In a lengthy argument the Supreme Court laid out the reasons for siding with the original decision. Like other states, New Jersey started with the English common law definition of rape as "carnal knowledge of a woman against her will." As elsewhere (see discussion in Chapter 5), over time New Jersey added the requirement of force, "apparently in order to prove that the act was against the victim's will." As of 1796, the New Jersey law defined rape as "carnal knowledge of a woman, forcibly and against her will." These three elements of rape—carnal knowledge, force, and nonconsent—remained the essential elements of the crime of rape in New Jersey until 1979.[18]

As we have already seen, such elements placed on the victim the burden of showing not only that she had actively indicated nonconsent but that she had done so "to the utmost limit of her power," as a New York decision interpreted the element of force in 1918.[19] As true elsewhere, the resistance standard was relaxed but not abandoned as the century progressed. For example, a 1965 New Jersey appellate division court stated, "We only require that she resist as much as she possibly can under the circumstances." According to this decision the resistance had to be "in good faith and without pretense, with an active determination to prevent the violation of her person, and must not be merely passive and perfunctory."[20]

Rape law reform argued that the requirement of even this amount of resistance put the victim on trial. Not only did the victim have to prove nonconsent, she had to show also that force used by the defendant was sufficient to overcome her will.[21] Rape reform in New Jersey, as elsewhere, was designed to shift the focus from the victim's behavior to the defendant's conduct, "particularly to its forceful and assaultive, rather than sexual, character."[22] Along these lines the 1978 reform law in New Jersey relabeled rape "sexual assault" and broadened its scope by referring to "penetration" rather than "sexual intercourse." It emphasized the assaultive character of the offense by defining sexual penetration to include "insertion of the hand, finger or object into the anus or vagina" as well as penetration with the penis. Consistent with the assaultive character of the offense, the statute renders the crime gender neutral so that both sexes can be "actors or victims."[23]

In interpreting the meaning of "physical force," in its M.T.S. decision the Supreme Court tried to remain true to the legislative intent of the reform law. This intent, as interpreted by the court, was to emphasize "the affinity between sexual assault and other forms of assault and battery." Thus, as would be true in any other kind of assault, the victim is not required to resist. Furthermore, his or her responsive or defensive behavior upon being assaulted is immaterial. On the basis of this reasoning, the court concluded:

> We are thus satisfied that an interpretation of the statutory crime of sexual assault to require physical force in addition to that entailed in an act of involuntary or unwanted sexual penetration would be fundamentally inconsistent with the legislative purpose to eliminate any consideration of whether the victim resisted or expressed non-consent.[24]

Based on this reasoning the court's attention shifted to affirmative consent. The court concluded that "any act of sexual penetration engaged in by the defendant without the affirmative and freely-given permission of the victim to the specific act of penetration constitutes the offense of sexual assault." Thus, the court stated, the definition of "physical force" is satisfied under New Jersey's law "if the defendant applies any amount of force against another person in the absence of what a reasonable person would believe to be affirmative and freely-given permission to the act of sexual penetration."[25]

This decision was in keeping with the legislature's recasting of rape law to protect women's common law right of privacy and bodily control. Its conclusion with respect to privacy provides a historic statement of the relevance of the law of sexual assault for protecting personal autonomy.

> Today the law of sexual assault is indispensable to the system of legal rules that assures each of us the right to decide who may touch our bodies, when, and under what circumstances. The decision to engage in sexual relations with another person is one of the most private and intimate decisions a person can make. Each person has the right not only to decide whether to engage in sexual contact with another, but also to control the circumstances and character of that contact. No one, neither a spouse, nor a friend, nor an acquain-

tance, nor a stranger, has the right or the privilege to force sexual contact.[26]

In 1993 this precedent-setting decision was quoted by the prosecutor during the gang rape trial of four high school athletes from Glen Ridge, New Jersey, accused of gang raping a mentally retarded schoolmate. In closing arguments, Glenn Goldberg said that the jury could find the four young men guilty even if they concluded that the young woman did not actively resist the alleged sexual assault. According to Goldberg, "the victim does not have to say no." Nor does she have to resist. "If she just lies there and says nothing, if she doesn't give affirmative consent, you can find them guilty."[27] After eight days of deliberations the jury convicted three of the defendants on counts of first-degree aggravated sexual assault, which under New Jersey law is synonymous with rape. The fourth defendant was convicted of third-degree conspiracy.[28]

The New Jersey Supreme Court decision in the case of M.T.S. is not alone in holding that a demonstration of affirmative consent is required. This requirement exists in other states as well. In 1980, the Wisconsin Supreme Court upheld a conviction for sexual assault despite the defendant's contention that parties can enter into consensual sexual relationships without showing "freely given consent in words or acts."[29] The Wisconsin sexual assault law defines consent as "words or overt actions by a person who is competent to give informed consent indicating a freely given agreement to have sexual intercourse or sexual contact."[30]

The Illinois sexual assault law defines consent to mean "a freely given agreement to the act of sexual penetration or sexual conduct in question." The Illinois statute explicitly states that "lack of verbal or physical resistance or submission by the victim resulting from the use of force . . . shall not constitute consent." "The manner of dress of the victim at the time of the offense" is also mentioned as not constituting consent.[31] Another state stressing affirmative consent is the state of Washington.

According to its revised code, " 'Consent' means that at the time of the act of sexual intercourse or sexual contact there are actual words or conduct indicating freely given agreement to have sexual intercourse or sexual contact."[32]

According to Lynn Hecht Schafran, director of the National Judicial Education Program, standards requiring a yes or its equivalent steer jurors away from looking for evidence of physical resistance. She provides a persuasive rationale for why we must go beyond no means no. The requirement of affirmative consent, Schafran says, makes an important distinction between consent and "frozen fright." "Frozen fright" means that the "victim cannot physically or verbally resist at all." However, her silence and passivity does not mean that she is responsive in any positive sense, only that she is unable to resist. Thus, silence can never be interpreted as consent, because it may mean dissent or forced submission.[33] The affirmative consent standard bypasses the mistaken tendency on the part of some men to assume that silence means consent, when in fact silence could mean something quite different, as Malik and M.T.S. found out.

AFFIRMATIVE CONSENT: VERBAL OR EXPRESSED?

The New Jersey Supreme Court decision in the case of M.T.S. and the state statutes mentioned above do not require affirmative consent to be verbal. According to the New Jersey Court, for example, permission can be "indicated through physical actions rather than words." The court claimed that permission would be determined "when the evidence, in whatever form, is sufficient to demonstrate that a reasonable person would have believed that the alleged victim had affirmatively and freely given authorization to the act."[34]

This approach raises a host of questions regarding the definition of a "reasonable person" and of "freely given authorization." As Susan Estrich points out, "reasonable" could mean either the assumption that no means yes and anything goes, or, the assumption that " 'no means no' and . . . extortion for sex is no more justifiable than extortion for money."[35]

As long as the old stereotypes remain current, the safest approach would be to require affirmative verbal consent. Although he doesn't suggest verbal consent, Professor George E. Dix of the University of Texas Law School raises considerations that lead me to this conclusion. Dix criticizes the M.T.S. decision on the grounds that it ignores the accused's state of mind. Raising the issue of intent, Dix points out that a basic principle of criminal law is the requirement of awareness "of the operative facts as a condition of imposing criminal liability." In other words, a man has to be aware that he is committing a rape in order to be liable for criminal conduct.[36]

This issue was also raised by Stephanie Gutmann, but Dix resolves it differently. He does not conclude that the prosecution must show that the accused was conscious that the victim was nonconsenting. "Liability can quite reasonably be imposed for recklessness," he suggests, "which requires awareness of only the risk." Since one way of being aware of the risk would be in the event that the victim said no, Dix believes that it would be wrong to eliminate nonconsent from modern rape and sexual assault statutes. Referring to the Pennsylvania case of David Berkowitz, he concludes that if the complainant said no, a defendant could properly be found guilty "by a jury convinced that he was aware of a considerable likelihood that the complainant was—given her protestations—not consenting."[37]

Other legal thinkers suggest that we must go beyond no means no. In an article written for the *University of Pennsylvania Law Review,* Lani Anne Remick, a Penn law student at the time, argues persuasively for verbal consent as a way to solve the interpretation and intent problems. She holds that a man "who has not established the willing participation of his partner by obtaining her verbal consent" must shoulder the risk of punishment if it should turn out that she was not consenting. Remick comes to this conclusion by weighing the relative value of two interests: her sexual autonomy on the one hand and his freedom "not to trouble himself with inquiring as to his partner's consent" on the other. According to Remick, "a woman's interest in sexual autonomy is greater than a man's interest in engaging in sexual activity without having to bother to inquire as to consent." Obtaining verbal consent, she suggests, is "the clearest and most unambiguous form of consent."[38] As one set of commentators quoted by Remick state: "Given the severity of the harm and pain that rape victims experience, the obligation positively to inquire so that unequivocal consent is obtained seems a minimal requirement indeed."[39]

The legal developments and the debate on college campuses promise to bring into being a new form of female sexual subjectivity and agency. Sexual subjectivity means being able to define one's desire first to one's self and then with a partner. Sexual agency means being in control of one's body, feeling free and confident in expressing desire without fear of being branded as bad, rejected as a sexless prude, or ignored altogether. Since sex beyond masturbation is always a kind of exchange, sexual subjectivity and agency for women means entering a sexual relationship as a fully equal partner in the give-and-take of pleasure. More than any other development in the twentieth century, the legal expectation placed on males of getting affirmative consent promises to end unquestioned male sexual dominance.

If affirmative consent becomes a cultural norm, we will see more than just an end to the problem of sexual assault; a new cultural understanding of female sexuality will emerge, encouraging women to explore diverse paths of sexual subjectivity. Some of the possibilities are suggested in the stories told by Clarissa Pinkola Estes, to flesh out the various aspects of female sexuality. Although I do not agree with her assumption that buried deep in the female psyche lies the essential wolf woman (desire for some women may be better reflected in the lusty song of the delicate but joyous Carolina wren), the stories she tells in *Women Who Run With the Wolves* take us out of the hunt-pursuit-capture mentality.[40]

Although widely criticized by feminists for its depiction of sex as a form of exchange in which the female serves the sexual interests of the male in return for money or marriage, the movie *The Piano* presents a unique female desire. The main character of the film, Ada, stubbornly resists the usual sexual regime by not speaking. Through silence she nurtures an inner life which she expresses by playing the piano. What she says in her music reaches deep into those who hear it. As one character comments in the movie, her music is like a mood that passes into you.

Ada is not sexually immune to the men she meets in New Zealand, where she goes to embark on a contract marriage. At first she rejects both her husband and Baines, the man who understands that he can reach Ada sexually only through the piano her husband had forced her to abandon by the sea because it does not fit his concept of the wifely role. Baines rescues the piano from the encroaching waves and sets it up in his house as a lure to attract Ada. The two strike a deal. She can revel in her music while he revels in her body. The deal is that after a certain number of notes in exchange for sex, Ada will earn back her piano. By agreeing, she enters into a second sexual contract. With both her husband and Baines, however, Ada holds back sexually. She performs wifely duties for her husband but gives him no sex, and plays the piano for Baines while reluctantly displaying her body at his request.

Even as she begins to feel attracted to Baines, seduced as much by her own music as by his advances, Ada resists him. Baines returns the piano when he begins to understand and love Ada. Ada's passion for Baines is sparked by this action and by the realization that he is not frightened by her music, the symbol of her uniqueness, which has frightened the other men in her life—the father of her child and her new husband.

Ada's music is a metaphor for the sensuous exploration of an inner world of fantasy and feeling. As Susan Griffin has shown in her book *Pornography and Silence,* this world is silenced by the pornographic obsession with sex as power, conquest, and outlet.[41] Through *The Piano* we come to know one woman's sexual subjectivity. The story raises in my mind several questions. How can a woman ever know her own music and name her desire if she must be on constant guard, ready to parry an unwanted sexual thrust? Isn't all sex a form of exchanging pleasure for pleasure? These questions apply to men and to same-sex partners as well. The issue is how we define and express pleasure. My pleasure may not be your pleasure. Like language, sex is a form of exchange, of communicating interest and desire. Without language, sex all too often reverts to the default definition learned from peers, movies, or pornography.

I find another clue to female sexual agency in the ancient story of Baubo, the goddess who brings the light of laughter back to the bereaved Demeter by making a sexual gesture.[42] Laughter is elemental, passionate, vitalizing, and arouses feelings that are not consistent with the model of passive-aggressive sexuality prescribed by Ellis and Freud. Laughter, Clarissa Pinkola Estes says, "is a kind of sexuality that doesn't have a goal." "It is a sexuality of joy, just for the moment, a true sensual love that flies free and lives and dies and lives again on its own energy."[43]

Possibilities for sensuous exploration and sharing proliferate once the mind leaves the prison of the hunt-pursuit-capture model of sexual expression. Sexuality is an electrifying energy that courses through the body and mind, bringing intense pleasure, even ecstasy. The pleasure can be altruistic and deeply compassionate. Sometimes the pleasure is shared with a lover, in and out of bed, sometimes not. Part of the fun and excitement of life is exploring the world and finding that pleasure and the person with whom it can be shared in the most unusual places and in one's own way.

THIRTEEN

CONCLUSION

As we move into the twenty-first century, it is useful to place the meaning of sexual aggression in the context of social progress and human evolution. As much as Darwin stressed competition, he also stressed cooperation or acting in behalf of what he called "the general good." Darwin suggested that "it would be advisable . . . to take as the standard of morality, the general good or welfare of the community, rather than the general happiness."[1] Increasingly in today's world, the general good is ignored in the interest of competition, individualism, and freedom without rules, with the result that American life is becoming a war zone.

Many students of human evolution believe that the hallmark of humanity is "sociality." Sometimes called altruism, sociality refers to the capacity for cooperative behavior, which humans share with social mammals in general. Throughout our evolutionary history, Richard Leakey and R. Lewin note, "There must have been extreme selective pressures in favor of our ability to co-operate as a group: organized food gathering and hunts are successful only if each member of the band knows his task and joins in with the activity of his fellows." These authors conclude that the pressure toward sociality is so strong and operated over such a long period of time (at least three million years and probably longer) "that it can hardly fail to have become embedded to some measure in our genetic makeup."[2]

Keeping women in a state of fear with the threat of rape may increase social bonding among men but it is unlikely to have contributed to the evolution of the species. Fear splits the sexes into ranked camps and reduces the overall level of cooperation. By increasing levels of stress in females, fear may reduce fertility rates and a female's capability to bear children. It also reduces the ability of the sexes to coordinate food-gathering activities. It is hard to imagine how the combination of fearful, dependent females and aggressive, belligerent males could have helped us through the many evolutionary crises created by changing environmental circumstances and widespread extinctions on the long road toward humanity. Indeed, one could easily argue that male aggressivity hastens extinction because of its tendency to create a culture of violence, where death rather than life excites men.

The American consensus that rationalizes male sexual aggression by attributing it to "boys will be boys" has helped create an atmosphere of violence that is all too familiar. Hate, rape, homicide, spousal abuse, child abuse, incest, and, most recently, right-wing self-appointed warriors planting bombs that kill scores of their fellow Americans are the news of the day. Such widespread breakdown in sociality, affecting all levels of American society, and even our children, could eventually lead us to social extinction as a society at war with itself falls apart. The appropriate question, then, is not whether sexual aggression is biologically determined but whether the current high level of aggression, with its consequences for social breakdown, threatens our survival as a species.

When the rhetorical dust settles from the date-rape backlash, several facts will remain. Acquaintance rape is a problem. Men as well as women —legal scholars, legislators at the state and national levels, feminists, professionals, and students—are increasingly concerned about sexual violence against women as one of the problems that must be addressed in combatting violence in general.

As far as the numbers go, the latest national study confirms trends revealed since the mid-fifties. On average, one in five American women are victims of forced sex. The problem will not go away by arguing over statistics and blaming feminism. It is time to stop the sexual politics of the backlash and start thinking about change. The first step is changing attitudes.

We all live with a certain mindset about sex, a set of stereotyped reactions to sexual situations we confront, hear of, or read about. I call this the default position, as when your computer switches on to one particular program unless otherwise instructed. But this doesn't mean there aren't other programs, other sets of propositions and assumptions, other ways of thinking about sex. In this book I have shown how the mainstream default position, with its typical stereotypes, has been biased against women accusers through the centuries of American rape jurisprudence.

Beginning in the 1960s, the mainstream stereotypes came under significant challenge by feminists. The anti-rape movement that developed is not about legislating values, but about change and opening up options for both sexes. With this book I am not suggesting that everyone hold the same values, but that everyone has the right to protection of bodily integrity in sex. Those who like rough sex may choose it. Those who reject rough sex for themselves have the right to prosecute the individual who forces it upon them in violation of the law. If a woman likes to be swished up the stairs by a Rhett Butler and forced, that's her prerogative. Hopefully, she won't then take the man to court if her submission was consensual. But if she did not submit, and did not consent, the legacy of Scarlett O'Hara should not keep her from justice in the courtroom.

The point is that sex does not spring full flowered out of male hormones like Athena from the head of Zeus. Sex is what we make of it. Sexual aggression in any society is curtailed or enhanced by the prevailing sexual ethos and by the social response to rape. The idea that male sexual aggression is natural is ingrained in the American sexual ethos. While I do not deny a biological component to aggression, how societies channel the human sex drive is of greater consequence. All human societies have instituted codes for appropriate and inappropriate sexual expression. Sometimes these codes encourage male violence against women. Often these codes punish male sexual violence.

As I have shown, codes for sexual expression curtailing or encouraging male sexual aggression are derived from philosophical assumptions about the nonhuman world. For example, in the U.S. we conceive of nature primarily as a competitive struggle for survival, where animals prey on each other. In this alleged struggle, as we conceive it, male animals display their dominance not only vis-à-vis other males but also by their sexual dominance of females. Applying this model to the human world, we think of the male as sexual hunter and the female as prey. We make the human male the supreme winner in nature's vast struggle because of his superior weaponry, physical strength, and mind. This way of thinking, reduced to its most simple form, not only motivates stalking and male sexual aggression, it determines in part the way we respond to a woman's allegations of rape.

In other societies, such as the Minangkabau of West Sumatra, Indonesia—an advanced modern, literate society of six million people, not the tribe in the jungle, where people think most anthropologists work—the conception of nature is very different. For several years I studied the Minangkabau worldview as it related to the low incidence of rape and aggression in general. With the Minangkabau, nature is not a scene of competitive struggle, but of slow growth nurtured by the mother in the case of animals, and by the sun and rain in the case of plants. As plants grow from seedlings, trees from transplanted branches, rivers from a trickle of water, and mountains from a clump of earth, so do people. Like the seedlings of nature, people and emotions must be patiently fed so that they will flower in their fullness. Applied to sex, this approach rules out aggression because aggression weakens rather than strengthens the body's tie to nature and society.

These two widely different social approaches to sexual expression reaffirm one of the most important lessons of twentieth-century anthropology, namely that there is enormous variability in the ways humans have found to channel basic drives. This finding applies to the sex drive as much as to any other. In order to understand sexual behavior in any society, we must turn to the social and cultural forces that shape its expression. As anthropologist Bronislaw Malinowski said long ago, based on his study of the sex life of the Trobriand Islanders, "Sex, in its widest meaning . . . is rather a sociological and cultural force than a mere bodily relation of two individuals."[3]

I agree with Malinowski's conclusion. Human sexual behavior cannot be divorced from the larger cultural system of beliefs, values, and attitudes, which determine the sexual ethos and motivate the social response to rape. Nor can sexual behavior be separated from the social relations in which it is embedded. To assume or assert otherwise is to fall into the trap of biological essentialism and to remain mired in destructive sexual myths.

Changing sexual attitudes and building a national consensus about what is appropriate and inappropriate sexual behavior are possible if we are willing, among other things, to rethink sexuality according to new models for pleasure. I emphasize change rather than celebrating the status quo. I do not see male sexual aggression as a manifestation and celebration of Western power. If what many young women have told me about the excess visited on their unyielding and resisting bodies is an example of the power of the West, I can only respond that the West, if typified by American sexual aggression, is in decline. The expression of male sexual primitivism without regard to women's feelings not only bespeaks sexual anarchy, it is a violation of basic human rights. It is also symptomatic of a society plagued by violence of other kinds. The situation we find in America can be compared with other rape-prone societies, where a high incidence of interpersonal aggression is associated with a high incidence of rape.

I believe that change is essential. A society that doesn't protect its women and guard its children from sexual abuse jeopardizes its future. In the interest of national pride, we must move from a society divided against itself to one that unites for change. Some sort of national consensus is needed not just on where to draw the line between sex and rape, but on how to punish those who cross it. Although our rape laws define the line and the punishment, these laws are useless if juror attitudes are affected by ancient sexual stereotypes. We must see these stereotypes for what they are—attitudes that encourage male violence. We can no longer afford to blame feminists for a problem that lies with our social definition of masculinity and femininity.

The combined experience of the many individuals who speak in these pages teaches us that it takes a strong personality and a courageous mentality to combat the current trends. As far as sex goes, we are in the midst of a still unnamed revolution. But then, strength and courage are the stuff of revolution.

NOTES

PROLOGUE

1. Angela's story is based on testimony presented on the witness stand during the pretrial hearings in 1990, the two trials in 1991 and 1992, and from an interview with Angela in May 1991.

2. *Newsday,* June 26, 1991.

1. THE ST. JOHN'S CASE GOES TO TRIAL

1. Parrot (1991:369).

2. The name Tawana Brawley was synonymous in the New York area with false accusations of rape. Tawana Brawley was a young black teenager who claimed she had been abducted and raped in 1987 by white racists and dumped in a garbage bag, her body smeared with excrement. A New York State grand jury concluded that she was a false accuser and her appearance self-inflicted. Only one of the grand jurors believed that something happened to Tawana Brawley. He was one of two black jurors. *The New York Times* reporters who covered the case wrote a book suggesting that the whole affair had been concocted as a form of blackmail.

3. Katz and Mazur (1979:214).

4. *The New York Times,* May 15, 1990.

5. For example, Joseph Fried of *The New York Times* wrote, "they made the woman perform oral sex." *Times,* June 11, 1991.

6. LaFree (1989:217–20).

7. In the same study a juror admitted arguing for acquittal in a case involving a black victim on the grounds that "a girl her age from that kind of neighborhood probably wasn't a virgin anyway." LaFree (1989:220).

8. *The New York Times,* May 1, 1990.

9. *Daily News,* May 11, 1990.

10. *The New York Times,* May 1, 1990.

11. *Daily News,* May 11, 1990.

12. Quoted in article in *Newsday,* July 21, 1991, while the St. John's jury was deliberating.

13. Varchaver (1991:17;21).

14. *Daily News,* July 25, 1991.

15. Varchaver (1991:17;18).

16. Ibid., p. 19.

17. Ibid., p. 20.

18. Theodore Lynch's account of the trial comes from an interview for this book in the spring of 1991.

19. *Newsday,* July 24, 1991.

20. Ibid.

21. Ibid.

22. *U.S. News & World Report,* August 12, 1991.

23. *Newsday,* July 24, 1991.

2. BIRTH OF THE FALSE ACCUSER: THE CASE OF MARGERY EVANS

1. Marcus (1983:296–97).

2. Ibid., p. 293.

3. Ibid., pp. 300–1.

4. Ibid., p. 304.

5. Ibid., pp. 305–6.

6. Ibid., p. 313.

7. Geis (1978:42) notes that Justice Bazelon said in a 1978 federal decision that Hale's cautions are "one of the most oft-quoted passages in our jurisprudence."

8. Marcus (1983:295).

9. Ibid.

10. Leah Marcus (1983:313–15) suggests that the case of Margery Evans was settled either in the summer before the masque was performed or was still pending. She believes the masque dramatizes the story of Margery Evans. Barbara Breasted (1971) believes that the masque was a commentary on another case, the Castlehaven scandal, involving a member of the Earl of Bridgewater's family. The masque was performed on September 29, 1634, three years after the Margery Evans and the Castelhaven affairs. Whichever case provided the model for the masque, the message that justice must be meted out fairly applies to both of these cases.

11. This summary of *Comus* is taken from Corson (1899:126–64).

12. Ibid., p. 108.

13. In her analysis of *Comus* and the Margery Evans affair, Leah Marcus (1983:321) likens Sabrina to the Earl of Bridgewater in a manner that can be applied to those who must judge acquaintance rape in today's world. Sabrina is a figure of compassion who does not judge the victim of abduction, but seeks to extricate her from that which has ensnared her, "offering the victim not judgement but grace," Marcus says. Sabrina sees through the situation confronting the Lady, as does the Spirit who informs the brothers of her plight. This quality of "seeing" is essential in rape cases. As Leah Marcus says, jurors must "become good judges of equivocal evidence," "in which the same witnesses, words, or events can be made to support opposite interpretations and carry opposite moral implications, depending on how they are viewed and the context in which they are placed."

14. Bracton as translated by Thorne (1968:415). See also Sir William Blackstone (1902, Bk 4:211) and Block (1992:13–14).

15. Friedman (1985:20–21) points out that William Blackstone's *Commentaries on the Law of England,* "a great bestseller, both in England and America," became available to colonials in the 1750s. Hale's approach to rape is found in Blackstone's (1902) treatment of English common law with respect to rape.

16. Hale's definition of rape is quoted by Block (1992:11). See also Hale (1800:627). Blackstone (1902:215) quotes Hale's cautions.

17. Simpson (1986:108).

18. Ibid., pp. 108–9. See also Simpson (1984:281).

19. Simpson (1986:109).

20. Ibid., p. 121.

21. Quoted by Geis (1978:40).

22. Quoted by Simpson (1986:108). See also Blackstone (1902:215).

23. The scorned woman was a popular literary image of the seventeenth century, appearing in plays by Dryden and Colley Cibber. Some believe that Congreve's famous lines were prompted by Dryden's "Rage has no bounds in slighted womankind," from his play *Cleomenes.* Others find the analogue in Colley Cibber's "We shall find no fiend in hell can match the fury of a disappointed woman," from the play *Love's Last Shift,* which appeared the year before *The Mourning Bride.* See Aubrey Williams (1979:176). See also Bartlett (1980:324).

24. Lines quoted from the play are taken from Davis (1967:317–85). For more on Eve in sixteenth- and seventeenth-century popular culture, see Catherine Belsey (1985:168).

25. Quoted in James (1981:7).

26. Geis (1978:40).

27. Ibid., pp. 29–30.

28. Ibid., pp. 29–30. Such sentiments were characteristic of the anti-female polemical tradition of the medieval and Renaissance periods. See Woodbridge (1984).

29. I am indebted to G. Geis's analysis of the trial (1978:30–40).

30. Ibid., p. 35.

31. The analysis by Marcus (1983:293) suggests there were relatively few convictions for rape. Executions for witchcraft was a vastly different story. According to information reported by Geis (1978:35–37), in one county in England, 107 women were executed for witchcraft, compared with 7 men.

32. Geis (1978:36–38).

33. Ibid., pp. 39–40.

34. *Encyclopaedia Britannica* (1967, vol. 10:1,130).

3. THE ENIGMA OF PURITAN SEXUALITY: RAPE IN EARLY NEW ENGLAND

1. For article by Camille Paglia see *The New York Times,* Dec. 14, 1990, Sec. A, p. 39. For article by Orlando Patterson see *The New York Times,* Oct. 20, 1991, Sec. 4, p. 15.

2. Laqueur (1990:4;159) calls this the "one-sex model."

3. Quoted by Laqueur (1990:43;48;64–65).

4. Thompson (1986:191;195).

5. Ibid., p. 51.

6. Morgan (1942:607;592–93).

7. Koehler (1980:9–10).

8. Ibid., p. 72.

9. Davis (1908:364–65). See also Koehler (1980:72).

10. Koehler (1980:72–74).

11. Flaherty (1971:206).

12. Koehler (1980:73;78–79).

13. Thompson (1986:82;135;140;196–97).

14. Ibid., pp. 3–15.

15. Adapted from the court record quoted by Thompson (1986:130–32).

16. Koehler (1980:86).

17. Thompson (1986:131–32).

18. Haskins (1968:150).

19. Powers (1966:265).

20. Ibid., pp. 264–67. Koehler (1980:94) reports several other areas that specified capital punishment for the crime of rape: New Haven in 1656, Plymouth in 1671, and New Hampshire in 1679.

21. Thompson (1986:12;80;217n.37).

22. Koehler (1980:92,98,100).

23. Ibid., pp. 91–92;94.

24. Ibid., pp. 92–96. See also Thompson (1974:237–38) and Lindemann (1984:79;81–82).

25. Koehler (1980:92–93;106).

26. Ibid., pp. 96–97.

27. Ibid., p. 97.

28. Ibid., p. 95.

29. Ibid., pp. 92–95.

30. Lindemann (1984:79;81–82). Lindemann bases her conclusions on a study of rape prosecutions in Massachusetts between 1698–1797. Lindemann found that most of the rape cases involved assailants of "a lower social order than the victim, or in which the victim was a married woman who forcefully resisted." Instances of coerced sexual relations between men of authority and lower-status women, she suggests, were probably not perceived as rape.

31. Flaherty (1971:235).

32. Ibid., p. 216.

33. Evans (1989:22).

34. Ibid., p. 23.

35. Hosmer [Winthrop's Journal] (1946:234). Evans (1989:31–32).

36. Quoted by Evans (1989:32).

37. Flexner (1973:9–12). Hosmer [Winthrop's Journal, Vol. 1] (1946:240).

38. Evans (1989:32).

39. Koehler (1980:388–91). From 1638 to 1692, 103 individuals were accused of witchcraft, 25 males and 78 females. See Koehler's Appendix 5, pp. 474–91.

40. Ibid., p. 411.

41. Ibid., pp. 395–96.

42. Ibid., p. 389.

43. Ibid., p. 85.

44. Ibid., p. 404.

45. According to Koehler's (1980:474–91) Appendix 5, 81 of the 315 accused witches between 1620 and 1699 were males.

46. Powers (1966:503–5). See also Geis (1978:43).

47. Koehler (1980:421;430–33;435–36).

48. Evans (1989:34).

4. THE NO-MEANS-YES DEFENSE: RAPE AT THE BIRTH OF THE NATION

1. Slotkin (1973:4).

2. Hofstadter (1989:5).

3. Block (1992:36).

4. D'Emilio and Freedman (1988:49).

5. Flaherty (1971:247–48).

6. Ibid., p. 234.

7. James (1981:51).

8. Flexner (1973:21).

9. Flaherty (1971:234–35). See also Ryan (1983:79).

10. Thompson (1974:238).

11. Gilfoyle (1992:24–26).

12. Hunt (1993:30;36–37).

13. Trumbach (1993:253–54).

14. Ibid., p. 254.

15. Hunt (1993:44).

16. Thomas (1959:196).

17. Clark (1987:6).

18. Quoted in Rossi (1988:10–11).

19. Ibid., pp. 9–11.

20. Ibid., pp. 11;15.

21. Quoted by Norton (1980:242–43).

22. Cott (1978:221–23).

23. Laqueur (1990:150).

24. Cott (1978:226–27).

25. Stansell (1987:22).

26. Evans (1989:74).

27. See Laqueur (1990:149–93) for discussion of the two-sex model.

28. Cott (1978:220–21).

29. Stansell (1987:97–98).

30. Arnold (1989:37).

31. Blackstone (1902:211–12).

32. Summary of Hale's evidence requirements by Blackstone (1902:211).

33. Arnold (1989:37).

34. Ibid., p. 39.

35. Ibid., pp. 41;42–43.

36. See discussion in Chapter 3.

37. Arnold (1989:48).

38. Ibid., p. 48.

39. Ibid., p. 49.

40. Ibid., p. 49. See also Stansell (1987:23–25) for a discussion of this case.

41. Arnold (1989:49–50).

42. Quoted by Stansell (1987:24) from *Report of the Trial of Henry Bedlow for Committing a Rape of Lanah Sawyer* (New York, 1793). See also Arnold (1989:50–51).

43. Arnold (1989:40).

44. Ibid., pp. 50–51.

45. Ibid., p. 51.

46. Stansell (1987:25).

47. Quoted by Stansell (1987:25–26).

48. Stansell (1987:26).

49. Flexner (1973:15–16). See also Rossi (1988:16–18).

50. Norton (1980:251), James (1981:96), Kerber (1980:225).

51. Norton (1980:252–54).

52. Ibid., pp. 254–55.

53. Columbia College commencement oration "On Female Influence" (1795), excerpted in Wortman (1985:79).

54. Flexner (1973:16–17).

5. RAPE AND SEXUAL POLITICS IN THE NINETEENTH CENTURY

1. Welter (1966:313–15).

2. Gilfoyle (1992:24–26).

3. Ibid., pp. 18;29–30.

4. Wortman (1985:214).

5. Gilfoyle (1992:99;114–16;130–31).

6. Ibid., pp. 76–81.

7. Ryan (1983:73–74).

8. Ibid., p. 114.

9. Douglas (1988:73).

10. Ibid., pp. 12;73;57;61.

11. Ibid., pp. 8;10;12–13;58.

12. Smith-Rosenberg (1985:110–12).

13. Ibid., pp. 109;120;124;127.

14. Schneir (1972:154).

15. Pleck (1983:451).

16. Gordon (1990:111–13).

17. Wortman (1985:198–201).

18. *American Digest* (1897–1904).

19. Stansell (1987:278n33). Gilfoyle (1992:69).

20. Block (1992:42).

21. Nemeth (1980:215;218).

22. *People* v. *Abbot,* 19 Wendell's Reports (New York) 193–95.

23. Ibid., pp. 194–95.

24. Ibid., pp. 194–95.

25. Ibid., pp. 196–97.

26. Ibid., p. 201.

27. See Block (1992) Chapter V for a thorough discussion of this case.

28. *People* v. *Abbot,* op. cit., 196–97.

29. Block (1992:143–47). *People* v. *Jackson* 3 Parker C.R. 391 (N.Y. Sup. Ct. 1857). See also Nemeth's (1980:219–29) discussion of this case.

30. *Crossman* v. *Bradley* 53 Barb. 125 (1868). Nemeth (1980:220–21).

31. Nemeth (1980:220–21).

32. Ibid., p. 221.

33. Ibid., p. 225.

34. Ibid., p. 221.

35. Ibid. *Woods* v. *People* 1 T. & C. 610 (N.Y. Sup. Ct. 1873), 55 N.Y. 515 (1874).

36. Nemeth (1980:222).

37. Ibid., p. 222.

38. Ibid., pp. 222–23.

39. Ibid., p. 223. For case of homeless woman see *Brennan* v. *People* 14 N.Y. Sup. Ct. 171 (1876).

40. Block (1992:42–43).

41. Ibid., pp. 62–66, citing *State* v. *Crow,* 10 *Western Law Journal* 501 (1853).

42. Ibid., pp. 69–73, citing *People* v. *Crosswell* 13 Mich 247, 87 Am Dec 774 (1865), 435.

43. Ibid., pp. 73–76, citing *State* v. *Tarr,* 28 Iowa 397 (1869), 398.

44. Ibid., pp. 72–73.

45. Ibid., pp. 77–79, citing *People* v. *Quin,* 50 Barb (NY) 128, 133–34.

46. For cases involving fraud see *American Digest* (1897–1904: Sections I.9 to I.11).

47. Nemeth (1980:225).

48. Quoted by Nemeth (1980:224–25).

49. Sanday (1990:113).

6. CONSTRUCTION OF MODERN SEXUAL STEREOTYPES

1. Showalter (1990:46–49); Peiss (1989); Snitow, Stansell, and Thompson (1983:115–16).

2. Cott (1987:43–44) quoting from an article in *The Nation.*

3. Schlossman and Wallach (1978:86).

4. Langum (1994:17).

5. Peiss (1989:59).

6. Cott (1987:3). According to Cott (1987:14–15), the word "feminism" was coined in the 1880s in France and was used in England in the 1890s to denote women's struggle for independence. The first journalistic reference to feminism in the United States that Cott finds is a 1906 article in the New York offshoot of the London *Review of Reviews,* entitled "Feminism in Some European Countries."

7. Ibid., p. 42.

8. Ellis (1926:203–5).

9. Darwin (1936:872–73).

10. Quoted by Hofstadter (1992:40–41;50). See Degler (1991:11) for discussion of relevance of label "social Spencerism."

11. Gay (1993:47).

12. Krafft-Ebing (1965:33).

13. Ibid., 34–35; 41.

14. See discussion in Robinson (1976:23).

15. Quoted by Robinson (1976:19) from Havelock Ellis.

16. Ellis (1926:2–3).

17. Ibid., pp. 24–25.

18. Ibid., pp. 28–29.

19. Ibid., pp. 66–67.

20. Ibid., p. 69.

21. Ibid., p. 33.

22. Ibid., p. 82.

23. Ibid., p. 103.

24. Freud (1975:1).

25. Ibid., pp. 85–86.

26. Ibid., pp. 23–24.

27. Ibid., pp. 86–87.

28. Masson (1985:85–86).

29. Ibid., pp. 268–69.

30. From "The Aetiology of Hysteria," in Masson (1985:276–77).

31. Masson (1984:9).

32. Ibid., pp. 136–37.

33. Ibid., p. 110.

34. Ibid., p. 122.

35. Dora claimed that the vaginal discharge was due to her father's venereal disease and that he had passed it on to her by heredity. Despite the fact that Dora never claimed that her father violated her, nor did Freud ever hint at this possibility, her certainty that both she and her mother were suffering from his illness together with the symptom of the vaginal discharge suggest that her father may have abused her sexually. See Freud (1963:93–94) for his thoughts on the meaning of the vaginal discharge and the hereditary implications of Philip Bauer's venereal disease.

36. Ramas (1983:73). See also Freud (1963:41).

37. Freud (1963:131–32).

38. Ibid., p. 132.

39. Ibid., p. 75.

40. Freud (1957:54).

41. Cott (1987:38).

42. Schwarz, Peiss, and Simmons (1989:118–19).

43. Cott (1987:43–44).

44. Quoted by Simmons (1989:163).

45. Cott (1987:46).

46. Hale (1995a:269–70). See also Barko (1982:27) and Drinnon (1961:149–52).

47. Schlossman and Wallach (1978:86–87).

48. Lunbeck (1987:513). See Hale (1995b:74) on the establishment of the hospitals.

49. Lunbeck (1987:n.1.539).

50. Healy and Healy (1969:1;5). See Healy and Healy (1969:162–217) for chapter on "Cases of Pathological Accusations."

51. Healy (1969:231;403).

52. Ibid., p. 403.

53. Wigmore (1970:737).

54. Ibid., p. 736.

55. Ibid., p. 737.

56. Ibid., p. 737.

57. Ibid., p. 744.

58. Ibid., p. 747. See also Bienen (1983a:255–58).

59. Healy and Healy (1969:182). See also Bienen (1983a:250–51).

60. Wigmore (1970:742). See Healy and Healy (1969:187).

61. Williams (1983:957).

62. Ibid., pp. 973–75.

63. Ellis (1942:287).

7. THE GREAT AMERICAN SEX BUSINESS

1. By 1918, Hale (1995a:476) notes, "some 23 percent of all intellectual magazines favored 'sex freedom,' by 1928 some 56 percent. The corresponding percentages for the mass magazines were 13 percent in 1918 and 40 percent in 1928."

2. Quoted by Evans (1989:178–79).

3. Simmons (1989:168).

4. Freedman (1989:201).

5. Simmons (1989:163–64).

6. Hale (1995a:98).

7. Simmons (1989:164).

8. Quoted by Millett (1970:241). See Lawrence (1962).

9. Hamilton and Macgowan (1976:562).

10. Quoted by Jackson (1987:63). See also Van de Velde (1928:139), emphasis in original. See also Ehrenreich, Hess, and Jacobs (1986:47).

11. Schmalhausen (1976:355).

12. Ibid., p. 379.

13. Ibid., p. 355.

14. Ibid., p. 359.

15. Glueck (1937:318–20).

16. Freedman (1989:206).

17. Ibid., p. 200.

18. Ibid., pp. 201;209–11;213.

19. Freedman (1989:213).

20. Reich (1969:265–69).

21. Commenting on Kinsey's debt to Freud, Hiltner (1953:66–67) points out that Kinsey gave Freud credit "for suggesting the presence of sexuality in young children, for extending the concept of sexuality to suggest that 'all tactile stimulation and response are basically sexual,' and for the general movement toward a 'biologic viewpoint' on sex." Kinsey, however, saw no evidence for a "generalized pregenital sexuality nor for a 'latency period'; nor for the Oedipus complex," or for sublimation.

22. Kinsey (1948:216).

23. Ibid., p. 263.

24. Quoted by Trilling (1950:233).

25. Kinsey (1948:373).

26. Robinson (1976:55).

27. Kinsey (1948:204–5).

28. For a study conducted early in the twentieth-century see Exner (1915:6). For studies in the 1950s see discussion of those conducted by Kirkendall, Ehrmann, and Kanin at the end of this chapter. For later studies see discussion in Chapter 9.

29. Hefner (1962:166).

30. Ibid., p. 169.

31. Ibid.

32. Norman (1953:6).

33. Ibid., p. 7.

34. Ibid., pp. 7–8.

35. Wylie (1958:51).

36. Wylie (1955).

37. Wylie (1958:52–53).

38. Kirkendall (1961:238).

39. Ibid., p. 69.

40. Ibid., pp. 58;68–69.

41. Ibid., p. 100.

42. Ibid., pp. 93–94.

43. Ibid., p. 76.

44. Ibid., p. 92.

45. Ibid., pp. 109–12.

46. Ibid., pp. 80–83.

47. Ibid., p. 237.

48. Ibid., p. 114.

49. Kinsey (1948:348; 1953:330–31).

50. Ehrmann (1959:188–90;242–46).

51. Kirkpatrick and Kanin (1957:53,56).

52. Miller (1984:49–52).

53. See *Playboy,* "Saucy Sophomore," Sept. 1958, p. 41.

54. Quoted by Millett (1970:3). See Miller (1965:180).

55. As early as the 1920s, evidence had been reported that women did not necessarily benefit from male sexual aggression. A study discussed by Hamilton and Macgowan (1976:575) showed that few of the women who had experienced male sexual aggression in their youth were able to achieve orgasm as adults.

56. *Yale Law Journal* (1952:55–56).

57. Ibid., p. 55.

58. Ibid., p. 66.

59. Ibid., p. 66.

60. Ibid., pp. 67–68.

61. Ibid., p. 69.

62. Freedman (1989:216).

63. Based on a comparison of the acquittal rate listed for simple rape presented in Table 72 with acquittal rate for major crimes listed in Table 9, Kalven and Zeisel (1966:42;253).

64. LeGrand (1973:927). See also Clemens (1983:881).

8. FEMINISM IN THE SIXTIES AND THE ANTI-RAPE MOVEMENT

1. *Esquire,* July 1961, p. 96.

2. *Time,* January 24, 1964, p. 54.

3. *The Washington Post,* Oct 13, 1979.

4. Gebhard, Gagnon, Pomeroy, and Christenson (1965:108–9).

5. Hite (1976:312).

6. In interviews with 930 randomly selected women ranging in age from 18 to 80 in San Francisco, Russell (1984b:55) found that for women under 25, the rape rate increased from 15 percent in 1931 to 51 percent in 1976.

7. Based on Federal Bureau of Investigation *Uniform Crime Reports for the United States* (1970–1980).

8. LeGrand (1973:920).

9. Brown (1983), first published in 1962.

10. In this Friedan was very different from the other popular women's writer of the time, Margaret Mead. Although Mead had written in her early book, *Sex and Temperament* (1935), that sex roles were largely due to culture, in *Male and Female* (1949) Mead helped solidify the feminine mystique by arguing that men have a "natural springing potency," and women a "spontaneous slower-flowering responsiveness." Women are "essentially domestic," she suggested, while men need to "exercise their biologically given aggressive protectiveness or desire for individual bravery." Since male and female roles were biologically grounded in these traits, she suggested that men should explore outside of the home, go to the moon if need be, while women should bear children and tend the domestic fires to achieve a sense of fulfillment. For a discussion of these points see Sanday (1980:340–47).

11. Friedan (1974:78), first published in 1963.

12. Evans (1980:87).

13. Freeman (1975:57).

14. Evans (1980:198–99). See also Freeman (1975:60).

15. Evans (1980:200).

16. For statement of the Miss America protest see Morgan (1970:584–87). For Morgan's account of her role in the protest see Morgan (1992:21–29).

17. Morgan (1970:xxiii).

18. Dworkin (1994:14).

19. Ibid., p. 15.

20. *New York Post,* Thursday, March 11, and Monday, March 8, 1965.

21. *The New York Times,* March 6, 1965.

22. Griffin (1986:29). Griffin (1971) is a well-known early feminist essay on rape.

23. Lear (1972:63).

24. Sheehy (1971:28).

25. Connell and Wilson (1974:1).

26. Millett (1970:23).

27. Ibid., p. 23.

28. Ibid., pp. 29–33.

29. See Mead (1935) for variability in temperament in New Guinea, and Sanday (1981b) for a discussion of variability in female power and male dominance in a worldwide sample.

30. Millett (1970:44).

31. Ibid., p. 32.

32. Interview, Robin Morgan, Oct. 4, 1994.

33. This account of the New York Conference on Rape is taken from a feminist newspaper entitled *Everywoman,* Vol II, No. 9, June 18, 1971.

34. See Medea and Thompson (1974:127–28;144–50) for a discussion of the establishment of early rape crisis centers.

35. *Time,* December 18, 1972, p. 33.

36. Kling (1965:215).

37. *University of Pennsylvania Law Review* (1970:460).

38. Clemens (1983:871).

39. Sheehy (1971:28).

40. Lear (1972:11).

41. *Newsday,* July 21, 1991.

42. Williams (1983); *Yale Law Journal* (1952:56–57); Clemens (1983).

43. Kalven and Zeisel (1966:253;495).

44. Wigmore (1970:737–40); Freedman (1989:211).

45. Wigmore (1970:737–40).

46. Quoted by Clemens (1983:873–74).

47. Largen (1976:70–71).

48. Feild and Bienen (1980:153).

49. Ibid., pp. 153–54.

50. Bienen (1983b:139); Loh (1981:28); Feild and Bienen (1980:153).

51. Allison and Wrightsman (1993:214–15). Capital punishment in rape was never beneficial to rape victims because the penalty was almost always applied to black not to white defendants. According to one researcher (see Sagarin 1977:147), 89 percent of the 455 men executed for rape since 1930 were black. See also Bienen (1980:173).

52. Bienen (1980:172–75).

53. Largen (1988:276).

54. Information taken from *The Economist,* August 16, 1975.

55. Fairstein (1993:79).

56. Ibid., pp. 122–23.

57. Ibid., pp. 127–28.

58. Marsh (1988:388–99).

59. Largen (1988:283;289).

60. Bienen (1980:184).

9. NAMING AND STUDYING ACQUAINTANCE RAPE

1. Interview with anonymous college student, spring 1984.

2. McCluskey (1992:261–62).

3. For an excellent summary of studies of the heterosexual and homosexual assault of male victims, see Struckman-Johnson (1991:192–213).

For another source see Hickson et al. (1994), which describes a study of 930 homosexually active men living in England and Wales in which 27.6 percent said they had been sexually assaulted or had had sex against their will. Some of these men reported being abused by women assailants. Another source on male-male acquaintance rape is Mezey and King (1992).

For a study of partner abuse in lesbian relationships see Renzetti (1992).

4. Kalven and Zeisel (1966:254).

5. Amir (1971). See LeGrand (1973:922–23) on Amir and for other studies on proportion of stranger to acquaintance rape cases.

For still another study see Prentky, Burgess, and Carter (1986:73–98). These authors state that a sample of sixteen studies showed that the incidence of stranger rape ranged from 26 percent to 91 percent.

6. Amir (1971:245) and LeGrand (1973:922–24).

7. Brownmiller (1975:257).

8. Ibid.

9. Russell (1984a:11). First published in 1974.

10. Ibid., p. 12.

11. Ibid., p. 102.

12. Ibid., p. 136. A "train" is a sexual ritual in which a number of men line up to rape a woman in succession. See Sanday (1990) for a discussion of trains.

13. Ibid., pp. 107;137.

14. Ibid., pp. 31–34.

15. Russell (1984b:34;37–38).

16. Ibid., p. 35.

17. Ibid., p. 59.

18. Ibid., pp. 35–36.

19. Ibid., pp. 96–97;284.

20. Koss (1985:194).

21. The kind of behavior Brownmiller (1975:257) called date rape (see discussion in the text) corresponded to Koss's (1985:196) "low sexual victimization" category, which Koss does not label rape.

22. Two of the three questions used to determine the 13 percent asked whether actual or threatened physical force had been used in nonconsensual intercourse. The third question asked whether oral or anal intercourse or penetration with an object through the use of force or threat of force had been used in nonconsensual intercourse. Koss (1981: Table 4, p. 51). See also Koss and Oros (1982:455–57).

23. Koss (1981:21–27).

24. For Kinsey data see Kinsey (1953:330–31; 1948:348). From Koss's data, which she supplied to me, I calculated results from the responses to the question: "Have you ever willingly had sexual intercourse with a member of the opposite sex?" The percentages refer to those answering yes.

25. Hunt (1974:149–53).

26. For the first published version see Koss, Gidycz, and Wisniewski (1987:162–70).

27. Warshaw (1988:11). See also Koss (1988:15–16).

28. Koss (1988:15–16).

29. Koss (1992a:122–26). For more discussion of these statistics and how they were used in the backlash against Koss, see Chapter 11.

30. One and a half percent of the men said they had forced a woman into intercourse, oral or anal penetration, or penetration with objects by using threats or physical force; 4 percent of the men said they had intercourse with an unwilling woman by giving her drugs or alcohol. See Koss (1988:8).

31. Koss (1988:18–19).

32. Malamuth study summarized by Russell (1984b:159); Briere study in Russell (1984b:64). See also Malamuth (1981:138–157).

33. Scully (1990:27–28;159;163).

34. For a summary of these studies and others, see Koss and Cook (1993:110). For further discussion of acquaintance rape statistics, see Chapter 11.

35. For a summary of many studies, see Koss (1993:1,062–9). For the 1992 national study on rape, see National Victim Center (1992). Koss found that 16 percent of the women in her national sample said they had experienced nonconsensual sex due to a man's force, threat of force, or use of alcohol. When Koss excluded the question about alcohol, this figure was reduced to 11 percent; see Koss and Cook (1993:106).

36. Barrett (1982:50–51).

37. Warshaw (1988:101).

38. See discussion in Sanday (1990:1–2). See also Ehrhart and Sandler (1985).

39. O'Sullivan (1991:144;151).

40. Sanday (1990:74–75).

41. Ibid., pp. 5–7.

42. Ibid., p. 34.

43. Ibid., pp. 71–72.

44. Ibid., p. 72.

45. Koss and Leonard (1984:221;223).

46. The percentages reported here were computed by me from Koss's 1985 national survey data on acquaintance rape. The questions were asked so that students could check one of five responses: strongly disagree, disagree, neither agree or disagree, agree, strongly agree. The figures I report are based on the percentage of students checking "agree" or "strongly agree."

47. For example, only 13 percent of those who had been raped agreed that women like to be roughed up sexually, as compared with 11 percent of women who had not been raped (and 11 percent of the nonaggressive men). Six percent of the women who had been raped expressed agreement with the idea that women have an unconscious desire to be raped, as compared with 6 percent of women who had not been raped (and 8 percent of the nonaggressive men).

48. See "Afterword" by Mary P. Koss in Warshaw (1988:189–210) for description of the sample of college students holding these attitudes. The figures presented here were computed by me based on Koss's data with her permission. See note 46.

49. See discussion in Koss and Leonard (1984:213–31).

50. Koss and Dinero (1988:133–47).

51. Malamuth, Sockloski, Koss, and Tanaka (1991:670;672).

52. Sanday (1981a:5–27). In this study I defined a rape-prone society as one in which the incidence of rape is reported by observers to be high, or rape is excused as a ceremonial expression of masculinity, or rape is an act by which men are allowed to punish or threaten women. I defined a rape-free society as one in which the act of rape is either infrequent or does not occur. I used the term rape free not to suggest that rape was entirely absent in a given society but as a label to indicate that sexual aggression is socially disapproved and punished severely. Thus, while there may be some men in all societies who might be potential rapists, there is abundant evidence from many societies I have researched and from the one in which I conducted nearly two years of anthropological field work that sexual aggression is rarely expressed.

53. Koss (1988:11–12).

54. Quoted by Warshaw (1988:39).

55. For fraternity song, see *Together,* UCLA feminist newsmagazine, coedited by Katrina Foley and Sheila Moreland, March 1992.

56. Sanday (1990:140–41).

57. Koss and Gaines (1993:104–5).

58. Sanday (1990: Chapter 7).

59. For this remark see Bowden (1983). For discussion see Sanday (1990:34).

60. Millett (1970:167).

61. Morgan (1992:78–89).

62. Dworkin (1974:55–56).

63. Dworkin (1989:209), first published in 1979.

64. In a widely cited article, social psychologist Martha Burt (1980:217) coined the term "rape myth" to characterize "prejudicial, stereotyped, or false belief[s] about rape, rape victims, and rapists." Citing a number of studies, she shows that the cluster of attitudes that include rape myths create a climate both hostile to rape victims and conducive to sexual aggression. For example, some studies show that rape myths are part of the belief system of law enforcement officials who interact with rape victims, while other studies indicate that rape myths affect verdicts in mock-jury trials.

Koss and Leonard (1984:221–23) showed that the same constellation of beliefs and attitudes about rape ("rape myths") distinguish sexually aggressive from nonaggressive men.

65. Malamuth (1993:573–74).

66. Calculated through a Nexis search of major newspapers and magazines from March 1991 to December 1991.

10. THE CONTINUING POWER OF STEREOTYPES

1. Estrich (1987:4–7).

2. See Palm Beach Police Department (1991). Bowman's comments were in response to the questionnaire administered to victims of sexual assault by the Palm Beach Police Department.

3. Ibid. March 30, 1991.

4. Ibid.

5. Ibid.

6. Ibid.

7. Ibid., April 1, 1991.

8. *The Washington Post,* May 10, 1991.

9. Ibid.

10. *The New York Times,* April 17, 1991.

11. Butterfield with Tabor (1991).

12. Quindlen (1991).

13. Estrich (1991).

14. *The New York Times,* April 26, 1991.

15. *The Washington Post,* May 10, 1991.

16. Ibid.

17. Ibid.

18. *The New York Times,* May 11, 1991.

19. Jordan (1991).

20. Fromm (1991:580–81).

21. Ibid., p. 581.

22. Vatz and Weinberg (1991).

23. Clifford (1991).

24. *The Boston Globe,* Dec. 7, 1991.

25. Ibid., Dec. 3, 1991.

26. Quindlen (1991).

27. Dershowitz (1991).

28. *ABC News, Nightline,* Dec. 11, 1991.

29. Quoted by Barron (1991).

30. Ibid.

31. *Larry King Live,* December 13, 1992.

32. *The New York Times,* March 27, 1992.

33. Information on the St. John's trial was gathered by me through observation of testimony and behavior in the courtroom throughout the trial, as well as interviews with Judge Browne, Peter Reese, Vincent Gentile, and Angela on the day of the plea.

34. Shipp (1992).

35. Material based on Interview with J. Gregory Garrison, Indianapolis, November 1994.

36. Interview with deputy prosecutor Steve Tesmer, Indianapolis, November 1994.

37. Garrison and Roberts (1994:203).

38. *The New York Times,* January 31, 1992.

39. Garrison and Roberts (1994:223).

40. Ibid., pp. 223–25.

41. Ibid., pp. 227–31.

42. Ibid., pp. 219–21.

43. Ibid., p. 231–32.

44. Ibid., pp. 254–56.

45. *The New York Times,* Feb. 11, 1992.

46. Ibid., Feb. 8, 1992.

47. Garrison and Roberts (1994:248).

48. Ibid., pp. 248; 216.

49. Ibid., p. 294.

50. *The New York Times,* Feb. 11, 12, 13, 1992.

51. Ibid.

52. For a discussion of research on the frequency of false reports of rape see Allison and Wrightsman (1993:10–11;205–6) and Katz and Mazur (1979:207–8). Katz and Mazur summarize research based on interviews by social workers (or medical examinations), who estimate that between 1 and 6 percent of rape accusations are false. False reports must be distinguished from those classified as "unfounded" by the police. The percentage of unfounded reports of rape is generally higher, between 15 to 25 percent. A report may be classified as unfounded for reasons other than it being false. A study summarized by Katz and Mazur (1979:211) conducted in 1973 of Denver police records listed eleven reasons why a case might be classified as "unfounded." Some examples of reasons unrelated to falsity of the report were: victim moving away; lack of cooperation of victim; failure to keep an appointment; victim's uncertainty; victim being thought a prostitute; the crime occurring outside the jurisdiction.

53. *Commonwealth of Pennsylvania* v. *Robert A. Berkowitz,* J-139-1993. Decided May 27, 1994, in the Supreme Court of Pennsylvania Middle District. See pages 5 and 6 of decision.

54. *The Philadelphia Inquirer,* March 22, 1995. See also Senate Bill No. 2, Special Session No. 1 of 1995, of the General Assembly of Pennsylvania.

55. *The Philadelphia Inquirer,* March 28, 1995.

11. THE CRUSADE AGAINST ANTI-RAPE ACTIVISM

1. Cited in *Working Woman,* March 1995, p. 15.

2. Wiener (1992).

3. NOW's participation in drafting the act was publicly recognized by Biden when he thanked Helen Neuborne, executive director of the NOW Legal Defense Fund, for NOW's help. Biden expressed his gratitude to Neuborne when she appeared before the Senate Judiciary Committee in hearings on the nomination of Judge David Souter to the Supreme Court. Federal News Service, Sept. 18, 1990.

4. Senator Joseph Biden, Jr., Congressional Record—Senate. Legislative day of Monday, June 11, 1990. 101st Cong. 2nd Sess.

5. Ibid.

6. PR Newswire Association, Inc. November 13, 1990.

7. MacKinnon (1991).

8. From testimony given by Mary P. Koss at hearing on the Violence Against Women Act, quoted in *The Washington Post,* August 30, 1990.

9. Gutmann (1990).

10. Wiener (1992) chronicles the use of "inappropriate innuendo" as Swarthmore's alleged definition in several magazines and articles. In its cover story on date rape, *Time* (June 3, 1991) used the "inappropriate innuendo" quotation and referred to Swarthmore as an institution that "sees rape as a metaphor, its definition swelling to cover any kind of oppression of women." Wiener, a University of California history professor, whose article appeared in *The Nation* (January 20, 1992), notes that *Time* received a letter from the coordinators of the school's date-rape program stating that the training guide "did not intend to say . . . that verbal harassment or innuendo qualifies as rape, but rather that discussion of the issues

involved in sexual assault should not be limited to narrowly defined rape." *Time* did not print the letter, and used the quotation in another article in the October 14, 1991, issue. See Wiener (1992) for other uses of the "inappropriate innuendo quote."

Finally, in its November 11, 1991, issue, *Time* printed a letter from Michael Dennis, Swarthmore's student body president, who wrote that the training guide was no longer in use and that the Swarthmore policy on sexual assault "clearly defines acquaintance rape and does not equate it with other types of sexual assault or harassment, such as 'inappropriate innuendo.'"

11. Paglia's article appeared in *New York Newsday* on January 27, 1991, and the Felten article appeared in *The Washington Times,* on January 29, 1991.

12. Paglia (1992:50–51;63;53).

13. Paglia (1990:3).

14. Ibid., pp. 1–3.

15. Paglia (1992:53) and Paglia (1990:23;3).

16. Paglia (1992:51–53; 57; 63).

17. Ibid., pp. 63–65; 53.

18. Ibid., p. 58.

19. Ibid., p. 47.

20. Slotkin (1973:5).

21. Biden (1991).

22. See *U.S. News & World Report,* August 13, 1990, for "femino-puritanism" quotation. See Leo (1991) on Paglia and Gutmann. For more on Leo and Swarthmore see Wiener (1992).

23. Koss and Cook (1993:106).

24. See *Playboy,* October 1990 and November 1990.

25. Felten (1991).

26. Gilbert (1991b:60).

27. Gilbert (1991a).

28. Ibid.

29. Koss (1992b:63).

30. Ibid., pp. 63–64; 69.

31. Ibid., pp. 64–66.

32. Koss and Cook (1993:111).

33. Ibid., p. 106.

34. Ibid., p. 107.

35. Ibid.

36. For the specific references of the original studies see Koss and Cook (1993:110).

37. For a discussion of "validity," see Kinsey et al. (1953:67).

38. Koss and Cook (1993:110). For more on Kanin's surveys in the 1950s, see Chapter 7.

39. Michael et al. (1994:33;221). See also Laumann et al. (1994).

40. Michael et al. (1994:223).

41. Laumann et al. (1994:335).

42. Michael et al. (1994:221). For more on the Antioch Sexual Offense Policy, see Chapter 12.

43. *The New York Times,* Nov. 29, 1981.

44. Information based on interview with Myra Hindus, Storrs, Connecticut, November 1994.

45. Roiphe (1993:39).

46. Ibid., p. 57.

47. Roiphe (1991).

48. Roiphe (1993:66). See also Roiphe (1991).

49. Roiphe (1993:71–72).

50. National Victim Center (1992).

51. Roiphe (1993:172).

52. Estrich (1987:101).

53. Sommers (1994:216).

54. Ibid., pp. 22;33;35.

55. Looking cross-culturally at sex roles in a variety of societies, this approach recognizes that variation is much more evident than universal patterns. My own work, for example (see Sanday 1981a and b), has focused on the range of variation in male-female relationships in the sexual and social arenas. For more recent work by anthropologists emphasizing the cultural variability of sex roles and the intricacies of the relative status of the sexes, see Sanday and Goodenough (1990) and Lepowsky (1993). The basis for this approach is not new to anthropology. The concept of cultural selection and change with respect to sex roles was first introduced by Margaret Mead (see Chapter 8), based on Ruth Benedict's theory of cultural selection.

56. Sommers (1994:225).

57. Ibid., pp. 225–26.

12. AFFIRMATIVE CONSENT

1. United Press International, BC cycle, November 29, 1990, Domestic News. Nexus.

2. See video *Sex Without Consent* by Toby Simon, New York: Mumbleypeg Productions.

3. Material presented in this section based on interviews with Toby Simon and members of the Cast of Color as well as observations at the 4th International Conference on Sexual Assault and Harassment on Campus.

4. Interview with Melinda Kanner, Antioch College, spring and fall of 1994. Phone interview (May 1995) with Andrea Brown, a senior at Antioch in 1990–91.

5. Guskin (1995:25–27).

6. Interview with Karen Hall, November 1994.

7. Interview with Joan Chappelle, May 1994.

8. Interview with Andy Abrams, May 1994.

9. Interview with Sierra Levy, Antioch College, May 1994.

10. Interview with Kristine Herman, Antioch College, May 1994.

11. Interview with Tex Clark, Antioch College, May and November 1994.

12. Interview, Antioch College, May 1994.

13. State in Interest of M.T.S., 1992, 129 N.J. 425–46.

14. Ibid., pp. 427–28.

15. Ibid., pp. 429–30.

16. Ibid., pp. 428; 425.

17. Ibid., p. 444.

18. Ibid., pp. 431–42.

19. Ibid., p. 433.

20. Ibid., p. 434.

21. Ibid., p. 435.

22. Ibid., p. 438.

23. Ibid., p. 440–41.

24. Ibid., p. 443.

25. Ibid., p. 444.

26. Ibid., p. 446.

27. Quoted in *Newsday,* March 4, 1993.

28. *Newsday,* March 17, 1993.

29. Schafran (1994:8).

30. Wisconsin Statutes @ 940.225 (1994).

31. Illinois Compiled Statues Annotated. 720 ILCS 5/12-17 (1995).

32. Annotated Revised Code of Washington. (ARCW) @ 9A.44.010 (1994).

33. Schafran (1994:9).

34. State in Interest of M.T.S., p. 445.

35. Estrich (1987:98).

36. Dix (1993).

37. Ibid. See Chapter 10 for discussion of Berkowitz case.

38. Remick (1993:1133;1137).

39. Ibid., p. 1138, quoting Balos and Fellows (1991:618).

40. See Estes (1992).

41. Griffin (1981).

42. For a discussion of Baubo and the story itself see Estes (1992:334–40). For a wonderful historical summary of the Baubo image see Lubell (1994).

43. Estes (1992:342).

13. CONCLUSION

1. Quoted by Degler (1991:9).

2. Carrithers (1989:197). See Leakey and Lewin quoted in Howell and Willis (1989:21–22).

3. Malinowski (1929:xxiii).

BIBLIOGRAPHY

Allison, Julie A. and Lawrence S. Wrightsman
1993   *Rape: The Misunderstood Crime.* Newbury Park, CA: Sage.

American Digest
1897–   *Century Edition of the American Digest: A Complete Digest of All Reported American Cases from the*
1904   *Earliest Times to 1896.* Volume 42. St. Paul: West Publishing Co.

Amir, Menachem
1971   *Patterns in Forcible Rape.* Chicago: University of Chicago Press.

Arnold, Marybeth Hamilton
1989   " 'The Life of a Citizen in the Hands of a Woman': Sexual Assault in New York City; 1790 to
        1820." In *Passion and Power: Sexuality in History,* Kathy Peiss and Christina Simmons, eds., 35–
        56. Philadelphia: Temple University Press.

Balos, Beverly and Mary L. Fellows
1991   "Guilty of the Crime of Trust: Nonstranger Rape." *Minnesota Law Review,* Vol. 75:599.

Barko, Naomi
1982   "Lost Women: The Emma Goldman You'll Never See in the Movies," *Ms.,* 10(9):27–31.

Barrett, Karen
1982   "Date Rape: A Campus Epidemic?" *Ms.,* 11(3):49.

Barron, James
1991   "Experts on Rape Back Smith's Acquittal," *The New York Times,* December 12.

Bartlett, John
1980   *Familiar Quotations: A Collection of Passages, Phrases, and Proverbs Traced to Their Sources in Ancient
        and Modern Literature,* Fifteenth and 125th Anniversary Edition, Emily Morison Beck, ed. Bos-
        ton: Little, Brown and Company.

Bechhofer, Laurie and Andrea Parrot
1991   "What Is Acquaintance Rape?" In *Acquaintance Rape: The Hidden Crime,* Andrea Parrot and
        Laurie Bechhofer, eds., 9–25. New York: John Wiley & Sons.

Belsey, Catherine
1985   *The Subject of Tragedy: Identity and Difference in Renaissance Drama.* London and New York:
        Methuen.

Biden, Joseph R., Jr.
1991   "Combatting Aggression at Home: Violence Against Women Must Be Taken Seriously," The
        Atlanta *Journal and Constitution.* March 3.

Bienen, Leigh B.
1980   "Rape III—National Developments in Rape Reform Legislation," *Women's Rights Law Reporter*
        6(3):171.
1983a   "A Question of Credibility: John Henry Wigmore's Use of Scientific Authority in Section 924a
        of the Treatise on Evidence," *California Western Law Review,* 19(2):235–68.
1983b   "Rape Reform Legislation in the United States: A Look at Some Practical Effects," *Victimology:
        An International Journal,* 8(1–2):139–51.

Blackstone, Sir William
1902   *Commentaries on the Laws of England,* Book 4. William Draper Lewis, Ph.D., ed. Philadelphia:
[1765– Rees Welsh & Co.
69]

Block, Mary R.
1992   *"An Accusation Easily to Be Made": A History of Rape Law in Nineteenth-century State Appellate
        Courts, 1800–1870.* Master's thesis, Department of History, University of Louisville, Louisville,
        Kentucky.

Bowden, Mark
1983   "The Incident at Alpha Tau Omega," *Philadelphia Inquirer Magazine,* September 11.

Breasted, Barbara
1971   *"Comus* and the Castlehaven Scandal," *Milton Studies,* 3:201–24.

Brown, Helen Gurley
1983   *Sex and the Single Girl.* New York: Avon Books.
[1962]

Brownmiller, Susan
1975   *Against Our Will: Men, Women and Rape.* New York: Simon and Schuster.

Burt, Martha R.
1980   "Cultural Myths and Supports for Rape," *Journal of Personality and Social Psychology,* 38(2):217–
        30.

Butterfield, Fox and Mary B. W. Tabor
1991   "Woman in Florida Rape Inquiry Fought Adversity and Sought Acceptance," *The New York
        Times,* April 17.

Carrithers, Michael
1989   "Sociality, Not Aggression, Is the Key Human Trait." In *Societies at Peace: Anthropological Perspec-
        tives,* Signe Howell and Roy Willis, eds.; 187–209. London: Routledge.

Clark, Anna
1987   *Women's Silence, Men's Violence: Sexual Assault in England 1770–1845.* New York: Pandora.

Clemens, Margaret A.
1983   "Elimination of the Resistance Requirement and Other Rape Law Reforms: The New York
        Experience," *Albany Law Review,* 47:871–907.

Connell, Noreen and Cassandra Wilson, eds.
1974   *Rape: The First Sourcebook for Women. By New York Radical Feminists.* New York: New American
        Library.

Corson, Hiram, LL.D.
1899   *An Introduction to the Prose and Poetical Works of John Milton.* New York: Macmillan.

Cott, Nancy F.
1978   "Passionlessness: An Interpretation of Victorian Sexual Ideology, 1790–1850," *Signs,* 4(2):219–
        36.
1987   *The Grounding of Modern Feminism.* New Haven, CT: Yale University Press.

Darwin, Charles
1936   *The Origin of Species by Means of Natural Selection or the Preservation of Favored Races in the Struggle for
        Life and the Descent of Man and Selection in Relation to Sex.* New York: The Modern Library. *Origin*
        first published 1859; *Descent* 1871.

Davis, Herbert, ed.
1967   *The Complete Plays of William Congreve.* Chicago: University of Chicago Press.

Davis, William T., ed.
1908   *Bradford's History of Plymouth Plantation, 1606–1646.* New York: Charles Scribner's Sons.

Degler, Carl N.
1991   *In Search of Human Nature: The Decline and Revival of Darwinism in American Social Thought.* New
        York: Oxford University Press.

D'Emilio, John and Estelle B. Freedman
1988   *Intimate Matters: A History of Sexuality in America*. New York: Harper & Row.

Dershowitz, Alan M.
1991   "Two Rape Cases: Justice on Trial; Florida Scores Against Smith," *The New York Times,* July 26.

Dix, George E.
1993   "Date Rape: Defining When 'No' Means 'No,' " *Legal Times,* April 5.

Douglas, Ann
1988   *The Feminization of American Culture*. New York: Anchor Books.
[1977]
1995   *Terrible Honesty: Mongrel Manhattan in the 1920s*. New York: Farrar, Straus and Giroux.

Drinnon, Richard
1961   *Rebel in Paradise: A Biography of Emma Goldman*. Chicago: University of Chicago Press.

Dworkin, Andrea
1974   *Woman Hating*. New York: E. P. Dutton.
1989   *Pornography: Men Possessing Women*. New York: E. P. Dutton.
[1979]
1994   "Andrea Dworkin, 1946–." In *Contemporary Authors Autobiography Series* 21 (July–August):1–21.

Ehrenreich, Barbara, Elizabeth Hess and Gloria Jacobs
1986   *Re-Making Love: The Feminization of Sex*. Garden City, NY: Doubleday.

Ehrhart, Julie K. and Bernice R. Sandler
1985   "Campus Gang Rape: Party Games?" *Project on the Status and Education of Women*. Washington, DC: Association of American Colleges.

Ehrmann, Winston
1959   *Pre-Marital Dating Behavior*. New York: Henry Holt.

Ellis, Havelock
1926   *Studies in the Psychology of Sex, Volume III. Analysis of the Sexual Impulse; Love and Pain; The Sexual*
[1903]   *Impulse in Women*. Philadelphia: F. A. Davis Company.
1942   *Psychology of Sex*. London: Heinemann.
[1933]

Encyclopaedia Britannica
1967   "Sir Matthew Hale." In *Encyclopaedia Britannica,* Vol. 10, 1,129–30. Chicago: Encyclopaedia Britannica, Inc.

Estes, Clarissa Pinkola, Ph.D.
1992   *Women Who Run With the Wolves: Myths and Stories of the Wild Woman Archetype*. New York: Ballantine.

Estrich, Susan
1987   *Real Rape*. Cambridge: Harvard University Press.
1991   "The Real Palm Beach Story," *The New York Times*. April 18.

Evans, Sara M.
1980   *Personal Politics: The Roots of Women's Liberation in the Civil Rights Movement and the New Left*. New York: Vintage Books.
1989   *Born for Liberty*. New York: The Free Press.

Exner, M. J., M.D.
1915   *Problems and Principles of Sex Education*. New York: Association Press.

Fairstein, Linda A.
1993   *Sexual Violence: Our War Against Rape*. New York: William Morrow and Company.

Faludi, Susan
1991   *Backlash: The Undeclared War Against American Women*. New York: Crown.

Federal Bureau of Investigation, United States Department of Justice
1970–80 *Uniform Crime Reports for the United States*. Washington: U.S. Government Printing Office.

Feild, Hubert S. and Leigh B. Bienen
1980   *Jurors and Rape: A Study in Psychology and Law.* Lexington, MA: Lexington Books.

Felten, Eric
1991   "Seduction or Rape? Bad Manners or Harassment?" *The Washington Times,* January 29, 1991.

Flaherty, David H.
1971   "Law and the Enforcement of Morals in Early America," *Perspectives in American History,* 5:203–53.

Flexner, Eleanor
1973   *Century of Struggle: The Woman's Rights Movement in the United States.* New York: Atheneum.

Foner, Eric
1992   "Introduction." *Social Darwinism in American Thought* by Richard Hofstadter, ix–xxviii. Boston: Beacon Press.

Freedman, Estelle B.
1989   " 'Uncontrolled Desires': The Response to the Sexual Psychopath, 1920–1960." In *Passion and Power: Sexuality in History,* Kathy Peiss and Christina Simmons, eds., 199–225. Philadelphia: Temple University Press.

Freeman, Jo
1975   *The Politics of Women's Liberation: A Case Study of an Emerging Social Movement and Its Relation to the Policy Process.* New York: David McKay Company.

Freud, Sigmund
1957   "Five Lectures on Psycho-Analysis." In *The Standard Edition of the Complete Psychological Works of*
[1910] *Sigmund Freud,* Vol. XI, James Strachey, trans. and ed., 3–55. London: Hogarth Press.
1963   *Dora: An Analysis of a Case of Hysteria.* Philip Rieff, ed. New York: Collier.
1975   *Three Essays on the Theory of Sexuality.* James Strachey, trans. and ed. New York: Basic Books.
[1962]

Friedan, Betty
1974   *The Feminine Mystique.* New York: Dell.
[1963]

Friedman, Lawrence M.
1985   *A History of American Law,* 2nd Edition. New York: Simon & Schuster.
[1973]

Fromm, Barbara
1991   "Sexual Battery: Mixed Signal Legislation Reveals Need for Further Reform," *Florida State Law Review,* Winter:579–604.

Garrison, J. Gregory and Randy Roberts
1994   *Heavy Justice: The State of Indiana v. Michael G. Tyson.* Reading, MA: Addison-Wesley.

Gay, Peter
1993   *The Cultivation of Hatred: The Bourgeois Experience, Victoria to Freud,* Vol. III. New York: W. W. Norton.

Gebhard, Paul H., John H. Gagnon, Wardell B. Pomeroy and Cornelia V. Christenson
1965   *Sex Offenders: An Analysis of Types.* New York: Harper & Row.

Geis, G.
1978   "Lord Hale, Witches, and Rape," *British Journal of Law and Society,* 5(1):26–44.

Gelles, Richard J. and Donileen R. Loseke, eds.
1993   *Current Controversies on Family Violence.* Newbury Park, CA: Sage.

George, Linda K., Idee Winfield and Dan G. Blazer
1992   "Sociocultural Factors in Sexual Assault: Comparison of Two Representative Samples of Women," *Journal of Social Issues,* 48(1):105–25.

Gilbert, Neil
1991a   "The Campus Rape Scare," *The Wall Street Journal,* June 27:10.
1991b   "The Phantom Epidemic of Sexual Assault," *Public Interest,* 103:54–65.

Gilfoyle, Timothy J.
1992   *City of Eros: New York City, Prostitution, and the Commercialization of Sex, 1790–1920.* New York: W. W. Norton.

Glueck, Sheldon
1937   "Sex Crimes and the Law," *The Nation,* Sept. 25:318–20.

Gordon, Linda
1990   *Woman's Body, Woman's Right: Birth Control in America,* revised and updated. New York: Penguin
[1974] Books.

Griffin, Susan
1971   "Rape: The All-American Crime," *Ramparts,* 10(3):26–35.
1981   *Pornography and Silence: Culture's Revenge Against Nature.* New York: Harper & Row.
1986   *Rape: The Politics of Consciousness.* San Francisco: Harper & Row.

Guskin, Alan E.
1995   "A Response to Critics of Antioch's Sexual Consent Policy," in *Rape on Campus.* Bruno Leone and Katie de Koster, eds. 23–29. San Diego: Greenhaven Press.

Gutmann, Stephanie
1990   "Date Rape; Does Anyone Really Know What It Is?" *Playboy* 37(10):48–56.
1991   " 'It Sounds Like I Raped You!' How Date-Rape Re-Education Fosters Confusion, Undermines Personal Responsibility, and Trivializes Sexual Violence." In *Human Sexuality,* O. Pocs, ed., 217–21. Guilford, CT: Dushkin.

Hale, Sir Matthew
1800   *The History of the Pleas of the Crown,* 2 vols., George Wilson, ed. London: E. Rider, Little-Britain.
[1678]

Hale, Nathan G., Jr.
1995a   *Freud and the Americans: The Beginnings of Psychoanalysis in the United States, 1876–1917.* New
[1971] York: Oxford University Press.
1995b   *The Rise and Crisis of Psychoanalysis in the United States: Freud and the Americans, 1917–1985.* New York: Oxford University Press.

Hamilton, G. V. and Kenneth Macgowan
1976   "Physical Disabilities in Wives." In *Sex in Civilization,* V. F. Calverton and S. D. Schmalhausen,
[1929] eds., 562–79. New York: AMS Press.

Haskins, George Lee
1968   *Law and Authority in Early Massachusetts.* Hamden, CT: Archon Books.

Healy, William
1969   *The Individual Delinquent: A Text-Book of Diagnosis and Prognosis for All Concerned in Understanding*
[1915] *Offenders.* Montclair, NJ: Patterson Smith.

Healy, William and Mary Tenney Healy
1969   *Pathological Lying, Accusation, and Swindling: A Study in Forensic Psychology.* Montclair, NJ: Patter-
[1915] son Smith.

Hefner, Hugh
1962   "The Playboy Philosophy," *Playboy,* 9(12):73.

Hickson, Ford C.I. et al.
1994   "Gay Men as Victims of Nonconsensual Sex," *Archives of Sexual Behavior,* 23(3):281–294.

Hiltner, Seward
1953   *Sex Ethics and the Kinsey Reports.* New York: Association Press.

Hite, Shere
1976   *The Hite Report: A Nationwide Study of Female Sexuality.* New York: Macmillan.

Hofstadter, Richard
1989   *The American Political Tradition and the Men Who Made It.* New York: Vintage Books.
[1948]
1992   *Social Darwinism in American Thought.* Boston: Beacon Press.
[1944]

Hosmer, James Kendall, ed.
1946   *Winthrop's Journal: "History of New England," 1630–1649*, Vol. 1. New York: Barnes & Noble.
[1908]

Howell, Signe and Roy Willis
1989   "Introduction." In *Societies at Peace: Anthropological Perspectives*, Signe Howell and Roy Willis, eds., 1–28. London: Routledge.

Howell, Thomas Bayly, ed.
1809   *Cobbett's Complete Collection of State Trials and Proceedings for High Treason and Other Crimes and Misdemeanors from the Earliest Period to the Present Time*, Vol. III. London: T. C. Hansard.

Hunt, Lynn
1993   "Introduction: Obscenity and the Origins of Modernity, 1500–1800." In *The Invention of Pornography: Obscenity and the Origins of Modernity, 1500–1800*, Lynn Hunt, ed., 9–45. New York: Zone Books.

Hunt, Morton
1974   *Sexual Behavior in the 1970s.* Chicago: Playboy Press.

Jackson, Margaret
1987   " 'Facts of Life' or the Eroticization of Women's Oppression? Sexology and the Social Construction of Heterosexuality." In *The Cultural Construction of Sexuality*, Pat Caplan, ed., 52–81. London: Tavistock.

James, Janet W.
1981   *Changing Ideas About Women in the United States, 1776–1825.* New York: Garland Publishing.

Jordan, Mary
1991   "Willy Smith, the 'Independent' Kennedy, Anonymous No More," *The Washington Post*, May 10.

Kalven, Harry, Jr., and Hans Zeisel
1966   *The American Jury.* Boston: Little Brown.

Kanin, Eugene J.
1957–58 "Male Aggression in Dating-Courtship Relations," *American Journal of Sociology*, 63:197–204.

Katz, Sedelle and Mary Ann Mazur, M.D.
1979   *Understanding the Rape Victim.* New York: John Wiley & Sons.

Kerber, Linda K.
1980   *Women of the Republic: Intellect and Ideology in Revolutionary America.* Chapel Hill, NC: University of North Carolina Press.

Kinsey, Alfred C., Wardell B. Pomeroy and Clyde E. Martin
1948   *Sexual Behavior in the Human Male.* Philadelphia: W. B. Saunders.

Kinsey, Alfred C., Wardell B. Pomeroy, Clyde E. Martin and Paul H. Gebhard
1953   *Sexual Behavior in the Human Female.* Philadelphia: W. B. Saunders.

Kirkendall, Lester A.
1961   *Premarital Intercourse and Interpersonal Relations.* New York: Gramercy.

Kirkpatrick, Clifford and Eugene J. Kanin
1957   "Male Sex Aggression on a University Campus," *American Sociological Review*, 22:52–8.

Kling, Samuel G.
1965   *Sexual Behavior and the Law.* New York: Bernard Geis Associates.

Koehler, Lyle
1980   *A Search for Power: The "Weaker Sex" in Seventeenth-Century New England.* Urbana: University of Illinois Press.

Koss, Mary P.
1981   "Hidden Rape on a University Campus," National Institute of Mental Health, Final Report for Grant R01MH31618.
1985   "The Hidden Rape Victim: Personality, Attitudinal, and Situational Characteristics," *Psychology of Women Quarterly*, 9:193–212.

1988   "Hidden Rape: Sexual Aggression and Victimization in a National Sample of Students in Higher Education." In *Rape and Sexual Assault II,* Ann Wolbert Burgess, ed., 3–25. New York: Garland Publishing.

1992a   "Defending Date Rape," *Journal of Interpersonal Violence,* 7(1):122–26.

1992b   "The Underdetection of Rape: Methodological Choices Influence Incidence Estimates," *Journal of Social Issues,* 48(1):61–75.

1993   "Rape: Scope, Impact, Interventions, and Public Policy Responses," *American Psychologist,* 48(10):1,062–69.

Koss, Mary P. and Sarah L. Cook
1993   "Facing the Facts: Date and Acquaintance Rape Are Significant Problems for Women." In *Current Controversies on Family Violence,* Richard J. Gelles and Donileen R. Loseke, eds., 104–19. Newbury Park, CA: Sage.

Koss, Mary P. and T. E. Dinero
1988   "Predictors of Sexual Aggression Among a National Sample of Male College Students." In *Human Sexual Aggression: Current Perspectives. Annals of the New York Academy of Sciences,* Vol. 528, Robert A. Prentky and Vernon L. Quinsey, eds., 133–47. New York: New York Academy of Sciences.

Koss, Mary P. and John A. Gaines
1993   "The Prediction of Sexual Aggression by Alcohol Use, Athletic Participation, and Fraternity Affiliation," *Journal of Interpersonal Violence,* 8(1):94–108.

Koss, Mary P., Christine A. Gidycz and Nadine Wisniewski
1987   "The Scope of Rape: Incidence and Prevalence of Sexual Aggression and Victimization in a National Sample of Higher Education Students," *Journal of Consulting and Clinical Psychology,* 55:162–70.

Koss, Mary P. and Kenneth E. Leonard
1984   "Sexually Aggressive Men: Empirical Findings and Theoretical Implications." In *Pornography and Sexual Aggression,* Neil M. Malamuth and Edward Donnerstein, eds., 213–32. New York: Academic Press.

Koss, Mary P. and Cheryl J. Oros
1982   "Sexual Experiences Survey: A Research Instrument Investigating Sexual Aggression and Victimization," *Journal of Consulting and Clinical Psychology,* 50(3):455–57.

Krafft-Ebing, Richard von
1965   *Psychopathia Sexualis: a Medico-forensic Study,* Harry E. Wedeck, trans. New York: Putnam.

LaFree, Gary D.
1989   *Rape and Criminal Justice: The Social Construction of Sexual Assault.* Belmont, CA: Wadsworth Publishing Company.

Langum, David J.
1994   *Crossing Over the Line: Legislating Morality and the Mann Act.* Chicago: University of Chicago Press.

Laqueur, Thomas
1990   *Making Sex: Body and Gender from the Greeks to Freud.* Cambridge: Harvard University Press.

Largen, Mary Ann
1976   "History of Women's Movement in Changing Attitudes, Laws, and Treatment toward Rape Victims." In *Sexual Assault,* Marcia J. Walker and Stanley L. Brodsky, eds. Lexington, MA: Lexington Books.

1988   "Rape-Law Reform: An Analysis." In *Rape and Sexual Assault II,* Ann Wolbert Burgess, ed. New York: Garland.

Laumann, Edward O., John H. Gagnon, Robert T. Michael and Stuart Michaels
1994   *The Social Organization of Sexuality: Sexual Practices in the United States.* Chicago: University of Chicago Press.

Lawrence, D. H.
1962   *Lady Chatterley's Lover.* New York: Grove Press.

Leakey, Richard E. and Roger Lewin
1977   *Origins: What New Discoveries Reveal About the Emergence of Our Species.* London: Macdonald & Jane's.

Lear, Martha Weinman
1972   "Q. If You Rape a Woman and Steal Her TV, What Can They Get You for in New York? A. Stealing Her TV," *The New York Times Magazine* (January 30):11.

LeGrand, Camille E.
1973   "Rape and Rape Laws: Sexism in Society and Law," *California Law Review,* 61(3):919–41.

Leo, John
1991   "Don't Oversimplify Date Rape," *U.S. News and World Report,* February 11.

Lepowsky, Maria
1993   *Fruit of the Motherland: Gender in an Egalitarian Society.* New York: Columbia University Press.

Lindemann, Barbara S.
1984   " 'To Ravish and Carnally Know': Rape in Eighteenth-Century Massachusetts," *Signs,* 10(1):63–82.

Loh, Wallace D.
1981   "Q: What Has Reform of Rape Legislation Wrought? A: Truth in Criminal Labelling," *Journal of Social Issues,* 37(4):28–52.

Lubell, Winifred Milinus
1994   *The Metamorphosis of Baubo: Myths of Women's Sexual Energy.* Nashville: Vanderbilt University Press.

Lunbeck, Elizabeth
1987   " 'A New Generation of Women': Progressive Psychiatrists and the Hypersexual Female," *Feminist Studies,* 13(3):513–43.

McCluskey, Martha T.
1992   "Privileged Violence, Principled Fantasy, and Feminist Method: The Colby Fraternity Case," *Maine Law Review,* 44(2):261–313.

MacKinnon, Catharine A.
1987   *Feminism Unmodified: Discourses on Life and Law.* Cambridge, MA: Harvard University Press.
1991   "The Palm Beach Hanging," *The New York Times,* December 15.
1993   *Only Words.* Cambridge, MA: Harvard University Press.

Malamuth, Neil M.
1981   "Rape Proclivity Among Males," *Journal of Social Issues,* 37(4):138–57.
1993   "Pornography's Impact on Male Adolescents," *Adolescent Medicine,* 4(3):563–76.

Malamuth, Neil M., Robert J. Sockloski, Mary P. Koss and J. S. Tanaka
1991   "Characteristics of Aggressors Against Women: Testing a Model Using a National Sample of College Students," *Journal of Consulting and Clinical Psychology,* 59(5):670–81.

Malinowski, Bronislaw
1929   *The Sexual Life of Savages in North-Western Melanesia: An Ethnographic Account of Courtship, Marriage and Family Life Among the Natives of the Trobriand Islands, British New Guinea.* New York: Harcourt Brace Jovanovich.

Marcus, Leah Sinanoglou
1983   "The Milieu of Milton's *Comus:* Judicial Reform at Ludlow and the Problem of Sexual Assault," *Criticism,* 25(4):293–327.

Marsh, Jeanne C.
1988   "What Have We Learned About Legislative Remedies for Rape?" In *Human Sexual Aggression: Current Perspectives. Annals of the New York Academy of Sciences,* Vol. 528, Robert A. Prentky and Vernon L. Quinsey, eds., 388–99. New York: New York Academy of Sciences.

Masson, Jeffrey Moussaieff
1984   *The Assault on Truth: Freud's Suppression of the Seduction Theory.* New York: Penguin.

Mead, Margaret
1935   *Sex and Temperament.* New York: William Morrow.
1949   *Male and Female.* New York: William Morrow.

Medea, Andra and Kathleen Thompson
1974   *Against Rape.* New York: Farrar, Straus and Giroux.

Mezey, Gillian C. and Michael B. King, eds.
1992   *Male Victims of Sexual Assault.* New York: Oxford University Press.

Michael, Robert T., John H. Gagnon, Edward O. Laumann and Gina Kolata
1994   *Sex in America: A Definitive Survey.* Boston: Little, Brown and Company.

Millar, Robert Wyness
1955   "Pioneers in Criminology, VI. John Henry Wigmore (1863–1943)," *The Journal of Criminal Law, Criminology, and Police Science,* 46(1):4–10.

Miller, Henry
1965   *Sexus.* New York: Grove Press.
[1949]

Miller, Russell
1984   *Bunny: The Real Story of Playboy.* New York: Holt, Rinehart and Winston.

Millett, Kate
1970   *Sexual Politics.* Garden City, NY: Doubleday.
Morgan, Edmund S.
1942   "The Puritans and Sex," *The New England Quarterly,* 15:591–607.

Morgan, Robin, ed.
1970   *Sisterhood Is Powerful; An Anthology of Writings from the Women's Liberation Movement.* New York: Random House.
1992   *The Word of a Woman: Feminist Dispatches 1968–1992.* New York: Vintage Books.

Muehlenhard, Charlene L., Irene G. Powch, Joi L. Phelps and Laura M. Giusti
1992   "Definitions of Rape: Scientific and Political Implications," *Journal of Social Issues,* 48(1):23–44.

National Victim Center
1992   *Rape in America: A Report to the Nation.* Arlington, VA; Charleston, SC.

Nemeth, Charles P.
1980   "Character Evidence in Rape Trials in Nineteenth Century New York: Chastity and the Admissibility of Specific Acts," *Women's Rights Law Reporter,* 6(3):214–25.

Norman, Bob
1953   "Miss Gold-Digger of 1953," *Playboy,* 1(1):6.

Norton, Mary Beth
1980   *Liberty's Daughters: The Revolutionary Experience of American Women, 1750–1800.* Boston: Little, Brown and Company.

Novak, Maximillian E.
1971   *William Congreve.* New York: Twayne Publishers.

O'Sullivan, Chris S.
1991   "Acquaintance Gang Rape on Campus." In *Acquaintance Rape: The Hidden Crime,* Andrea Parrot and Laurie Bechhofer, eds., 140–56. New York: John Wiley & Sons.

Paglia, Camille
1990   *Sexual Personae: Art and Decadence from Nefertiti to Emily Dickinson.* New Haven: Yale University Press.
1992   *Sex, Art, and American Culture: Essays.* New York: Vintage Books.

Palm Beach Police Department
1991   *Crimes Management System Incident Report,* March–May.

Parrot, Andrea
1991   "Recommendations for College Policies and Procedures to Deal with Acquaintance Rape." In *Acquaintance Rape: The Hidden Crime,* Andrea Parrot and Laurie Bechhofer, eds., 368–80. New York: John Wiley & Sons.

Pateman, Carole
1988   *The Sexual Contract.* Stanford: Stanford University Press.

Peiss, Kathy
1989   " 'Charity Girls' and City Pleasures: Historical Notes on Working-Class Sexuality, 1880–1920." In *Passion and Power: Sexuality in History,* Kathy Peiss and Christina Simmons, eds., 57–69. Philadelphia: Temple University Press.

Pleck, Elizabeth
1983   "Feminist Responses to 'Crimes Against Women,' 1868–1896," *Signs,* 8(3):451–70.

Powers, Edwin
1966   *Crime and Punishment in Early Massachusetts, 1620–1692: A Documentary History.* Boston: Beacon Press.

Prentky, Robert Alan, Ann Wolbert Burgess and Daniel Lee Carter
1986   "Victim Responses by Rapist Type," *Journal of Interpersonal Violence,* 1(1):73–98.

Quindlen, Anna
1991   "Public and Private: A Mistake," *The New York Times,* April 21.

Quinn, Arthur
1994   *A New World: An Epic of Colonial America from the Founding of Jamestown to the Fall of Quebec.* Boston: Faber and Faber.

Ramas, Maria
1983   "Freud's Dora, Dora's Hysteria." In *Sex and Class in Women's History,* Judith L. Newton, Mary P. Ryan, and Judith R. Walkowitz, eds., 72–113. London: Routledge & Kegan Paul.

Reich, Wilhelm
1969   *The Sexual Revolution.* New York: Farrar, Straus and Giroux.
[1945]

Remick, Lani Anne
1993   "Consent Standard in Rape," *University of Pennsylvania Law Review,* 141:1,103–1,151.

Renzetti, Claire M.
1992   *Violent Betrayal: Partner Abuse in Lesbian Relationships.* Newbury Park, CA: Sage.

Roalfe, William R.
1962   "John Henry Wigmore—Scholar and Reformer," *The Journal of Criminal Law, Criminology, and Police Science,* 53(3):277–300.

Robinson, Paul
1976   *The Modernization of Sex: Havelock Ellis, Alfred Kinsey, William Masters, and Virginia Johnson.* New York: Harper & Row.

Roiphe, Katie
1991   "Date Rape Hysteria," *The New York Times,* November 20.
1993   *The Morning After: Sex, Fear, and Feminism on Campus.* Boston: Little, Brown and Company.

Rossi, Alice, ed.
1988   *The Feminist Papers: From Adams to de Beauvoir.* Boston: Northeastern University Press.
[1973]

Russell, Diana E. H.
1984a   *The Politics of Rape: The Victim's Perspective.* New York: Stein and Day.
[1974]
1984b   *Sexual Exploitation: Rape, Child Sexual Abuse, and Workplace Harassment.* Newbury Park, CA: Sage.
1993   *Against Pornography: The Evidence of Harm.* Berkeley, CA: Russell Publications.

Ryan, Mary P.
1983   *Womanhood in America: From Colonial Times to the Present,* 3rd Edition. New York: Franklin Watts.

Sagarin, Edward
1977   "Forcible Rape and the Problem of the Rights of the Accused," In *Forcible Rape: The Crime, the Victim, and the Offender*, Duncan Chappell, Robley Geis, and Gilbert Geis, eds., 142–60. New York: Columbia University Press.

Sanday, Peggy Reeves
1980   "Margaret Mead's View of Sex Roles in Her Own and Other Societies," *American Anthropologist* 82(2):340–48.
1981a   "The Socio-Cultural Context of Rape: A Cross-Cultural Study," *Journal of Social Issues*, 37(4):5–27.
1981b   *Female Power and Male Dominance: On the Origins of Sexual Inequality.* Cambridge: Cambridge University Press.
1990   *Fraternity Gang Rape: Sex, Brotherhood, and Privilege on Campus.* New York: New York University Press.

Sanday, Peggy Reeves and Ruth Gallagher Goodenough
1990   *Beyond the Second Sex: New Directions in the Anthropology of Gender.* Philadelphia: University of Pennsylvania Press.

Schafran, Lynn Hecht, Esq.
1994   "Understanding Sexual Violence," *The National Judicial Education Program to Promote Equality for Women and Men in the Courts.* State Justice Institute.

Schlossman, Steven and Stephanie Wallach
1978   "The Crime of Precocious Sexuality: Female Juvenile Delinquency in the Progressive Era," *Harvard Educational Review*, 48(1):65–94.

Schmalhausen, Samuel D.
1976   "The Sexual Revolution." In *Sex in Civilization*, V. F. Calverton and S. D. Schmalhausen, eds.,
[1929] 349–436. New York: AMS Press.

Schneir, Miriam, ed.
1972   *Feminism: The Essential Historical Writings.* New York: Vintage (Random House).

Schwarz, Judith, Kathy Peiss and Christina Simmons
1989   " 'We Were a Little Band of Willful Women': The Heterodoxy Club of Greenwich Village." In *Passion and Power: Sexuality in History*, Kathy Peiss and Christina Simmons, eds., 118–37. Philadelphia: Temple University Press.

Scully, Diana
1990   *Understanding Sexual Violence: A Study of Convicted Rapists.* Boston: Unwin Hyman.

Sheehy, Gail
1971   "Nice Girls Don't Get Into Trouble," *New York*, 4(7):26–30.

Shipp, E. R.
1992   "Tyson Gets 6-Year Prison Term for Rape Conviction in Indiana," *The New York Times*, March 27.

Showalter, Elaine
1990   *Sexual Anarchy: Gender and Culture at the Fin de Siecle.* New York: Viking.

Simmons, Christina
1989   "Modern Sexuality and the Myth of Victorian Repression." In *Passion and Power: Sexuality in History*, Kathy Peiss and Christina Simmons, eds., 157–77. Philadelphia: Temple University Press.

Simpson, Antony E.
1984   *Masculinity and Control: The Prosecution of Sex Offences in Eighteenth-Century London.* Ph.D. dissertation, Dept. of Sociology, New York University, New York.
1986   "The 'Blackmail Myth' and the Prosecution of Rape and Its Attempt in 18th-Century London: The Creation of a Legal Tradition," *The Journal of Criminal Law & Criminology*, 77(1):101–50.

Slotkin, Richard
1973   *Regeneration Through Violence: The Mythology of the American Frontier, 1600–1860.* Middleton, CT: Wesleyan University Press.

Smith-Rosenberg, Carroll
1985   *Disorderly Conduct: Visions of Gender in Victorian America.* New York: Oxford University Press.

Snitow, Ann, Christine Stansell and Sharon Thompson, eds.
1983   *Powers of Desire: The Politics of Sexuality.* New York: Monthly Review Press.

Sommers, Christina Hoff
1994   *Who Stole Feminism? How Women Have Betrayed Women.* New York: Simon & Schuster.

Stansell, Christine
1987   *City of Women: Sex and Class in New York, 1789–1860.* Urbana, IL: University of Illinois Press.
[1982]

Struckman-Johnson, Cindy
1991   "Male Victims of Acquaintance Rape." In *Acquaintance Rape: The Hidden Crime,* Andrea Parrot and Laurie Bechhofer, eds., 192–213. New York: John Wiley & Sons.

Tanner, Leslie B.
1971   *Voices from Women's Liberation.* New York: New American Library.

Thomas, Keith
1959   "The Double Standard," *Journal of the History of Ideas,* 20(2):195–216.

Thompson, Roger
1974   *Women in Stuart England and America: A Comparative Study.* London: Routledge & Kegan Paul.
1986   *Sex in Middlesex: Popular Mores in a Massachusetts County, 1649–1699.* Amherst: University of Massachusetts Press.

Thorne, Samuel E., translated with revisions and notes.
1968   *Bracton on the Laws and Customs of England,* Vol. 2. Cambridge: Harvard University Press.

Trilling, Lionel
1950   "The Kinsey Report." In *The Liberal Imagination,* 223–42. New York: Viking Press.

Trumbach, Randolph
1993   "Erotic Fantasy and Male Libertinism in Enlightenment England." In *The Invention of Pornography: Obscenity and the Origins of Modernity, 1500–1800,* Lynn Hunt, ed., 253–82. New York: Zone Books.

University of Pennsylvania Law Review
1970   "The Corroboration Rule and Crimes Accompanying a Rape," *University of Pennsylvania Law Review,* 118:458–72.

Van de Velde, T. H., M.D.
1928   *Ideal Marriage: Its Physiology and Technique.* London: Heinemann.

Varchaver, Nicholas
1991   "Inside the St. John's Jury Room," *Manhattan Lawyer,* 4(7):16–21.

Vatz, Richard and Lee S. Weinberg
1991   "The Smith Case: An End to Rape Shield Laws?" *The Washington Post,* September 3.

Warshaw, Robin
1988   *I Never Called It Rape: The* Ms. *Report on Recognizing, Fighting and Surviving Date and Acquaintance Rape.* New York: Harper & Row.

Welter, Barbara
1966   "The Cult of True Womanhood: 1820–1860," *American Quarterly,* 18(Summer):313–33.

Weyr, Thomas
1978   *Reaching for Paradise: The Playboy Vision of America.* New York: Times Books.

Wiener, Jon
1992   "Rape by Innuendo," *The Nation,* 254(2):44.

Wigmore, John Henry
1970   *A Treatise on the Anglo-American System of Evidence in Trials at Common Law,* Vol. IIIA, Chadbourn
[1940]   Revision. Boston: Little, Brown and Company.

Williams, Aubrey L.
1979   *An Approach to Congreve.* New Haven: Yale University Press.

Williams, Susan N.
1983   "Rape Reform Legislation and Evidentiary Concerns: The Law in Pennsylvania," *University of Pittsburgh Law Review,* 44:955–75.

Woodbridge, Linda
1984   *Women and the English Renaissance: Literature and the Nature of Womankind, 1540 to 1620.* Urbana: University of Illinois Press.

Wortman, Marlene Stein, ed.
1985   *Women in American Law, Volume I: From Colonial Times to the New Deal.* New York: Holmes & Meier.

Wylie, Philip
1955   *Generation of Vipers.* New York and Toronto: Rinehart.
[1942]
1958   "The Womanization of America," *Playboy,* 5(9):51.

Yale Law Journal
1952   "Forcible and Statutory Rape: An Exploration of the Operation and Objectives of the Consent Standard," *The Yale Law Journal* 62(1):55–83.

ACKNOWLEDGMENTS

I owe a significant debt to many individuals in the writing of this book. My husband, Serge Caffie, my agent, Geri Thoma, my editor, Betsy Lerner, and my colleague and friend Ruth Goodenough, played significant roles in the conceptualization and editorial stages of the evolution of this book. Their support, patience, and editorial expertise are gratefully acknowledged.

In view of the current backlash against women's studies programs and scholarship, I particularly want to stress my debt to this scholarship. Without it I would have been unable to place the topic of acquaintance rape in the broad historical and cultural perspective that I feel is essential to understanding why justice has so often failed American women.

Of the many individuals I interviewed for this book, several took extra time and care to read parts of the manuscript: Mary Koss, Diana Russell, Andrea Dworkin, and Robin Morgan helped me reconstruct the development of the anti-rape movement in the late-1960s and 1970s. Laura X also provided information on the historical development of the issue of date rape.

For information on the current sexual revolution, I am indebted to visits with students, faculty, and administrators during the past five years on more than thirty campuses. Most particularly, I want to thank Melinda Kanner, anthropologist at Antioch College, who introduced me to Antioch students, and Toby Simon, associate dean at Brown University, who introduced me to members of Brown's Cast of Color. Carol Tracy, executive director of the Philadelphia Women's Law Project, and Julie Goldsheid of NOW's Legal Defense and Education Fund provided important material on the legal and legislative developments regarding affirmative consent, the defining sexual issue for today's students.

Rick Pringle of Goucher College helped me in the statistical analyses I report and provided insight based on his experience of the evolution of coeducation at this formerly all-women's college. Myra Hindus of the University of Connecticut, formerly at Princeton, was generous with her time in conveying an understanding of the anti-rape movement at Princeton. Jodi Gold and Erica Strohl, students who started the peer-education program at the University of Pennsylvania, were also an inspiration, as were Eli Dilapi, Gloria Gay, and Susan Villari, whose longtime work at Penn, where I teach, nurtures student initiative. To all these individuals and the many others who patiently answered my questions, I am extremely grateful, as I am to Rashida Holmes and Molly Roth, who spent many tedious hours typing the taped interviews.

Another essential source in the writing of this book came from interviews with the complainant in the St. John's trial, which took place in Queens, New York, in 1991–92. I would like to dedicate this book to Angela (not her real name), but I know she wants to get on with her life and put her ordeal behind her. I am grateful to John Santucci, the Queens district attorney at the time of the trial, and his top assistants, Daniel McCarthy and Phil Foglia, who granted me lengthy interviews. Peter Reese and Vincent Gentile, the trial prosecutors, were also generous with their time. From Reese, Gentile, and McCarthy I received a quick education in courtroom procedure and rape law, which helped me to understand what happened during the St. John's trial. Other important individuals contributing to my understanding of the St. John's incident were Dr. Anne Burgess, who testified as an expert witness on post-traumatic stress, Dr. Loretta Devoy, professor of philosophy at St. John's; Sonya Markes, a student; and the detectives who worked on the investigation.

For my account of the verdict in the St. John's trial I am indebted to Theodore Lynch, a juror at the trial, and Nicholas Varchaver, who interviewed several jurors. I also want to thank Meredith Stiehm and Peter Demereth, who helped me to record trial testimony, and Anjali Arondekar and Julie Crawford, Penn graduate students, for their editorial help with the final manuscript.

Over the years several colleagues have been particularly supportive of my work. In particular I want to mention Francis E. Johnston, Sandra Barnes, Ward Goodenough, Gregory Possehl, Louise Shoemaker, Anu Rao, and Helen Davies, of the University of Pennsylvania, and Cathy Winkler and Nicole Sault, colleagues at other universities. Without their help and support, I don't think I would have been able to sustain the many years of writing and researching the unpopular, controversial subject of the cultural context of human sexual aggression.

I dedicate this book to Serge Caffie out of respect for his 1967 book on Simone de Beauvoir, written while he was serving in the French army in Algeria in protest against another culture of violence and in support of freedom with responsibility.

INDEX